Lewis Alfred Wickes, Cynthia Wilcox Wickes

The Life and Letters of Rev. Lewis Alfred Wickes

being a brief narrative of his life, and the letters connected with his labors in

revivals in northern New York

Lewis Alfred Wickes, Cynthia Wilcox Wickes

The Life and Letters of Rev. Lewis Alfred Wickes
being a brief narrative of his life, and the letters connected with his labors in revivals in northern New York

ISBN/EAN: 9783337018047

Printed in Europe, USA, Canada, Australia, Japan

Cover: Foto ©ninafisch / pixelio.de

More available books at **www.hansebooks.com**

THE LIFE AND LETTERS

OF

REV. LEWIS ALFRED WICKES.

BEING A BRIEF NARRATIVE OF HIS LIFE, AND THE LETTERS CONNECTED WITH HIS LABORS IN REVIVALS OF RELIGION IN NORTHERN NEW YORK.

"Go ye into all the world and preach the Gospel to every creature."—MARK 16: 15.

COMPILED BY HIS WIDOW, MRS. CYNTHIA WICKES.

CHICAGO:
FAIRBANKS, PALMER & CO.
1884.

COPYRIGHTED BY
MRS. CYNTHIA WICKES,
1883.

CHAS N. TRIVESS, PRINTER.
CHICAGO.

TABLE OF CONTENTS.

CHAPTER I.—Narrative. Birth, Early Education and Conversion. 9
CHAPTER II.—Commencement of Ministerial Work.............. 12
CHAPTER III.—Pastoral Labors. At Stows Square and Antwerp. 20
CHAPTER IV.—Correspondence during His Early Ministry, from 1830 to 1833................................... 26
CHAPTER V.—Correspondence during Pastoral Work, from 1833 to 1841....................................... 50
CHAPTER VI.—Beginning of Evangelistic Work. Revival at Norfolk... 80
CHAPTER VII.—Revival Meeting at Massena. Removal of Family to Stows Square................................. 95
CHAPTER VIII.—Meeting at Canton and Waddington............ 103
CHAPTER IX.—Revival Meeting at Morristown. Birthday Letter of 1841.. 127
CHAPTER X.—Meeting at Parrishville........................ 144
CHAPTER XI.—Meeting and Sickness at Hermon. Revival at De Kalb... 151
CHAPTER XII.—Revival Meeting at Ogdensburg. Texts......... 163
CHAPTER XIII.—Meeting at Huvelton and De Puyster.......... 174
CHAPTER XIV.—Meeting at Lisbon and Birthday Letter for 1842.. 183
CHAPTER XV.—Meetings at Woodville, Copenhagen, and Rodman. 207
CHAPTER XVI. Meetings at Belleville and Adams.............. 218
CHAPTER XVII.—Revival at Mansfield........................ 226
CHAPTER XVIII. Meetings of 1844 at Huvelton, West Potsdam, and Madrid....................................... 235
CHAPTER XIX.—Second Meeting at Massena and Chateaugay, 1845... 247
CHAPTER XX.—Meetings at Burke, Lawrenceville, Moira. Birthday Letter of 1845................................. 262
CHAPTER XXI.—Meetings at Malone and Gouverneur........... 278
CHAPTER XXII.—Meeting at Oswego.......................... 295
CHAPTER XXIII.—Birthday Letter, 1848...................... 308
CHAPTER XXIV.—Revival Meetings at Boonville, Brownville, LaFargeville. Birthday and Letter to Mother.. 315
CHAPTER XXV.—Revival Meetings at Depauville, Cape Vincent... 335
CHAPTER XXVI. Meeting at Copenhagen and Last Sickness...... 348
CHAPTER XXVII.—Funeral Sermon and Testimonials. Closing Words.. 355

PREFACE.

In compliance with the urgent solicitations of many respected and dear friends of the deceased L. A. WICKES, and hoping to benefit those now living, who once enjoyed and were benefited by his life, and also as his memory is still sacred, that it may continue to be cherished by children and grandchildren.

It is attempted in a brief narrative to present some of the arduous labors selected from numerous letters concerning the successful revivals of religion where God in His kind providence marked out the path for our faithful and beloved friend to labor. Being well aware of the difficulties, at this late hour, to do justice to what the Lord wrought by His instrumentality, yet it is desired to encourage others to trust in the Lord, as His servant did, knowing the promises are sure to the obedient in His blessed cause.

We therefore send out some incidents of a faithful life, praying that to the inquiry "Who is on the Lord's side?" many may respond as did the subject of this memoir, unreservedly "Here Lord *am I*. What wilt thou have *me* to do?"

AN INTRODUCTORY NOTE TO SUBSCRIBERS.

A PEN PICTURE OF MRS. WICKES.

As most of the subscribers for the Life and Letters of Rev. L. A. Wickes will expect a portrait of Mrs. Wickes also, it is due them, to say, that at the exceedingly low price which she offered her book and the great personal sacrifice at which she has been, in order to have it printed at all, forbid any more expense.

And so it has been thought by some of her nearest friends that a brief pen sketch of her life would satisfy your expectations. Owing to her natural diffidence and failing health it has been by a great deal of persuasion that she has yielded to have this sketch written, and only acquiesced at the thought that it might be of encouragement and benefit to others and advance the cause of her Lord whom she desires above everything else to honor. Her parents were of puritanic stock and emigrated from Connecticut to northern New York when there was only a bridle path from Utica northward. Cynthia Wilcox was born Feb. 3, 1804. Her first recollection was learning to walk and of sitting in the foot of the cradle rocking her sister thirteen months younger than herself. Then when she was two and a half years old of riding to school on horseback with her father and being lifted off by the teacher. Being of a very religious turn of mind she recollects, when a very small child, of holding a blade of grass in her hand and wishing the Lord would turn it into a needle (as her mother had but few and could only procure more by sending to Utica, fifty miles away) so she might sew together some pieces that had been given her. At the age of seven years her first religious conviction of sin began on being told by a young cousin who was visiting at her father's house and who had a New Testament which she read with C., that she was a sinner, that everybody were sinners. She thought her father and mother could not be but the cousin said yes ALL were sinners, that Jesus had died for all who would repent and believe on Him. Two or three years after the cousin died and left as a parting gift to C. the New Testament, which she valued highly and spent much of her spare time in reading and committing to memory many passages. She remembers being much impressed by sermons preached by the Rev. Isaac Clinton in 1808. About the year 1816, under the ministry of Father Nash, her parents united with the Church and brought all their children (then seven in number) forward for baptism. Some weeks after, while visiting at their house, questioning C. about her religious faith Father Nash asked her if she loved the Savior. She replied, "He was the one altogether lovely." He asked her if she would not like to unite with the people of God and she assented. So when all Christians of all denominations were gathered together in the old school house where the church usually met for Sabbath worship, she was requested to stand up on a bench and "give in" her "religious experience," which she did," and Father N. asked all present who thought it a Christian experience to hold up their hands. From that time she spent much time reading such books as Baxter's Saints' Rest, Dodridge's Rise and Progress and Mrs. Hannah Moore and such like works. A ladies' Missionary and Library Society was organized and C. was chosen secretary and served as such for years. In 1820 a young man who united with the church at the same time C. did, and was studying for the ministry started the idea of a Sabbath School and organized one with twenty-five members. She being the oldest of the scholars was asked to hear a class, as their exercises consisted chiefly in reciting Scripture verses from memory. And from that time to this there has never been a time, unless prevented by very severe illness, that she has not gathered a class about her upon the Sabbath for instruction in the Bible. A few years ago, a former pupil of hers at Stows Square, while on a visit to her western home and speaking of that Sabbath School said; "The best S. S. ever was." The children were always nearly all converted while in her class; her constant aim was to guard them and bring them into the fold of the Good Shepherd. About 1826 the temperance movement commenced in the East, and people began to see bad effects from the use of malt or distilled liquors, and a pledge against such liquors was circulated.

One was brought to Miss C., while she was sitting at her loom weaving her day's work for family wear, and she immediately wrote her name. Afterward, the Washingtonian movement swept over the land and her father and mother with the older members joined it and received certificates of membership.

During the years 1821 and 1822 Miss C. attended school at Lowville Academy, then under the preceptorship of Prof. Taylor. During the year 1831 while teaching the day school at Stows Square a revival broke out among the children and nearly all the school "indulged a hope in the Savior." At this time Mr. Wickes came to Stows Square, the result of which is found in the narrative.

Diffident to attract public notice, it was not until after her marriage that she broke over the custom of "women keeping silence in the churches." He encouraged her to feel "that clothes stuffed with straw would not hinder her from praying before them, and *men* were but lumps of clay covered." She entered heartily and with an eye single to God's glory into every reform that presented itself, signing with her husband upon marriage, a pledge of total abstinence from all kind of liquor, tobacco, tea and coffee, which pledge she ever kept. Though she well remembers when ministers and deacons joined with all others in drinking from the full bottle and pitchers that were ever kept ready on the sideboard for all callers. After her husband commenced his evangelistic labors she with her little children returned from Antwerp to her father's house, where she made her home for nearly five years, attending prayer and maternal meetings, and having always a class in Sunday School, but when at all consistent with other duties, she accompanied her husband in his arduous, but to them delightful labor of leading souls to Christ. During this stay with her family at Stows Square, temperance and anti-slavery causes became greatly agitated, and were made by herself and friends subjects of special prayer, but the minister and leading members of the society were exceedingly "conservative and *forbid them to bring such subjects into their social meetings*, treating them with coldness by shutting the door in their faces or closing the meeting before giving them opportunity to take any part, consequently they thought best to quietly remain at home. Some sympathizing friends coming in each Sabbath to have a prayer meeting, or read a sermon, or anti-slavery lecture, as many stirring articles were being widely published, and so as a family they were strongly enthused by these and kindred subjects, and that no farther trouble should be made by the society, they wrote and sent in a "Withdrawal."

[Mrs. W. never ceased her work of teaching the Word of God both in S. S., and in a week day evening Bible class attended for years by adults and young people.]

But "the society" were not content to let them leave thus peaceably saying "Our S. S. is all run down, w can't afford to lose their support," so sent them a citation to "appear before the church for covenant breaking."

Mrs. W. had already arranged to assist her husband in a very interesting revival, and as a number of the family had planned to attend a large Abolition Convention at Antwerp, and accompany her on her way; feeling *that* the more important occasion, they did not attend the "Church meeting." The "Church" however met, and by an *ex parte* trial by vote of sixteen "cut off" ten of the absentees, but as Mrs. W. had a good excuse to go to assist her husband they put off her trial, and after several postponements, and an appeal to the Presbytery, where an earnest effort was made to have her vindicated and truth alone made to appear. Mr. W. sympathizing with his wife in all reformatory causes thought that justice would be done if the facts and truth were known. And while not willing to hinder the revival meetings in which he was engaged, hoped to carry on by writing and brother ministers, a satisfactory conclusion of the matter. But the clerical brethren were fearful that the anti-slavery cause would divide their churches, and so did not allow *all* the facts to appear. And at a special called meeting of "the Church" the then pastor pronounced her (5 against 4) "Cut off from all Church fellowship with man, *and no doubt with God."* The Presbytery at length decided *"There is nothing against Mrs. Wickes' Christian and moral character, and if she will recall her "Withdrawal," she may be re-instated into Church fellowship,"* but no word was promised of Christian liberty on the great moral questions of the day, and she felt to say, "What I have done I have done."

As Mrs. Wickes had only done what she felt as her duty to do, she had no regrets, or apologies to make. The long experience she had passed through and believing that "If ye know these things happy are ye if you do them," and "Happy is he that condemneth not himself in the things that he alloweth," led her to see, more and more, that the fellowship of Christians was one thing and man-made churches and sects another, and the more she was made the object of scorn the more she was led to close reading of the Bible and prayerful meditation. When the glorious liberty of the Gospel revealed itself still more fully to her consciousness she realized that he that *loveth is born of God* and " Through One Spirit" we all have access to the Father, and "There is no other name given under heaven among men whereby we can be saved," "But he that believeth on the Lord Jesus Christ shall be saved," "and to him shall be given a new name that no man knoweth save him to who it is given." And therefore, "the Bride, the Lamb's wife," is known by the Bridegroom, and as no voting by brothers or sisters, or strangers, can make a child belong to its parents, so no human power can create the relation of a child to God and if born of God all *are* by the "spirit of adoption," already "members of the General Assembly and Church of the first born" and members one of another. "Growing in grace and in the knowledge of our Lord and Saviuor Jesus Christ." "Not forsaking the assembling of yourselves together." Finding in the written word of God an all sufficient guide for "All Scripture is given by inspiration of God and is profitable for doctrine, reproof, correction, and *instruction* in righteousness, that the man of God may be thoroughly *furnished* unto every good work." Truth never acting in opposition to itself. And as the "law of the Lord" is exceeding broad, extending to every thought " so no condition or reform but will find direction or guidance in the blessed Bible, therefore made her courageous to accept and put in practice all reforms when made clear to her conscience. While visiting a daughter, in Fulton, Ill., in 1859, she was cordially invited to the charge of a Bible class, which she did to the acceptance of the members. After returning home where a feeble grand child needed her sympathizing care, being a naturally skillful nurse, her attention was drawn to the dress of women as affecting the lives and health of not merely themselves but their children, and she adopted the dress reform costume which she has worn for the last twenty-four years.

The subject of equal rights was very forcibly brought

to her notice by an incident soon after her husband's death. The pathmaster called to warn her of her road tax. According to New York law, Mr. W. had never been taxed, and she asked why she should be, as a widow. The answer was, "Not being a minister and holding property it must be taxed." "But," said she, "I am not as able as was my husband." "Can't help it, ITS THE LAW" was the reply, "And I warn you on the road to-morrow at 8 A. M. with such tools as you use in your garden." And so amid the tears of her children, accompanied by a little orphan boy staying with her, and whom she directed to take his Testament along to study his S. S. lesson, she was set at work on the road *by the side of the burying ground where her husband lay*. Was ever place more fitting to think of enactments that require "TAXATION *without representation*." It was with her, and her daughters, a life lesson. The anti-slavery question had expanded to one of human rights, regardless of sex. "In Christ Jesus there is neither male or female for all are one."

In 1863 she accompanied her children and their families to Iowa and settled in Humboldt Co. She has ever sought to exemplify her belief by her life, " that others seeing her good works may glorify God, and finding in every loving heart a brother or sister. She is now in her eightieth year. Her memory and faculties of mind are clear. Heart warm and in sympathy with the young people about her. Interested in all that interests the children and grandchildren, and the one little great granddaughter. Though suffering daily the most intense bodily pain, she sends out her little book hoping in the life she has tried to portray, an example that may be the means of winning many souls to Christ, and her oft repeated expression is "And now Lord, what wait I for, my hope is in Thee." "Who shall separate us from the love of God, which is in Christ Jesus our Lord." Truly of her may well be said as of another

> "*Humility*, religion's choicest grace,
> Adorned her life throughout her earthly race;
> *Meekness*, through life her tender soul inspired,
> While holy *zeal*, her ardent spirit fired.
> *Sectarian pride* and selfish *party zeal*
> Her free-born soul disdained to feel.
> Her liberal mind, her wide expanded soul,
> Loved all the saints, and fellowshiped the whole.
> Pure love for souls oft made her spirit yearn,
> While she in tears prayed sinners to return.
> Long will "*The Church*" her absence sad deplore;
> But, ah! 'tis ours to tremble and adore
> Jehovah's ways. We'll humbly kiss the rod,
> And bow submissive to the hand of God."

CHAPTER I.

BIRTH AND EARLY EDUCATION.

LEWIS ALFRED WICKES was born at Hyde Park, Dutchess County, N. Y., December 8, 1809. He was the eldest of ten children, and remarkable for his natural vivacity and affectionate disposition. His opportunities for Christian instruction in early life were rather limited, as his parents were not professedly religious.

He often spoke of his grandfather's taking him with him to meeting and seating him upon a low seat before the altar, and of standing, when very small, in the orchestra and singing, as he had an excellent voice and liked to join that part of worship on the Sabbath.

After several removals, his parents settled in Troy, N. Y., where he was surrounded with many temptations, as youths of his age, of convivial affinities in cities, always are. When his dear parents became Christians, espousing the cause of Christ, and erected a family altar, Lewis' heart rebelled against such an idea as being summoned to come daily around that altar. He told his brother he would run away from such a place. As he was his mother's main dependence in assisting about household affairs, she had very severe trials on this subject with him. His father was constantly engaged in business, and could not be with his family during the day.

His mind was not wholly at ease on the all-important subject of his soul's salvation. His father's prayers and his mother's warnings often aroused his consciousness of sin. While procrastinating, he tried in vain to shield himself under the doctrine of Universalism.

In 1826 Rev. C. G. Finney held a protracted meeting in Dr. Beman's church, the society with which his parents were connected at that time. Under the presentation of Divine truth he became fully convicted of his guilt as a sinner against God. So absorbed were his thoughts on his own sinfulness that he imagined the preacher speaking his name out audibly while he sat in the crowded gallery.

He was so sure it was so that he tried to stifle his feelings, and, aiming to conceal them, hastened home and asked his mother, who had been anxiously praying for him, why the minister mentioned *his name*. His parents were not blind to see the workings of the truth upon his heart, and prayers went up unceasingly in his behalf. For *several days* his agony seemed almost unbearable. Satan was not willing to give up his slave, but in mercy the Lord heard prayer; the chain was broken, the captive set free. He came out an emancipated, praying soul, *consecrating* ALL to God, and was faithful in the performance of every duty that was made known to him. With other young converts, he became an active member of the church and society, engaging in the Sabbath School and Temperance cause.

<small>Conversion.</small>

His father had apprenticed him to learn the carpenter's trade. He soon felt anxious to acquire an education, that he might be prepared to labor more efficiently and extensively for the cause of his Savior and the salvation of precious souls.

<small>Resolve to work for the Master.</small>

This was his constant theme of prayer. Christian friends encouraged him to make this aim his life-work. Accordingly, he bought his time of his employer, gave his note for one hundred dollars, hoping a kind Providence would enable him to pay, which in after time he satisfactorily accomplished.

In the month of May, 1826, with several of his associates who desired to study for the ministry, he went to Whitesborough and commenced his studies in the seminary at that place, their tuition being partly paid by a society of ladies in Troy. His parents furnished him with an outfit for present necessities, as bedding, clothing and books. For about two years he shared with the others in the funds supplied by the ladies for their tuition, paying the amount lacking by his own labor. He also gained the confidence of his teacher and fellow-students. While attending the seminary he went out into the neighborhoods, engaged in Sabbath schools and prayer-meetings, also assisted pastors and ministers when revivals of religion prevailed in that section, and was said to be "missed" when not present in prayer-meetings.

Straitened circumstances.

In April, 1830, his parents sent for him to return home, and bring all his things with him, as, with their increasingly large family and limited means, they could not, without incurring a debt, help him in things necessary to continue longer in school.

CHAPTER II.

EARLY MINISTRY.

<small>Called home.</small>
<small>Discouraged.</small>
<small>Way opens.</small>

IN May, young Mr. Wickes complied with his parents' request and returned to Troy, but with reluctance at leaving the revival work in Oneida County, in which his whole soul was engaged. He was dispirited, and in suspense as to the course the Lord would have him take; but he trusted Him to direct his steps, and He shortly opened his way, as the following, selected from many letters received from interested persons at Remsen, shows, who felt they had received benefit from his influence and labors.

Letter from Rev. Mr. Waters, June 15th, 1830. NEW HARTFORD, Tuesday morning, June 15, 1830.

MR. WICKES.

DEAR SIR: I last evening returned from Remsen, seventeen miles north of Utica, where I have preached for the three Sabbaths past. I hasten this morning to answer your letter, and would remark that my situation as a minister of the Gospel would not admit of discharging the duty of instructor; neither would my temporal domestic arrangements admit of such a place as you would need Yet, Sir, as I feel interested in your case, and very ready to afford you all the aid in my power, and as I perceive you are determined on leaving Troy, I will remark that in Remsen, where it is most probable I shall preach this summer, there is an academy, the preceptor of which has lately been converted, and in that place there is now a revival. Should you see fit to come right on, I should be glad to see you, and would find you some work there in the vineyard. Board is but $1.00 per week, tuition $4.50, and I think it very likely I might find you some way of earning your board. * * * Should you think of visiting R., you had better walk out from Utica to my house. You have friends in this neighborhood who will be glad to see you.

The work in Floyd continues, and has become powerful in Holland Patent and Trenton. There is now a precious line of revival from Floyd to Remsen.

Yours affectionately,
J. WATERS.

Young, with a limited education and an empty pocket, but with the prayers of his parents for his usefulness in the vineyard of the Lord, he set out on his journey, not knowing, like Abraham, whither he was going.

He found friends in the families of Revs. Waters and Foot, much interest being taken in and shown him while laboring in connection with them in the extensive revivals of religion that prevailed throughout all that region. In the town of Trenton he became acquainted with a Rev. Mr. Stowe and a Miss Mary Fowler, (she afterward becoming a missionary of the A. B. of F. M. to India), both of them from Oxbow, Jefferson County, N. Y. They earnestly requested him to go to that place, and assist in meetings in that vicinity. But a severe attack of typhoid fever prostrated him, during which time he was faithfully and kindly cared for

Began to labor.

in the family of a Mr. Wiser. After his recovery, being repeatedly solicited, he decided it was the Lord's will that he should go to Oxbow. Arriving there in the month of October, he assisted in organizing a temperance society, also conference and prayer-meetings, with great success.

In the month of March, 1831, he went to the village of Antwerp, was cordially welcomed, and ever afterward kindly entertained in the family of Mr. A. Whitford, an officer in a small Presbyterian society, which at that time had no minister, and was dependent on the Home Mission Society for preaching, but seldom had any. It was a place noted for all kinds of immorality, especially on the Lord's day. *Visited Antwerp.*

He did not expect to remain but a few days in that place, but, having found a destitute society, that had been organized in 1819 with eight members, desiring to see a better state of things both in and out of the church, being earnestly solicited, he commenced house-visiting and holding meetings, giving exhortations, and lecturing on the subject of temperance. An increasing interest, as well as numbers, became manifest in the meetings, notwithstanding the frivolities, carousals and drinking so prevalent among the inhabitants. He remained there until the month of May, and there were some fifteen or sixteen hopeful conversions. He then attended several protracted meetings in that region, at Evans' Mills, Brownville, and other places. *Assisted in revival work.*

The friends in Antwerp were very reluctant to have him leave. He had such hold on the affections of the people, especially the little church, they hoped and prayed his return might be speedy to them. Letters were addressed to him while attending the meetings at the above-named places, urging his return. In the month of August his health became so poor it was thought advisable to take a trip across the lake to Canada, which, though attended with severe sea-sickness, proved beneficial. He was invited to take part in meetings at B., in Lower Canada, from which afterwards a Christian brother wrote to have him come over and become their minister. He returned to Sackett's Harbor, from which place he wrote to his good friend, Mr. Whitford. On his way back he stopped at Chamount Bay. While there he wrote a letter to his parents, and another to his sister, A. M., whom he had recently heard had become a Christian. His affectionate, winning manners, and extensive opportunities to become acquainted with human nature, made him successful in obtaining access to the heart and conscience of those with whom he conversed, together with faithful devotion to his precious Bible (which he called his "sword"), and unceasing secret communion with God, as well as prayer and exhortation in every place where he could be a witness in the cause of Christ. These were all instrumental of his success in that village. We learn the result of his labors in his letter to his dear parents. He continued his studies until the month of March, 1831. He wrote to his parents, wishing them to request a letter of dismissal, and of his standing in the church of Troy. He obtained his request. The church in Antwerp gave him a call to become their minister. On his return, in the month of May, 1831, he applied to the Black River Association for, and obtained a license to preach. He commenced his

[margin notes: Health failed. On page. Licensed to preach by Black River Association.]

labors in Antwerp, and, with his usual enthusiasm, engaged in visiting from house to house, and three meetings on the Sabbath, and as many or more during the week. A gracious work of grace seemed to hover over the whole community. The place of worship became so thronged the people began seriously to talk about a meeting-house. They felt they were poor, but it was thought best to proceed and do what they could. A subscription was drawn up, a building committee chosen, and their minister chosen their agent, which was a great addition to his labors, both of body and mind; for he still felt he must pursue his studies, and the salvation of souls must not be neglected. However, he entered into the work, remembering the Savior worked as a carpenter, and "came to minister, and not to be ministered unto." The work went on; the church found the Lord on the giving hand, ready to open the windows of Heaven and pour out a blessing when the hearts and hands were open to the requirements of their spiritual wants.

September 5th, 1831, he passed a critical examination before the Black River Association, and was accepted as a licentiate of that body, to preach in all the churches the Gospel of the Lord Jesus Christ. They ever afterward found him to be one of the most efficient laborers in the vineyard of the Lord. His counsels and prayers will long be remembered as a true brother in the ministry, denying himself to promote the spiritual good of all the churches where Providence called him to labor in the cause of Christ. He was eminently successful in Sunday-schools and in the cause of moral purity, and all his energies were called out in the promotion of the temperance and anti-slavery enterprises.

Accepted as Licentiate.

Always discountenancing profanity, consecrating the Sabbath as a day blessed of Heaven, especially in the dispensation of Divine truth for the conviction and conversion of souls to God; *remembering* ALWAYS *to pray without ceasing for the aid of the Holy Spirit.* He continued his active labors in Antwerp until the meeting-house was finished, and an ordained minister was employed. He then pursued his studies, following the leading of Providence. In the month of May, 1832, he was requested to go to Stow's Square, Lewis County, The church in that place had no minister. The Sunday-school was languishing; the Superintendent, discouraged, said "it was no use to try to keep it up on the Sabbath, as they had no preaching; the parents would not come out to reading meetings and bring their children." Some members had gone to other societies, numbers had moved away, and some esteemed "pillars" had died. Truly, prospects looked dark and forbidding. On his arrival, a notice was given out in the week-day school that a young licentiate would preach at the meeting-house on the Sabbath, and also meet with the Sabbath-school after service; and though a stranger in the place, it may well be imagined a good congregation assembled, and their anticipations were more than realized or gratified, and the Sabbath-school greatly encouraged. "The Lord was there," aiding in the dispensation of truth, and stimulated Christians to pray. Meetings were appointed for prayer and conference, and soon a cloud of mercy betokened a refreshing from the presence of the Lord. The young preacher visited and prayed, expostulated with indifferent professors in his affectionate manner, and warned the impenitent by timely exposition of

Arrival at, and labors in Stow's Square.

Scripture, desiring them to listen to the providences of God, which were frequently occurring in the voice of mortality around them; the uncertainty of life; the certainty of death, the need of securing "the one thing needful," which NOW was freely offered them, which was the only accepted time. (His labors were arrested for a few days by his being taken down with the fever and ague. This increased the anxiety of the community, having become considerably enlisted in the all-important subject of religion; but a kind Providence soon permitted him to ride, and carry the good news of peace on earth and good will to men.) A day of fasting and prayer and confession of sin was appointed; a protracted meeting was suggested; an invitation was sent to Rev. Mr. Burchard to come and lead the sacramental host of God. The people all united harmoniously in prayer and in increased effort, and in every way to be ready for the conflict at hand. The spirit of God pervaded the mass of mind. The house of worship was thoroughly cleansed. A room and seats for all inquirers were prepared, with provisions for light, etc. The day appointed to commence Mr. B. did not arrive, on account of sickness, but the meeting was opened with prayer, and the work of the Lord went on. It was evidently His own work; there was no halting. Ministers around came in. They were surprised and astonished. Some consecrated themselves, and entered the work.

Extensive work of grace. There was no unusual noise. The enemy stood aghast. "The slain of the Lord were many." "For Thy name's sake, oh, Lord God of Israel!" went up from the sanctuary, from every altar of prayer in the social circle, and around the family altar. Truly, every room was a consecrated spot, from the cellar to the attic. In the barns, in the orchards, and in the woods, all were vocal with the voice of supplication, the very air echoing the sincerity of the petitions that were offered. During the entire convocation there was no unnecessary confusion apparent. It seemed like the glorious Advent, when the shepherds were watching their flocks by night. On the fourth day Mr. and Mrs. Burchard arrived, and entered immediately into the work. A room was appropriated for her use, and the little children flocked around her for religious instruction. The Holy Spirit graciously blessed her endeavors to draw them to Jesus. How precious the promises appeared to the little ones, and their thirsty souls were ready to drink the truth; while at the same hour it came rolling down from the pulpit, just as the moral law came issuing from Mount Sinai to the wondering multitudes at the foot of the mountain. In the crowded anxious room Mr. Wickes and Mr. Monroe, with laboring Christian brethren, faithful to their trust, were with prayerful interest leading inquiring sinners to the foot of the blessed cross of their Divine Lord. There had been repeated revivals and protracted efforts, in which great good had been done in the cause of Christ, at Stow's Square. God had blessed and graciously given success to the honored instruments, whose memory is still "like as ointment poured forth;" but such as was now in progress had never before been witnessed—so extensive, so harmonious. And when the multitude from abroad dispersed at the close of the meetings, Christians felt the importance of the Savior's command to "watch and pray, lest ye enter into temptation, and be not weary of well-doing."

CHAPTER III.

PASTORAL LABORS.

MR. WICKES continued his incessant labors with this people, except at intervals, when called to attend other successful protracted efforts. Father Dutton of Champion exchanged pulpits with him, to receive a large accession of members into the church, who then saw the importance of having an ordained minister.

They accordingly requested the Black River Association to ordain Mr. W., and with several other candidates he was ordained Feb. 6th, 1833. The important and solemn vows then made had a great influence on his spiritual life in after years, as well as usefulness in building up the cause of the Redeemer's kingdom. Faithful labors were much needed.

Ordination.

The Lord Jesus taught his disciples to pray "the Lord of the harvest to send forth laborers into his harvest, for the harvest was great but the laborers were few." The instruction of young converts, the Sabbath School, also the eradicating intemperance from the church as well as the community, and the intolerable crying sin of slavery demanded that ministers of the gospel "should lift up their warning voices and cry aloud and spare not."

The Sabbath preceding June 18th, 1833 Mr. Wickes invited the entire congregation to be present on

Marriage.

Tuesday evening at the solemnization of the marriage ceremony which was to take place.

Long before the appointed hour, every available spot was filled about the church with vehicles of every imaginable description from all the surrounding country. The Rev. C. D. Pickens of Lowville took his place in front of the tall old fashioned pulpit, as Mr. Wickes and Miss Cynthia Wilcox, daughter of Capt. Jesse Wilcox, and preceded by Mr. Townsend and Miss Maria Brigham took their places facing the congregation, Mr. Pickens pronounced the words which made them husband and wife, when to the surprise of all but a few, Mr. Wickes and bride turned around and the second couple took their places and were by him united in marriage. The four then took their seats when Mr. Pickens ascended to the pulpit, and delivered a discourse* from the text Matt. XIX: 6. "What therefore God hath joined together let not man put asunder." With the following heads:

I. God hath joined together church and ministry.

II. God hath joined holiness and happiness, let no man separate them.

III. God hath joined sin and misery, and no man can separate them.

IV. God hath joined man and wife. Let none sever the holy wedlock that God sanctions. The happiness of families, neighborhoods, communities and nations depends on the sacredness of this institution.

Visit to Parents. *Pastorate.* They immediately made a short visit to his parents at Albany, N. Y. He remained in Stows Square over four years, the last of which he spent a portion of his time as secretary for the Sabbath School Union Society of Lewis Co., and when winding

* This was culled from memory of the author.

up his labors, the State Secretary of S. S., wrote him not to "*leave* at his peril;" the children throughout the county knew and were drawn to him by his friendly manner to them.

Among other calls, was the earnest repeated solicita-tions of the church in Antwerp, to come back to that place. After much prayer and fasting, he concluded it was the Lord's will that he should turn his steps that way. In Sept., 1836, he moved there with his family. This change was a new era in his life. When he went to Antwerp in 1831, he was but a strip-ling, David like, with only his "sling and stone." Now he had become somewhat acquainted with the campaigns of war, and though he had a great desire for the good of the place, yet to lay a new siege when the enemy had barricaded it on every side, looked rather formid-able. The church still depended on the Home Mission-ary Society for aid. Through Mr. Wickes influ-ence, being one of the trustees of the Black River Religious Institute, Mr. Whitford had been appointed Professor of Mathemathics and was just moving his family to Watertown, whose counsels and sympathy had been like parents, and the loss of their important help he severely felt, still there were other dear friends and the Lord who had been his helper was the same, his cause was just as dear to him and where he looked for help in every approaching trial.

<small>Call to Ant-werp.</small>

<small>Loss of friendly aid.</small>

The church and society soon began to gird themselves up for the work, though iniquity had, and was, rolling in like a flood, it was evident "the Lord did lift up a standard against it," for soon they were enabled to support the gospel without the aid of foreign

<small>State of Society.</small>

help. Immoralities and errors in practice and doctrine began to disappear before the light of truth. Christians of different names became more harmonious, ran together for prayer and conference. Four years and a half, not a month and but a few weeks passed it was thought but there were conversions to the Lord Jesus.

Mr. W. gave frequent lectures on temperance and anti-slavery, in the neighborhoods around. Sometimes in late hours become so weary he would fall asleep on his way home in his vehicle, while the sagacity of his faithful horse would take him through diverging cross roads, and snow banks in safety, or give some signal for direction. In those indefatigable labors there were good brethren in the church that often accompanied and strengthened him in the work of the Lord.

Indefatigable Labors.

Sabbath School Work. The Sabbath School numbered some over a hundred and fifty while he was superintendent.

Reformatory Labor. Preaching on the seventh commandment to the annoyance of some fastidious persons, one of the trustees told him he had preached the bread out of his mouth; his reply was, that he must preach the truth whether men would hear or forbear. A clerk in one of the stores said to one of the elders a day or two after, Mr. W. had preached most immodest language and to prove it took out of his pocket a slip of paper on which he had penciled several sentences, the elder showed him they were passages from the Bible, he was speechless. Mr. W. was threatened with being rode on a rail, etc. The ladies met and organized a Moral Reform society auxiliary to the parent society in New York. In a few months there were a hundred names enrolled, and twenty copies of the Moral Reform Advocate and Family Guardian subscribed for and distributed monthly, also a sufficient sum raised for a life membership for their pastor's wife. "The pure in heart shall see God" said our blessed Saviour. They did not cease their efforts, the ladies repeatedly sent delegates to the conventions at Utica also Mr. W. was sent as a delegate at the same time and place, to the anti-slavery convention.

CHAPTER IV.

CORRESPONDENCE, DURING HIS EARLY MINISTRY.

THE following extracts from correspondence during the early ministry of Mr. Wickes are given as showing the blessed outpouring of the Holy Spirit while engaged in his arduous labors, and his entire dependence on God during the years of his pastoral work.

Written to L. A. Wickes from ANTWERP, May 16th, 1831.

DEAR SIR.

Letter from Antwerp. You will doubtless be willing and perhaps desirous to hear concerning the Sabbath here, I send a few lines inclosed in your bundle. Elder Grey was here, and the largest congregation was assembled that has met during this season, but from what I could gather from the conversation of many nearly all were disappointed. The day was fine, and the weather extremely warm, but the north wind which was blown upon the soul from the mouth of the Greenlander so chilled the hearts of the children of God that it caused many to shake. Our prayer meeting in the evening was conducted with the same spirit. The house was crowded with the vain and giddy youth, and many of the professors felt an anguish of soul for their lost condition when they entered the house. But Satan came also. Our leader opened the meeting with a lengthy prayer, and immediately commenced talking and continued his cold heartless conversation for near an hour. The effect was visible upon every heart, upon the impenitent as well as upon the professor. Many of the impenitent left the house before he had done speaking. The prayers which were afterwards made seemed to partake of the climate and air that surrounded them. Our meeting broke up and the congregation dispersed, but not with that satisfaction which was visible the Friday evening previous. We had a funeral discourse delivered last Thursday by Br. H., well calculated to keep up the courage of the wicked to persevere in their wickedness. I think that S. himself could not have done better. He (H.) has left another appointment for the next Sabbath to preach all day. You will doubtless understand why he means to preach here on Sabbath; we have gathered a little of the reasons from some of his society but I forbear to mention them, God can bring good out of evil. And now, dear sir, we wish you to consult the Lord, and see if it will not be for His glory and for the interest of the blessed Redeemer that you should be here next Sabbath at least. Much anxiety prevails among the professors and there is manifested a very great disappointment among the impenitent. Oh that God would direct. I am sensible that some are willing to trust the Lord but how many put their whole trust in Him, He alone knows. If you should attend the meeting at Brownsville I beseech you to have us remembered in your prayers. We hope your return will not be long protracted.

Yours in the Lord,

L. A. WICKES.   ARCHD. WHITFORD.

ANTWERP, May 23rd, 1831.

DEAR BROTHER.

<small>Situation in Antwerp.</small> I this moment received your letter of the 18th, having received the one you wrote the 20th, on Saturday last, first having been mislaid, I did not receive in season. The reason why I trouble you with a letter so soon, is because I find no mention made in either of your letters concerning your having received the clothing you sent for by R. Randall, but on the contrary it appears from the date of the 18th, that you had not received them. They were sent agreeable to your request by the stage on Monday the 16th, and until this morning I had supposed you to have received them. With regard to the contents of your letter as respects the coldness of our church you will know when you get here, and if you think it not best to stay with us may the Lord direct you, much anxiety prevails for your return nevertheless. If you do not stay and it is the Lord's will we must submit.

Yours in haste,
ARCHD. WHITFORD.

SACKETS HARBOR, July 20th, 1831.

DEAR BROTHER WHITFORD.

<small>Answer to above</small> I take a moment's opportunity to inform you, that I am alive as yet although my health is very poor. My lungs are in a very precarious condition, I can not talk but a very few minutes without injuring them very much. I have taken a trip to Kingston, U. C. On my return I was so sea-sick that I stood over the side of the steam boat about twenty miles, I think it will be for my good, but it was a hard medicine. But as is the old

saying, "no smart no cure." I attended a prayer meeting in Kingston and you may judge whether I kept my tongue still or not. I received many pressing invitations to stay at Brockville, the minister of that place was at Kingston. He acted as tho' the thunderings of the Almighty were breaking over his head. He said he could "not get more than six or seven of his church together, for a prayer meeting." I told him he had not got the carcass there, for where the carcass was the eagles would be gathered together. I told them there was not smell enough, to draw them together, for probably one eagle might eat up all his meat.

The church in Antwerp is not the worst yet. I am glad Mr. W. has accepted the invitation which was written to him in behalf of the church. I hope he will suit all, for if he does, you can have a meeting house. Although he may not be as powerful as some other men, yet he will be a leader for you, and is able to give you good *doctrine*, and you know if you only PRAY, his words will be blessed, and your church will be built up. And Dear Brother you MUST *pray* for there never was a time, when this county was in such commotion as at the present, for the *devil* is on his stilts, trying to raise the flag-staff of hell. If there ever was a time when Michael and his angels were contending with the devil, and his angels, it is now. And if ever the church was called upon to pray it is now.

<small>To the Church in Antwerp.</small> And to the church I would say, do not let a moment pass unoccupied, for a moment gone is gone to all eternity. If, beloved friends, God has brought you from darkness to light, let that light shine and break forth into a great flame, for the children of God are

the light of the world, a city that is set on a hill which can not be hid." If *you* have the *Lord* for *your* portion who can be against you. The enemy of souls would delight to have *you* sleep, but you are of the day, (if you are God's by regeneration,) and therefore must not sleep, but be up and doing, the more you devote yourself to God the greater will be your blessing, and as I have often told you (and yourself also know) that salvation must come out of Zion. Do not rest 'till she shall bring forth sons and daughters unto God. Take the same *promise* that God gives, and hand it back to him as an argument why he should bless you. "When the enemy shall come in like a flood, the Spirit of the Lord shall lift up a standard against him." This promise you may plead in Antwerp. Do not be discouraged, if you do not SEE the rain descending, for Elijah prayed *seven times* and kept his servant running to the top of the mountain to see if the cloud arose. But do not pray *once*, and then *stop*, but continue praying for one thing until you get it. And be careful that you do not *limit* God by asking him for little things, and thinking He will not give great things, for the greatest thing for which you can ask, is but a small thing for Him to give, and pray with *all* your soul. I do not always forget you when I go to God in prayer. Tho' my body may be absent from you, yet my spirit is often with you. Perseverance in prayer, will accomplish almost anything, that is if you pray in the Spirit. Therefore go forth breaking your pitchers, holding up the light, and sounding the trumpet, that is breaking the heart, the light of the gospel may be seen. I often feel as tho' I could not stay away from you. But beloved friends I do not know as God will ever let me speak to you again. But I shall visit you, how soon I can not tell, but I shall come as soon as God will. And now tho' I am far from you, yet feeling a great interest in the eternal welfare of that people, I would make a request, that in every petition which you offer to God, to remember the dear *youth* of Antwerp, and I do endeavor to do the same, probably when they are resting on their beds of ease at midnight. And always remember to pray for your most unworthy friend and unfaithful brother in the Lord.

To ARCHD. WHITFORD.   LEWIS A. WICKES.

About a month later he writes to his parents from

CHAMOUNT. Aug. 12th, 1831.

MOST AFFECTIONATE AND DEAR PARENTS:

Aug. 12, 1831. Chamount.

You undoubtedly feel anxious to hear from me by this time, as the last letter which I wrote was on the steam boat on Lake Ontario. I visited Kingston, and returned to Sacketts Harbor, and was as sea-sick as I want to be. Since that I have been traveling from place to place and my health has improved very much, especially since I came here. The bay separates the village, (if village it may be called.) It lays about half way between Brownville and Cape Vincent, on the stage road. It is called a sickly place, but thus far it has been a benefit to *my* health, whatever it may prove hereafter. There has been a seven days meeting here, and the number attending was very small. I presume there were not over one hundred impenitent souls who attended the meeting. Out of that number about thirty were hopefully converted, which we think was encouraging, taking all things into consideration. The preaching was in a *small barn half filled* with *hay* and some of the people had not a Bible in their houses, and some hardly knew enough to read one if they had it. Some houses where I visited, the pigs, geese and children were all in the straw together. But this is not a fair specimen of all the inhabitants, for there are some quite intelligent and very nice people, and fine stone buildings. There are Presbyterians, Congregationalists, Close Communion, Open Communion, Free Will and Seven Day Baptists, Methodists, Christians, Universalists, Deists, Atheists, Nothingarians and Everythingarians, in this town (Lyme). I have rowed from place to place, so much from one side of the bay to the other I have made several blisters on my hands. Yet it is pleasant to work where the harvest is already ripe and the Lord is going before us. I often feel that the task, or rather the *work*, is too great for me to touch. Yet God uses the feeble means which men would despise, to build up his own cause and in so doing may be seen more visibly the power and glory of God. It may be said that the harvest truly is great and the laborers are few, pray YE therefore the Lord of the harvest to send forth laborers into the vineyard. I have had so many invitations from one place and another that my greatest trial is to find out what duty is. I expect to go to Cape Vincent Tuesday next to attend a four days meeting and as requests are quite urgent, may continue the meeting some days longer, if the providence of God seem to favor it. The Lord is at work through this whole region, and the devil rages with all his might. He is walking on his stilts, and swinging his hat, and the dialect of hell rolling from his lips. I would write much more but time will not permit. As soon as I can get time I have a sheet full for sister A. M. Give my love to all and tell them to pray for your most unworthy son.

LEWIS A. WICKES.

P. S. We have been here about three weeks and formed a Presbyterian church of about thirty members, besides what go to the Baptist and Methodist, and I formed a Sabbath school of forty children.

L. A. W.

Letter to sister, Oct. 11, 1831. The promised letter to his sister seems so full of Christian experience and so well adapted to instruct the young it will be its own apology for its appearance in full.

ANTWERP, Oct. 11, 1831.

MY VERY DEAR SISTER:

I thought that this evening should be devoted to writing a short letter to you, but my room has been filled with company till this very moment (now about half-past eleven o'clock). But if I do not avail myself of this opportunity I know not when I shall find time to write, for I am busy from morning to morning generally. God, I believe, grants me his helping hand. * * * And I will keep my promise to write to you. I am told, Dear Sister, "you have found an interest in the Blessed Redeemer since I left Troy." This is the greatest blessing which the Lord could have given you, if it is founded upon *the Rock*.

I find the best thing I can do is to often *commune with my own heart and converse with God*. You are not altogether unacquainted with your heart, if you are a Christian, yet you cannot know *too* much about it and a little advice I here would give you, if you will accept of it from so unworthy a brother as I am.

And in doing this, I would recommend that you

become acquainted with a few things which I will mention, and the reasons why:

And, First, you should *become* ACQUAINTED with the *character of God.* You will find, the more you see of the beauties and holiness of God, the more lovely it will appear and the more you will desire to see of His excellencies, and therefore you will see more of your own vileness and sin, which will cause you to be oftener at the throne of grace, till you may feel, when comparing with God's purity, to say with Job, "I abhor myself and repent in dust and ashes." And the more of your sins you see, the nearer you will approach to God, till life shall end. You will feel more of the obligations you are under to God and the easier you will discover the hidings of God's face. For when a Christian lives in the dark, he is entirely insensible of his real condition.

And in the second place, I would advise you to become well acquainted with your own heart. The heart is deceitful above all things and desperately wicked. One great reason why so many persons imbibe error is because they have no real knowledge of their own hearts. They do not love the idea of looking into their hearts. But the Christian may live so as to have the Grace of God so apparent that it may be his spiritual barometer to guide his spiritual life.

Some people wonder why it is that the nearer the Christian comes to the Spirit of the Savior the more wickedness there is in his heart. But their wonder is not in the right channel. There is no more wickedness, but more light coming in shows what is contained in the heart. To illustrate my meaning, take a simple comparison. For instance, you sweep a dusty room which is perfectly dark and you discover no dust at all. You open a shutter and let in a little light you will discover some dust, you open another shutter and let in a little more light and you see more, you open a third and still more, and so on, till so much light comes into the room that the dust appears so dense that it seems almost impossible for you to breathe. Now there is no more dust in the last case than in the first, when the room was perfectly dark, but the light has shown what was in the room. Just so with the Christian's heart. The more Gospel Light there is shining into it the more the pollution of his heart it presents to him, yet it *creates* none, but is the instrument of driving sin from its throne. And in becoming more acquainted with your heart it will cause you to be more *devoted* and, my Dear Sister, a praying Christian is worth all other kinds of Christians. But this subject comes in more fully bye and bye. I shall therefore close for this time, as it is now about half-past one. Should this be my last hour to-night, how should I appear before God's awful bar? A glorious thought that enters the whole soul and runs through the mind. God is just and all will be well and my trust is all stayed on His Almighty Arm, who says: "Fear not, I am thy shield and thy exceeding great reward."

Wednesday morning, Oct. 12th. Another and Third subject you should acquaint yourself with is the Devil. If an enemy is about to break into a house and you wish to guard against the attack you will want to understand the manner he is expected to attack or break in, for then you will be prepared to meet him. If you are not acquainted with the devices of the Devil, he may enter into the heart and damage the furniture there before you are aware. And here I would say, if I may be allowed to express my mind: A cold, stupid, professor's head is the best workshop the Devil ever had, and you will find, the more you acquaint yourself with the character of the Devil, the better prepared you will be to guard against his wiles. And he is a *subtile fellow* and tries every way possible to enter into the heart of the Christian. But if you will only watch and pray you will be able to discern his character. But without prayer you will be so completely under the direction of his diabolical influence that you will oppose much of the *real piety* with which every Christian should be endowed. This is the reason why so many professors are found quarreling with the dealings of the Almighty. They have not grace enough to take as low a station as God delights to bless. And because God delights to bless those who appear and really are humble, they will often raise their reproachful hand against the child of God. And now, sister, let these few suggestions not be wholly lost. They are the commencement of a few hints that may run off the point of my pen.

I might have been more lengthy on each topic, but time will not permit. I have been appointed agent of the building committee for building a meeting-house in this place and it occupies considerable of my time. And it now is time for me to subscribe myself Your most unworthy and sinful but sincere and affectionate brother,
LEWIS.

Give my love to parents, brother and sisters, grandparents, uncle, aunts, cousins and in short to all inquiring friends. Tell Mrs. B. a young man, one of her young friends, while I was at Chamount, *indulged a hope.* Write soon. L. A. W.

ANTWERP, Dec. 9, 1831.

MY DEAR PARENTS;

Birthday Letter to Parents. 1831. It was my intention to have written yesterday. I had so much to do it was impossible, it being Thanksgiving day (so called by way of distinction), and the religious exercises of the day were laid upon me. Besides, I had an appointment about three miles from the village, so that I did not return till quite late and my room was too cold to write. These are my reasons why I did not write on my birthday. Yesterday brought me to my twenty-second year. Time, how fast it flies! Since my letter of Dec. 8, 1830, I have passed through various scenes, both temporal and spiritual, as my letters have already shown. I scarcely know how to express my feelings in reviewing the past year. Oh, the ingratitude there is in my heart! It seems at times that there is not so unworthy a creature on the footstool of God as I am. But these feelings are transitory, for soon my proud heart will rise up to such a height in wickedness that I almost forget *where* or what I am. I try to learn the devices of the Devil that I may be able to meet him in his attacks and it seems the more I see of my heart the less I know about it. It is a wonder to me how people can be Armenians when they look into their hearts. I once thought that the work of being prepared for eternity was all done at the time they thought they gave their affections to Christ. But I am convinced of the truth of Whitfield's remark "that the tearing down of the old man and the building up of the new is a work till *death*." The Enemy of souls does not care what degree of feeling a person arrives at if they will only be satisfied, for *he* knows that they will soon come down if they will only make a stop, for there is no neutrality in the cause of Christ. I often begin to reason with myself about being a Christian and I think, what good can I do? I am sure that I do but little, if anything for him, and how can he use me in his immense building? But my prayer is to the Lord: "Make me anything for thine own glory and do with me what seemeth to thee good," and it is my only desire, if I know my own heart, to live to his honor and glory, and when this is not my object may the Lord give me grace to see my crime and enable me to live to him. Since I have been in Antwerp I have had various things to encounter. The prejudices of the people have been very great against the Presbyterians, from the fact that there have been so many ministers in this place who have acted so much like the ungodly that it was almost impossible for me to get near them when I first came here, but now quite a different aspect may be seen, and my leaving causes no small talk among them. Since I returned from the short tour I took for my health in August, it has been improved considerably and my labors have been very numerous. I have raised about $800 here towards a meeting house, got the timber for the frame on the ground and framed, purchased 10,000 feet of lumber, helped measure it out myself and got it partly drawn, and dug the greatest part of ten cords of stone and attended three meetings on each Sabbath, three or more during the week and visited a little from house to house; formed a temperance society of seventy members, etc. For which I would give all the glory to the Lord of Hosts. I have often reflected on my leaving Troy. The feeling that I could not stay there, in consequence of which I started,

not knowing where I went, and to see where the Lord
has led me has been a source of wonder and joy mingled
together with me. For me to say that God has not
blessed my efforts would be saying that which I do not
believe and which would not perhaps be acknowledging
the mercies of God, yet I know, yea, I feel that I am unworthy. Since I have been here there have been between fifteen and twenty hopeful conversions. I will
notice one fact. All seemed to think and did talk as
though nothing could be done and ministers had given it
up for lost, before I ventured here, and in four or five
months the moral aspect had changed so much there
were *three* different ministers that wanted to get in here.
The people said: "We have got one kind minister and
we had rather keep him than run the risk of getting another which perhaps will not suit, etc., etc." I hope my
dear parents will not censure me for boasting. Forbear
with me a little in my folly, for if I glory it is in the
Lord. Yet my glorying will be entirely in vain except
it be blessed by the eternal God. As to temporals I
have nothing particular to say. I have enough to eat
and to drink and am comfortably clothed. They will
raise sixty or seventy dollars for me in this place. It is
more than I expected, for their situation is rather peculiar and I felt it would help the cause of Christ and
therefore I was willing to do all that I could that it
might be built up. They seem to be determined that if I
go away I shall come back again, which I am willing to
do, if it is God's will, but if it is not his will I shall not
come. I saw a notice of a protracted meeting at Mr.
Beman's church; please write the particulars.

I have long felt an inclination and a determination to

write to Grandfather B., but I did not know where he was. Oh, that he might be brought from darkness to light, and have a "new song put in his mouth even praise to God." I feel as though I must see my relatives in Troy, but I must leave it for God to decide. It rejoices me to hear of the conversion of our cousins. I should be pleased to receive a letter from them. I have just had my hair cut, and I will send you a lock of it, that you may see that I am not gray headed yet. Give my respects to all inquiring friends. Tell all to pray for me. And remember your most unworthy son,

LEWIS A. WICKES.

ANTWERP, March 8, 1832.

DEAR PARENTS:

Letter to Parents. The return of this day brings to me the expectation of my parents in receiving a letter. My time is fully occupied, or ought to be. I find it very important to attend to every duty in its appropriate time, and if it is not attended to then, it will be put off too long, both in temporal and spiritual concerns. You know much depends on my motto, "Onward," and the thing will be accomplished. *So in the cause of Christ what ought to be done, can,* SHOULD *be done.* There is much precious time lost among Christians in standing and looking at the work so long, before they take hold of the cause, and then they handle it as careful as they would eggs. But yet how foolish and inconsistent to see Christians so afraid of doing too much for the Lord of Glory. Why is it that the church of God are so dormant. They are truly unfaithful servants. There have been some hopeful conversions since I wrote, no very uncommon cases, however, although they are interesting because they excite interest in Heaven among the angels of God, for there is more joy over one sinner that repenteth, than over ninety and nine just persons that need no repentance; and it should cause joy among the children of God on earth. When the cause of Christ lays near the heart, it will cause the soul to bless the Lord for his wonderful works to the children of men. But when the heart is cold, to hear of the conversion of sinners, has no great effect at all, only to say, "Well!" The Devil is trying his uttermost to conquer the children of God. My heart aches within me, when I think how little the cause of Christ is loved by many of the friends, or rather the *professed* friends of Christ, and—Oh, how little it is loved by them! Yes, how little it is loved by *me* to what it should be.

But yet I think it does look too *dear* to be trampled under foot. And if there is any cause that should be lifted high it is surely the cause of Jesus Christ. You will please to answer this soon, and especially the letter referred to before. Give my love to all inquiring friends, especially brothers and sisters. Remember your son around the domestic altar. I do not forget you about 7 o'clock in the morning. Mrs. Whitford, with whom I board, sends love.

<small>A request for a letter from Dr. Beman's Church in Troy.</small>

I am your affectionate son,

L. A. WICKES

After leaving Antwerp he stopped in Stow's Square, where was a church surrounded by a farming community, and from which he writes as follows:

STOW'S SQUARE, July 13, 1832.

DEAR PARENTS:

Labors Commenced at Stowe's Square, July 13, 1832. Letter To Albany.

I expect you are anxious to hear from me, as I have told you a little about my sickness. My health is improving very fast, far beyond the expectation of every one, although I can feel the effects of it when I exert myself considerable either in mind or body. O, my dear parents, it would be the delight of my heart to visit you, and have a delightful visit with you. But stop! shall I leave dying sinners to grieve away the Spirit of God, and go down to hell for the sake of gratifying one's self? Blessed be God that he has made these lungs strong enough to heave his praises once more and beg for dying sinners' salvation. It is better to wear out in the service of God than to rust out. O, may God keep me from ever laying down its cares till I am laid in the grave! which I often feel will be soon. But blessed be the name of the Lord, he will take his own time. There is some feeling here, but not as much as there should be; sinners are enquiring, and some Christians do feel a *little*. But some of the old members do try my patience, and one old Deacon has a daughter who was as hard as a rock. I talked and prayed with her 'till it seemed as though the father would have me not say another word. But I was determined to obey God rather than man. And God heard and answered prayer, and when she felt so much as to go and ask her father to pray for her, he thought it was only *animal* feeling, and would follow her father in prayer, and yet he would not believe that the Spirit of God was striving with her. She now comes out and takes up her cross in social meetings, and visits her young friends and talks and prays with them, and he begins now to think he does not know, but she *may* be under *Conviction*. O, that God would convert such a Deacon. The young people are beginning to tremble; yesterday God was indeed in our midst at a prayer meeting. We do not have many meetings but what more or less desire the prayers of Christians. They come to the birth, but not enough strength in Zion to bring forth. Do pray that Zion may be strengthened in this place; that sons and daughters may be born unto God. But I must stop writing, for it is most time to commence Bible Class, and as soon as that closes prayer meeting convenes, and I expect God will be in the midst of us, and may the wind of the Holy Ghost blow upon all of us and fill us with faith.

Remember and pray for your unworthy son,

L. A. WICKES.

The following letter from his father shows his wish for the council of his parents on the important step he was meditating of taking.

TROY, Dec. 4, 1832.

DEAR SON:

From Father Wickes on Matrimony. Your last, and undoubtedly the most important letter you ever addressed to your parents, has been received, and when we attempt to answer it we are sensible that it will be only in part. I have not your letter before me, and shall not reply systematically. You inform us that you contemplate marrying, and having mentioned your situation and the character of the person, you ask counsel. What may be written on the subject will not change your purpose or confirm you in the enterprise, perhaps. Ministers have in common with other men, the privilege of marrying, but in all cases the welfare of Christ's kingdom should be the object and end, but very probably while the minister has been engaged in maturing and arranging the connection, souls have been neglected, and finally lost. You say that you have prayed over the subject. Remember my son, that there is no situation in which persons generally are more deceived, than in relation to some desirable and pleasant object they may have in view; their feelings are excited; the whole current of their wishes accompany their petitions, and from the fervor and earnestness exhibited, they are ready without making any allowances for circumstances, to say, I have indications that my contemplated project is favored by Heaven. I say to you, that it will be advisable, and be your bounden duty to marry, provided it will enable, and actually cause you to be a more devoted and an entirely devoted minister of the Gospel; if it will increase in your own soul devotion and active piety; if it will make you more studious in gaining knowledge of God's word, and will make you more indefatigable and laborious in the service of God and the church; more anxious and earnest to be the agent of Christ in pulling sinners out of the fire; if it shall have a tendency to elevate you in every christian and ministerial duty and employment, I say, marry. But if there is the least evidence to be gathered, that it will subtract from your devotedness, as a minister; if it shall lessen active piety in your own soul or life; if it shall divide your affections, and turn them off in any degree from the church, or cause the wretched condition of sinners to be less felt and realized, an exertion in any degree relaxed for their salvation, I say, do not marry. Remember among the excuses made by those who were bidden and invited to come and eat of the supper or feast, one is represented as saying, " I have married a wife," etc. If the tendency should be (which is hardly possible), not to affect in any of these, and other particulars that might be mentioned, your usefulness, neither to add nor diminish, it is then very questionable whether it would be proper. If I could see the person you name, I should say to her, that if she did not intend to excite you to faithfulness, diligence, consecratedness, heavenly mindedness, engagedness and consistency of ministerial character, etc.; if, in fine, she did not intend, by her influence and example, to make you a better man, a better minister, I would enter a solemn protest, and lodge it with the Master of the Assembly of the church in Heaven.

* * * * JONAS WICKES.

MY SON:

You no doubt are waiting anxiously for an answer to your letter, and your father has at last wrote a few lines, but you know he says he had rather write six deeds, than one letter, therefore it always devolves on me; but in relation to your letter, he has said *all that is necessary*, and has left room for me to tell the family news, which is that all enjoy good health, except myself, and I am much better. I have reason to bless the Lord for his mercy towards me in raising me twice from sickness, within four months. It is very healthy in the city at present. * * *

Rev. Mr. Finney is in the city. He preached on Sabbath. Mr. Beman is in New York. I cannot write more now, my hand trembles so it is difficult for me to hold my pen. Will write again soon, if I get strength.

I want you to write. Tell us whether you will visit us this winter.

Your Affectionate Mother,
S. B. WICKES.

STOWS SQUARE, DEC. 10, 1832.

MY DEAR PARENTS:

Birthday Letter of 1832 — Time has rolled another year around, and my business was so pressing on the 8th that I could not attend to writing, therefore I take the earliest opportunity to do it. In looking over the back year, and viewing my life, it looks dark, and every moment of time filled up with sin. Oh, how shameful for a follower of Christ! But the dealings of God towards me have been very kind, and his forbearance— Oh, how great! But my ingratitude to God, how surprising! Two years and a half have rolled away since I left your kind, affectionate, and paternal roof, with the expectation of probably going into some secular employment. And, (though not worthy of having such a comparison) like Jacob, went out not knowing whither I went. The money I had with me at that time was $7.00. On that I started my pilgrimage with a heavy heart, and so downcast a look that the stage passengers marked it, and asked the occasion of it. I then had my eye on the western region, though only known to myself, with the intention of never again visiting the city of Troy. Not that I any less esteemed my parents' roof. No, never! never! My heart has always felt for you, my dear parents, above every object, and shall ever continue till life shall end. Although I have for a moment thought that Pa by his never writing, said, "You may be your own counselor." But soon hushed to silence those wicked thoughts, with the most minute reflections; his family is large, his riches are none, and his *fingers* support them. But I did feel, and do still feel, that my sphere of usefulness in Troy would be nothing, and perhaps it is altogether best that it should be so, and I think I can say I bless God it has been so. Whatever my former *intentions were*, God has brought me where I very little, nay, never thought of being. "How wonderful are His counsels, and His ways past finding out!" He has never left me without friends, at least *professedly* so. I have never been naked, and he has always stood by me in trouble, and so far helped me through, and it is my determination to obey his commands as far as I know them, and when I have done all, I shall only be an unprofitable servant. To enter into a minute detail of the past year, I cannot at this time, neither would it be advisable. But I find in looking back a year, I find much to be lamented over, though I have not been left to commit any outbreaking sins. Yet I find it is the feelings of the heart God looks at, and therefore it is to have the *whole life* before God, such as would be pleasing to Him. I am well aware that there are many things in my life which can, and under God, shall be loped off. For I find it is utterly impossible for me to have access to God, without living in some faint degree up to his requirements. I believe one great reason why Christians do not enjoy higher attainments, is they do not *aim* at high and holy attainments. They take the character of Christians that have gone before them, whereas they should take the Lord Jesus Christ, and I know of no other way by which they can possibly attain to that qualification which is required, (perfection). I know for me to live near to God, I shall have to make a great effort, and that too, against a very light and trifling nature, that takes delight in sin. And I say to myself sometimes, when shall I be delivered from this *body* of death. If to be a good man, it was necessary to be a *great* man, I should ever faint of ever, yea, *despair* of ever gaining the point. But as goodness has nothing to do with greatness, I set my face towards the former, praying God to assist me for His great name's sake. If the Lord will use me to tear down the devil's kingdom, I am willing he should do it, and bless his name for it. If the Lord holds me up, I shall not fall, yet I often think that it is actually requisite for me to be knocked down to humble the pride of my heart. For God sets people low, that He may lift them up, but the devil lifts people up, that He may throw them down, (Matt. 4). And I know if I will only abase myself, God will exalt me, and I find no better place than at the foot of the cross, yea, infinitely beneath the *dust* that the cross rests upon. Oh, it is sweet communing with God, when I can lose myself in the glorious *will* of Heaven. My heart often makes me think of the bottomless pit; open the doors, and it is a black looking place, and the smoke of sin ascends from it, into all parts of the system, and spreads a stench all around, yet the fire of the Holy Ghost can purify and make it clean. It is true "the heart is deceitful, and above all things desperately wicked," and mine is "like a cage of unclean birds, or like the inside of one of the ancient sepulchers." My health is good as can be expected, for one that is all the time on the *go*. I have thought sometimes that if I was engaged in any other employment, I could not endure it. To let you see how much God enables me to do, (and I hope for His glory), I will give you the appointments of this week: 9th, Conference, 6 o'clock, meeting house; Monday, meeting three miles off, in the evening; Tuesday, Tracts Distributers meeting; Wednesday, Bible Class; Thursday, Thanksgiving, 10 o'clock preaching—evening, Union Meeting; Friday, Conference, mile off; Saturday evening, meet the young people three miles off northwest, to form another Bible Class, besides some small appointments, and visiting more or less every week, besides the duties of the Sabbath, and preparations for it. So the Lord enables me to go from one week to another. I have a severe cold, which seems to be inclined to settle on my lungs, and makes me very hoarse. I have yet to ride three miles, and attend a meeting in a very wicked neighborhood. The Lord can work even there, for since I commenced having meetings there, there have been six family altars erected, for which I would bless the Lord. The Universalists and Christians form one broad phalanx against us. But the devil is a conquered devil. Christ bruised his head. If I can only have my Saviour with me, I fear not what wicked men shall do to me. "Trust in the Lord and do good," and God's promises are sure, they are, yea, and amen in Christ Jesus.

Please write soon, and give my love to all friends, and pray for your affectionate, though unworthy son.

L. A. WICKES.

CHAPTER V.

CORRESPONDENCE DURING PASTORAL WORK FROM 1833 TO 1841.

THE following very interesting letter to his parents shows his natural affectionate cheerfulness, consecration to his work and solicitude for his friends.

STOWS SQUARE, Feb. 13th, 1833.

MY DEAR PARENTS.

I have but a short time to write but I will improve that. I have been very busy ever since I wrote you in preparing for Ordination which took place on the 6th of February. I had often thought of the solemnities of such a time, but *never did in any measure realize the intense interest of such a time.* Oh! my parents you can know nothing of the peculiar feelings of one kneeling down, and hands of the Ambassadors of Christ placed on the heads, and lifting up their prayers to Almighty God for the descent of the Holy Spirit upon him. Jehovah looking down, angels witnessing the scene, and devils waiting the results. If ever I needed the agency of God's spirit it is now, and if ever your prayers were asked for it is *now*. Oh! withhold them not. The world is looking upon me, and expecting more from me now than they ever did before. Without the spirit of Christ I shall utterly fail of accomplishing my duty. Last night I stood in a different place than I ever did before. I was as people say " tying the knot." It was a large circle of friends and connections. I thought I should be very much " dashed " but I spent a season in prayer for help, and God heard and answered so that one old Dutchman present said to use his own language, " It vas done so schlick as von goos egg." Wine was not brought near the banquet but in lieu pure cold water had the place. Perhaps you may be surprised when I tell you it is the *third* wedding I was ever at. I am not fully prepared to say what duty is in many cases of matrimony, but I suppose that now is the time for me to know if ever. It is, whether it is duty to solemnize a marriage where one is a Christian and the other is not. I have been in hopes to see it discussed by some able pen, but as yet I have looked in vain. I have been reading a piece in the Evangelist on " Unhallowed Marriages," but the writer in my estimation does not touch the point where the greatest objection lies.

If it is wrong in every circumstance and condition for Christians and unbelievers to be connected then, surely, it is for a minister to connect them. Therefore the whole question comes to this, " Is there *any case* where it is lawful for believers and unbelievers to be joined in matrimonial connection ?"

I hope sister A. M. will not indulge the thought that she cannot write. Why she can do as well as I when first I wrote to H. It is practice that makes perfect, and perseverance accomplishes almost every thing. Am sorry C. has left the seminary; poor girl, tell her to apply her mind to something useful, and improve it for usefulness. I must close at present and go off three miles through a tremendous snow storm to attend a Bible class, where I have over fifty to attend and it takes me about three hours to get through it. I feel that I need more of the help of God, for the more I am promoted the more pride I have to fight against. You know what a proud family we are, and how the Lord works to humble us, and if I can be humble it is a great blessing. The state of religion is low, we think, but strangers think there is a great feeling, and I suppose there is compared with other places. I have many calls to help in protracted meetings. If I was loose from this people I would spend much of my time in them. Just now I do not feel it would be my duty. I have attended only six this year of from six to fourteen days continuance. May the Lord give me health to labor much more. Love to all the family. Pray much for your son

L. A. WICKES.

During his pastorate in Stows Square, Mr. Wickes was repeatedly called to assist in revival work in other neighborhoods, from one of which he writes to his home society as follows:

GREIG, Sept. 4, 1833.

DEAR BRETHREN,

Early labors. Meeting in Greig, Lewis Co., N. Y.

I know it is your desire to build up the cause of the Redeemer, and to have the kingdom of the Saviour advanced in every place, and duty seems pointed out very plain here for me. There is but a very little help here (that is, human help), but God is present, and the work has commenced.

The whole community seems to be on the move. Br. Crandal cannot be here but a little, and Sabbath is his communion, and cannot leave. And the whole charge of the meeting is resting upon your unworthy minister. Br. Porter and Br. Stevens say it is plain that I should not leave here in such a time as this. Br. Bush will preach for you a part of the day. While I am writing Br. C. is preaching. Some Christians are in the room below praying and agonizing with groanings and tears that God would bless the truth. Brethren you are remembered in every season of prayer. And do now get hold of God's arm and Salvation will come, and that it may deluge this whole region is the earnest prayer of your unworthy Servant. Brethren come over and help us, pray for us.

L. A. WICKES.

Assists in revival work.

Saturday morning. The harvest is truly great but the laborers are few. There are many sinners under great convictions. Several conversions and some backsliders brought back to their Father in Heaven we trust, and there is a prospect of a great work. O pray for us, for this is a heathenish place. May God make *this "wilderness* bud and blossom like the rose." Claim the promises of God and victory will turn on Zion's side. In haste,

L. A. WICKES.

Continued Greig, Lewis Co. N. Y.

GREIG, Sept. 7, 1833.

AFFECTIONATE DEAR WIFE,

I dropped you a line Saturday. I will give a little more encouragement. Yesterday we had all the

Early labors as an Evangelist.

wicked that the town contains. There were more Universalists together than I have seen together for years. I preached from the 23d verse of the 6th chapter of Romans. "Wages of sin is death," etc. I preached two hours. God helped me to present the truth more plainly from that text than I ever did before, (it suited my own mind better). And such a squirming I never saw before. It made me think of running a pole in a hornet's nest. They fought and quarrelled all the intermission. Christians were praying. They saw for the first time the justice of God in the damnation of sinners. Arrows of conviction flew thick and fast. I could feel the prayers of Christians running through every nerve and muscle of the soul and body. God seemed to say to many "This is the way; walk ye in it." In the afternoon I preached one hour and three quarters from Malachi 3d, 18. God was in the midst. And it was so late we did not have a meeting in the evening but appointed meetings in all their houses. Brothers Porter, Dea. Abby and myself had a precious time at the house where we put up. There were four conversions, one near 60 years old, God was here indeed. They were happy this morning (perhaps too much so.) They are singing the "Bower of Prayer" and "Old Ship Zion." God has strengthened me beyond my expectations, I can not tell how many have been converted and reclaimed. I know and can enumerate ten or twelve converted and fifteen or twenty reclaimed. The meeting will continue, how long I cannot say, several submitted right in preaching time yesterday. Error was dug up from the bottom. Pray for us, the immense field is ripe ready for the harvest and the laborers are few. I staid at Dea. Pinney's one night, preached in the evening, he got full to overflowing. I cannot tell when I shall be home. The Lord will bless you. I will write again if I stay long. Farewell.

Your Husband,

L. A. WICKES

WEST LEYDEN, Oct. 5, 1833.

DEAR WIFE: I am in a strait between two and I hardly know what to do, but as things now are, the decision of the church and all the brethren is that I must stay here as there is no help except Father Kimble. Mr. Sawyer must leave. There is a prospect for good. One we hope has given her heart to God. It was a very interesting case. I have not time to give the particulars. I expect Mr. Murdock will preach for you if he does not let the brethren have their meeting. Tell Bros. Bates, L. Stevens and A. Stevens to put on their armour and come up here, for God demands it of them. Tell the church to pray for their unworthy minister.

[Marginal notes: Early labors, West Leyden, Oct. 5th, 1833. Lewis Co. N. Y. Anxiety for work for souls.]

Your Husband.

L. A. WICKES.

P. S:—Dea. Dewey writes, Oct. 16, West Leyden, the work of the Lord still progressing. New and interesting cases occurring, says new voices heard in prayer he never heard before from some new converts and backsliders. There seemed to be a desire that the work should not cease. All united in requesting prayer.

STOWS SQUARE, Dec. 8, 1834.

DEAR AND BELOVED PARENTS: This morning brings me to that period when you expect that I will give you something of a history of the last year of the life of your unworthy son. But to give you a minute description of past events it will not be in my power, neither would I be doing you any kindness by giving so black a list. The two last years of my life are filled up with momentous responsibilities. When I reflect upon the voluntary obligations that I have taken upon myself I am almost ready to wish that I had never begun them. My ordination vows. The administering of the gospel ordinance, the responsibility of being "an example to the flock," the choice of a companion for life, with the duties that are connected, the solemnizing of marriage contracts, etc., are in my mind of no small moment. The past has now taken its flight into eternity, and with all the events of life are gone, and as to the effects the judgment must bring them to light. When I view them as a Holy God must look upon them they look like one, long, broad and deep catalogue that cannot be numbered. But yet blessed be God for his abounding grace that may have put now and then a very small white spot in the list. For it is only through the mercy of God, that I am permitted to do any good in this world. O, how humble I should be for the goodness that God has bestowed upon me. But alas, how hard and stubborn this heart is! How unwilling to walk on the ground that Christ has laid down for a servant of God to walk on! I have been led almost (like Jeremiah) to curse the day of my birth. How easy it is for me to point out how the Christian should live, what should be the manner of his

Birthday letter, reviewing 1834.

conversation, the path of virtue and happiness. But, O, how hard to put them in practice, I have to take hold of my heart with a rope and drag it after the duties that I know that I should do, I am sensible that I have no other way to live but by crucifying the "old man with his deeds," and this in opposition to the natural propensities of the heart. Among other things of great moment, it has pleased the Lord to make me a *parent*. To describe the feeling I *have* often, is a thing I cannot do. It is sometimes the hardest thing to believe I am a parent. When I get the child in my arms I often think I have one of my parent's children in my hand, that it is a brother or a sister of mine, and at other times it appears like one that God has placed under my protection and parental care. Thus I find myself greatly tried, for the example that I must set before the child must be one that directs its mind towards heaven and which will gloriously prepare it for heaven. In order to do it I find I have much to do, and much that will make me solemn and circumspect; my natural lightness and habitual levity with which I am addicted cause me a great deal of trouble, and then to have them affect our little daughter, as they probably will, is a thought that I do not relish at all. She is a candidate for another world, for heaven or for hell. Shall I be an instrument of adding to the number of damned souls or to the number of the rank of Satan? May God forbid it! I believe as God has placed this immortal under my care that its salvation or damnation in a greater or less degree is devolving on me. God is ready on his part to save it, and if we as the parents neglect our duty the child may be lost! But I sometimes think I am over anxious as to its future prospects. 1st, I cannot bear that she should be of no use in the world. To train up a cipher in the world I think God would not be honored. 2nd, If I train her up and she enters the list of the opposers to the work of God and whose influence will be on the side of the devil and whose efforts will be to destroy the works of holiness, and whose eternity will be spent cursing God and blaspheming her Maker, are thoughts that I cannot harbor with composure. For I hate the devil too much to build up his kingdom. I am by *my own* efforts trying to destroy the works of the devil and I cannot bear to do more by one act to build up the enemies' ranks than I have done in all my life to pull it down. And then again I look at the prevalence which popery may have over our land and see the consequences that may follow if she lives a devoted child of God, I feel that it is only the power of an holy God that can sustain in such an hour. And should she relinquish her faith in Christ how much the cause of Christ would suffer and be reproached. I have other feelings and reflections that the church will look to me for an example how to bring up their families, and here if I make a mistake or be careless it might be the means of many being destroyed. These are some of the responsibilities that this year have been thrown upon me. With these I often have some joy. The opening of the mind, the embracing of new ideas, the imitation of every example that is set before her, the eloquence there is expressed in the bright dark eye, and the activity of the limbs, with the parrot talk of " Pa," all create sensation peculiar to itself. And the hope of her being a useful one in society and a follower of the lamb, of bringing others to a knowledge of Jesus Christ, the eternal felicity of heaven, honoring God and praising the Lamb causes a little respite from the deep anxiety that I often as a parent feel. But then faith in the promises of God surmounts the whole and is a lighthouse to all the trials arising from this source. O may I have more grace to accomplish the task that God has given. I want more knowledge, more faith and more of the spirit of God to guide me in all I attempt for the furtherance of the Redeemer's cause. If ever *mortal* had access to God I desire it. But I have another source of responsibility with which I sometimes am at a loss to know how and what to do. If it was in putting new only in the mind I should feel altogether different about it, but there is a work to do to eradicate the old principles which he had formerly imbibed, I mean the guardianship of a young lad. The momentous responsibility that I took upon me when I took the guardianship of him was far greater than I anticipated. You know what a rogue I was, and "set a rogue to catch a rogue" is the old proverb. His habits drove me to God with all my soul to pour my heart out unto him for guidance and direction. I talked and entreated and it did not affect, it seemed necessary to use correction; it pained my soul but it must be done; I prayed and God heard and blessed be his name the work was accomplished in part. To keep him too close may dispirit him, to let him run too much may be ruination of his usefulness. I often wish I had you here to ask your counsel and then perhaps you would not know what to do. You would be surprised to see the change there is in him thus far. The thought that he will yet be a useful man in the world, causes me some consolation in the midst of anxiety. He is now turning his mind to his studies and he now prays with us every day and in prayer meetings takes an active part.

Yesterday I preached two Missionary sermons. This morning I heard him praying that God would open a way that he might be prepared to fill the place of a missionary. I feel thankful to God that he ever induced you to pray that he might be sent here. But I have not time to particularize any further. With all that God has laid upon men, I have not sank under but have been permitted to rise above them all. I have not had to leave the pulpit yet from ill health, though sometimes my voice has been very weak and unpleasant to the ear. The number of meetings are as many as the days of the year into ten. God has thus far led me through ways almost unknown to any one but himself! Who thought five years ago I should have been preaching on my third year as pastor of one church. Truly "God's ways are not as our ways." The most laborious work that I ever did is to labor in protracted meetings. In them I have spent about two months or more this year. It is a continual stretch of the mind, the anxiety that is thrown upon the mind is great, the honor or dishonor of God in all, the salvation or damnation of immortal souls keep the feelings stretched like the cable of a ship anchored in a storm, and that is the reason why God blesses them so. I now commence a new year birthday of my life, it is known only to Him who holds me in existence whether I shall ever see the close of it, or how far I may advance in it. This may be the last commencing of a new birthday year I may ever see, if so, O, glorious news to my soul. But whether I live or die I wish to spend my life in the service of God. As it respects my eternal destiny, I am not disposed to query with my heavenly Father, for he will do all things as he pleases. I believe I can say with Peter "Lord thou knowest that I love thee." Why then should I be concerned about my state that I cannot effect only to serve him while on this earth. May God grant you my dear parents more faithful children to serve God, and may each of us be ornaments to your gray hairs in the hours of dissolution. I must close as I have to go ten miles to deliver a temperance address. That you may be sustained in all the vicissitudes of life, I subscribe myself,

Your unworthy son

L. A. WICKES.

STOWS SQUARE Dec. 8th, 1835.

Being the 27th year of the earthly existence of Lewis Alfred, eldest son of Jonas and Sarah Wickes.

MY DEAR AND MOST AFFECTIONATE PARENTS :

Birthday review of 1835.

It is with pleasure that I have the privilege of writing to you this day, not because of the *worth* of my letters, or the power of communicating anything instructive to you, but of showing my *regard* to those ever dear and honored parents, who were the instruments of my life, who watched over me when a *helpless* child, clothed and fed me when an *ungrateful child*, instructed and prayed for me when pushing through countless blessings down to *eternal woe*. It seems but a day in comparison since I wrote my first birthday letter, date 1831. I know it should be my care to fill up every inch of time in such a way " that I may *give* some *good* account at last." O, that God's gracious influence may be ever exerted to bind my wandering heart to

Jesus and his cause. I must of necessity be brief. I have been blessed with a good degree of health, so that I have been able to fulfill my engagements and appointments. I have conducted two protracted meetings *out of this town.* There were several conversions to God. To God be all the glory given. When I see how little good I do it weakens my faith, and then God, of course, *cannot* bless, " for according to your faith be it unto you." And when God does bless, I get so proud, that he has to abase me. O, for a great share of humility and faith in the promises of God. I preached the funeral sermons of four individuals, and they were all men, and older than myself. How soon God may call me I know not. I want to be prepared to *live,* and then I shall be ready to *die.* I am sensible that the life of a private Christian ought not to satisfy me. I know that it is my duty to live nearer to God, and set a more holy example, than a private member of the church. I have been set apart for the office of the sanctuary of God, and have sworn to be wholly consecrated to the work of the Lord, not serve tables. And besides ministers are to be an example for others to follow. And *Christians are expecting* to find in ministers an example of holy life (comparatively I mean), and the world to find ministers ever ready to warn, admonish, and entreat for the cause of Christ. But oh how far short have I lived! and what an untoward example have I set! Some of the wicked tried to injure me, but I can hardly say that it was for Christ's sake. But I have felt that

"Mine enemy is oft my friend, though wrathful and severe.
He helps to perfect that great end, for which I linger here."

Labors of the year. I have preached during the year one hundred and thirty-six sermons, admininistered the Lord's Supper three times, attended about one hundred and thirty prayer and conference meetings, attended five meetings of ecclesiastical bodies, delivered three temperance addresses, attended two Sabbath school celebrations, solemnized four marriages, and written one hundred and twenty letters. Thus I have given you but a brief sketch of the last year of my life. It is gone, and gone to all eternity. It may be reviewed, but it can never be *recalled*. The only remedy is to live more to the glory of God, in whatever times I may have to live, in the coming year; I now have commenced. I may not close it in this world, or if I am permitted to live, I know not what is before me. Oh, for a *heart* to say as well as lips: "Let the morrow take care for the things of itself." Sufficient unto the day is the evil thereof. I know it is easy to *plan out* how to spend my time, but it is another thing to live out the plan. I think God wants us to work for the present advancement of his kingdom, and the present conversion of sinners. May the Lord give me that "wisdom which is from above," that I may be enabled to promote the cause of the Lord Jesus Christ.

That your last days may be days of usefulness, of peace and joy, and that every child which you have brought up may be to you a crown of joy and blessedness, is the prayer of   Your Eldest Son,

L. A. WICKES.

Written to his wife during her absence to her parents (where she met Mrs. Ermina N. Worcester, a missionary to the Indian tribes, and daughter of Father Nash, of saintly memory,) giving his thoughts on his pastoral life, fearing the results from his natural volatility and levity in conversation. ANTWERP, Oct. 19, 1837.

DEAR LOVE.—It is near 12 o'clock at night, and I have but just got back from meeting, where we felt God was. There is indeed some little feeling, and yet how small. The cause is suffering for the want of helpers. But how scarce they are who really feel for the salvation of souls. I sometimes feel that I am more in the way than all the others. Oh, for a heart to be filled with the Holy Spirit, to have God direct me in the path in which I should walk. It is in vain for us to expect that we can do anything without the Spirit of God. And we may as well stay away from Antwerp as to live here, and not walk in Christ. How much there is contained in that expression of Paul: Gal. 5:7, "Stand fast in the liberty, wherewith Christ has made us free and not be again entangled in the yoke of bondage." The liberty which we enjoyed was that of the sons of God, and that which Christ maketh free, is free indeed. Free from every bondage, and every corruption, and all unbelief. Truly, to be Jesus Christ's free man is a great blessing indeed, and O, how few of us do really enjoy it. The more I see of my heart, the more I feel that I mistook my calling in choosing the ministry of reconciliation. How little like Christ do I feel, and how much do I pattern after the image of hell. O, for a crucifixion to the cross of Christ, and to be crucified to the world. But may I be an example to others. Do pray for this place and get hold on the arm of God. Make an occasional call at your old closet and see what God would say there, compare your present faith with what you once had, and how you once claimed the promises of God. I am quite anxious to hear from you. I have just had a visit from Brother Lawrence, who has tarried all night with us, and has been up to meeting with me, he is a good brother. He preaches in L. next Sabbath. If there is no preaching on the S., you had best to go and hear him. Love to all. But I must close. Pray, pray.

As ever yours,
L. A. WICKES.

There is an omission here of two years. The following letter from Rev. Isaac Clinton, regarding the early history of the church of Antwerp, attests Mr. Wickes' labors and interest in his work.

LOWVILLE, Dec. 26th, 1837.

REV. AND DEAR SIR:

Your note of December 5th, was duly received, and the reason why it has not been answered sooner, has not been because of any neglect, but because of low and feeble health. I well recollect that I did organize the church at Antwerp, and to the best of my remembrance, one Elder and one Deacon were elected and ordained, and the Lord's Supper administered and some baptisms. A record of all the transactions was made on a loose sheet of paper and left with the officers of the church, who were directed to procure a blank book suitable to record the doings of the church sessions, and into which they were directed to transcribe the record which I left them—I believe it was about as long ago as you speak of, viz., eighteen or twenty years—and if the record which I left them has been lost, I do not see how that can in any way effect the existence of the church, as that has been recognized by the Presbytery, received under their care, and their records often examined and approbated. About the time of the organization of that church I was often there, and was well acquainted with most of the people, but for some twelve or fifteen years past I have been there but seldom. At the formation of the church the scene was solemn, and deeply impressive, and not easily to be effaced from my mind. And if, as you say, it was organized in a ball room and the ordinances of Christ administered, I do not know how that could any way affect the legality of those transactions. It was an upper chamber, and many associated many pleasing recollections and precious thoughts concerning the first administrations of the Sacred Supper by our Lord Himself. And as there was not at that time even a school house where religious meetings could be held, it was certainly very kind in Mr. Copeland to offer and open his chamber for such a meeting, and as often as preaching could be obtained. In reading the history of the Free churches in New York, I find that for a while one of them used the Masonic hall, another a theatre, and another a brewery, and I have never been disposed to censure them for that. If evil had ever been done in those places or in Mr. Copeland's chamber, I do not see in that circumstance any justifiable reason why good should not be done in the same places. As I said, the scene was solemn and deeply affecting. The church felt it and others appeared to feel it. I believe Christ was there. Since that time the church has had many trials many have died, many have moved away, and others, strangers to me, have been united to it. Changes have

taken place, but the church lives. It is, I trust, a vine
of the Lord's planting, and God has not forsaken it.
Yes, that church as well as many others, which I have
been the humble instrument of organizing, still lives and
blessed be God, it lives in my *heart* and *affections*, and
has a lively interest, and an affectionate remembrance in
my prayers. Again, you say the church in Antwerp
was organized in a *ball* room! Be it so, but did that
circumstance vitiate, or in the least degree affect the
legality or the sacredness of the transactions? Nothing
from without a man, defileth a man, but that which is
from within, which proceedeth from the heart, being pure,
is acceptable unto God, but being impure, that defileth a
man. Present my best respects and regards to the
church at Antwerp; tell them it is my devout and
ardent prayer that they may be forgetting the things that
are behind and pressing forward unto those things that
are before, unto the mark of the prize of their high calling of God in Christ Jesus. And may God make all grace
abound towards them. May they be abundantly blessed
with copious showers of divine influence, be increased in
numbers, and enriched with all spiritual gifts and graces.
Yes, may grace, mercy and peace from God, the Father,
and from the Lord Jesus Christ, be multiplied unto them.

N. B.—I wish, sir, that when you make your statement on the first Sabbath of the year, you have the goodness to read this letter to the church and congregation.

Yours, in the faith and fellowship of the Gospel,

ISAAC CLINTON.

Being the twenty-eighth year of the life of L. A.
Wickes, the oldest son of ten children of Jonas and

Sarah B. Wickes, the husband of Cynthia and father of Aurelia Elizabeth, and Emma Maria Wickes:

Antwerp, Dec. 8th, 1836.

Most Affectionate Parents:

I suppose that by the twelfth of this month, you will be, according to custom, expecting what you call my "birthday letter." Well, were it not that I loved my parents, you would not see it. But having by experience, the feeling of a parent, I cannot refuse to do all in my power to make my dear father and mother happy. Though, perhaps, only to raise them to a higher summit, that if I should prove disgraceful to my parentage and the cause of Christ, to sink them deeper in sorrow and mourning, from which thing may heaven ever keep me.

If I recollect right, my first "birthday letter" was written in this town, the day that I was twenty-one years of age. That is seven years ago, to-day, in the house of Deacon Lacy, at what is called the Oxbow, in this town. Little did I then think that I should be here at so late a period. I commenced my public talking at the Oxbow, from which place I came here in March, 1831, when this place had been deserted by all ministers, and every thing bad was connected with the name of Antwerp. Here I stayed, conducted their public worship for eighteen months, during which time I laid the foundation of a church edifice, raised a subscription to build the house, and got nearly all the materials on the ground to complete the house. And on the 8th of May, 1832, I was licensed to preach the unsearchable riches of Christ, and on the 18th of May, I commenced my labors with the church of Stow's Square, which continued for four years, during which time I married me a wife, visited my parents, had two children born. And on the 1st of July, 1836, I came, after repeated invitations, to this place and commenced my present campaign, having been ordained on the first Tuesday of Feb., 1833. Thus God showed me "my ways were not His ways, and my thoughts were not His thoughts." When in this town before, I verily thought I never should be able to stand professedly on the watch tower of Zion, and that in all probability, I should, in a year or two, go to eternity. But I sometimes felt I did not care how soon. Yet here I am as rugged as ever nearly, and able to preach from seven to fifteen times a week. Truly, what a great debtor I am, and shall be, owing God for strength thus to work and labor. I know I have nothing to cancel it with, and except I can show a pardon sealed by the Savior, I must ever be imprisoned for debt, and that justly too. Oh, for an obedient heart. As to this year, I have nothing very special to write. As to the number of meetings that I have attended, the number of sermons, etc., I cannot tell, as I have kept no memoranda. I have held three neighborhood protracted meetings, and have witnessed the conversion of about fifty or sixty souls to God. Yet how small a number in comparison to what it should be. There is one neighborhood in this town that goes by the name of Arab settlement. This neighborhood, it has pleased God, to visit in mercy. We commenced a little meeting and continued for six or seven days, and I cannot tell how many have been converted to God, some of the most profane men, and women too, have bowed at the feet of Christ, and give a pleasing evidence of a change of heart. But I think it probable, that you could not hardly swallow some, of what the wicked call noisy meetings, yet you might as well take fire into your bosom and not make a noise in groaning, etc., as to make Christians hold their peace when they felt for souls. We begin to feel a little here that we do not accomplish much in a meeting, if we do not rob Satan of one of his children, and bring a wanderer home to his Father's house. Yet, how small is our faith, and how weak is our love to him. When I see one soul born to God in answer to prayer, I say that I never will doubt God again, and perhaps, the next time I bow before him, damning unbelief rolls up again, and then another combat with powers of hell to subdue. Oh unbelief! one of the strongest powers of Satan. But still Satan is a conquered foe, and by watchfulness, prayers and perseverance I can yet conquer, and my prayer, if only indicted by the Holy Spirit, can move this whole region, and make the wicked bow. Oh, what a difference there is in *making prayer, saying prayer and praying.* I suppose it is a difference that you have long known and felt, and what a happy thing it would be if the young would take the experience of the old, and go on towards perfection, and not have to begin again to lay the old superstructure that has been laid so many times. But instead of that we must all learn by our own experience, and then lament at every step that we take that we serve God no more faithfully. It has been a source of pain to me, that so few have felt for the welfare of souls and the church have laid down in their dens, as though they had nothing to do in the cause of God. "It is like children in the market places, who will neither lament or dance." Oh, what an apathy! Truly, it is to be dreaded more than thunder bursting over their heads. Yet there is a bright side to all the dark. There are a few who do feel for souls in this region. There are several places, where we have seen salvation, and where there are some revivals. May God add to their number and continue the work, until the angel shall stand one foot on the dry land and the other on the sea, and pronounce time shall be no longer. Oh, what a day will that be to those who have no God!!

Pray for your affectionate son,

L. A. WICKES.

ANTWERP, DEC. 11, 1838.

MY DEAREST PARENTS:

Birthday Review of 1838. You perceive by this date that it is three days after the usual time for my birthday letter, but it is the first opportunity that has offered itself for me to write, and now I have no time in comparison, that I can possibly devote to writing. This year has been a busy year with me. I have, however, held only three protracted meetings, one which lasted thirty days, and the others from two to three weeks, and many souls have, I trust, been born to God, for which He shall have the glory, for it is due to His great and holy name. But the multiplied duties of the minister's life have increased constantly, and the responsibility has also augmented and increased, and, Oh, that I but felt it still more, then might I act as becometh the child of God, and as the professed minister of Christ. But while some good has been done, the Lord only knows how much evil has been done by my unguarded, and my unholy walk. May the Lord direct me to the right path, that I may see the enormity of my own heart. The additions to the church have been many during the year, and here responsibility increases constantly around me. I am more and more convinced that God intends we should build up his cause, and that man is his co-worker.

There have been some interesting cases of conversion. Oh, how good it is to see men enlisting in the cause of the Redeemer, and sowing the seed of righteousness. I do not know why the word Thirty has such an effect on a person. But I now feel I am getting to be what is called a man of middle age, almost, having lived to commence my 30th year. Can it be possible? How short in appearance, is the time that has elapsed since I wrote my first birthday letter from this town, at the age of twenty-one, yet it has been some years. Neither does it look long since I commenced my studies. Nor is it beyond my memory when I removed from Reading to Troy; nor when I went to the West; when I used to wear the little checkered apron; nor do I forget being drawn to school by my dear Father on a little hand-sled, in Dutchess County; nor is the impression effaced from my memory of seeing a drunken man lay upon the floor in grandfather's bar-room, at Rhynebeck Landing; nor of going into the store-house to catch snow birds with some of my uncles; nor do I forget when I was taken to the Methodist Church and seated along with cousin, William Lemon, on the steps around the altar, and there taught to kneel as others knelt for prayer; nor have I forgotten on a visit to some of our connection (I cannot tell where), I received a little looking glass as a present, and a whipping with a *planting* rod from my mother; nor do I forget how many times I have compelled her to whip me since!

Truly how checkered has been my life, and scarcely have I thought of the passing of time, until I began to say, I am in my 30th year. Now I feel it is time to put away childish things. Who would have thought that I should have visited my parents but once in almost nine years. But so it is. I have been almost compelled to start for Albany, by the pleadings of little Aurelia and Emma, when they come into my study and say, " Pa, won't you go to Albany?" Why dears?" "Because we want to see Grandpa and Grandma Wickes." "Why do you wish to see them?" "Because we have never seen them, and if you will go we will give them a good kiss. Pa will you go when you get money enough?" There is a power in their pleadings that is stronger than any but a parent can know. We have during the last year enjoyed a good degree of health. Health is a great boon of Heaven. When the bodily health is good the mind is clear. Aurelia learns quite easily; she reads a great deal of the time, so much so, I am inclined to think it is not good for her. She is very thankful for the book you sent her, though it is quite hard for her to comprehend. I do not know what we may do about sending her to school; as yet, we do not think it best. Emma enjoys very good health as a general thing, and loves her books, but is one of the most uneasy things you ever saw, all the time on the move. She reads in her abs. I desire that their life and education may be for the glory of God, and the building up of his cause. And it is my earnest prayer that they may know what practical Godliness is in their early days How responsible and accountable is the station of a parent. How little do those who are about forming the marriage connection think of it, or even know about it. But glorious promise, "My grace is sufficient for you." Remember us to all the brothers and sisters, and may we all meet in Heaven, is the prayer of your son.

LEWIS.

(An extract).

ANTWERP, Dec. 9, 1839.

MY DEAR AND AFFECTIONATE PARENTS:

Birthday Review of 1839. You perceive that I date this one day after my birthday, yesterday being Sabbath, I could not devote to writing. How important so to improve time, that we may meet it at the bar of God with delight, feeling that we may meet with his blessed approval of "Well done *good* and *faithful* servant, thou hast been faithful over a few things, I will make thee ruler over many. Enter thou into the joy of thy Lord." Oh, how full of meaning is that text! What is a *good* servant, and what qualities does a faithful servant possess? I am very sensible that I cannot receive that appellation on my acts of obedience. The Lord has blessed me with a better state of health during the last year of my life, than for several years before. I have felt that God was taking charge of my body, and was strengthening me, but why, I can hardly tell, for I make such a poor use of my time, it must be but poor encouragement for God to thus bless. I sincerely ask forgiveness for all my unfaithfulness. I have had to groan over my negligence, until it has learnt me that obedience is better than sacrifice. I have held a protracted meeting since we returned from Albany in September. I preached every night for seventeen evenings, and twice a day for fifteen days more, and done talking and praying enough to preach two more each day, besides, and the Lord blessed to the conversions of immortal souls. Some hard hearts, by grace, were made to bow to the Savior. One man, that is a very intelligent man, a man worth some five or six thousand dollars, had been an awful drunkard, came out on the side of the Lord, as we have reason to hope. After attending the meeting some two or three days, I visited him at his house. He rose in the congregation and addressed Bro. A. Stevens, and said: " Mr. Stevens *I can forgive you to-night.* You recollect that about three years ago, you prayed for me, and in your prayer you prayed I might be broken off from my cups, for 'no drunkard should enter the kingdom of Heaven.' There was considerable fuss made about it, and you came to me, and said it was ill timed, and not proper at *that time* and *place*. I told you I would never forgive you as long as I lived. But I can do it to-night, and feel willing to get down at your feet and ask your forgiveness for the abuse I have heaped upon you. Your prayer was right, and I knew it. The Lord, my family, my friends, and my conscience were all on one side, and my appetite and the devil on the other. I followed the devil. My drunkenness from that time has cost me more than *one thousand* dollars. At the rate I have gone since that, in two years more I should land my family in Canton poor house, and myself in the drunkard's grave. My friends, I am determined to serve my God, if it costs me all I am worth. I know my besetting sin. Do pray for me, that the Lord will help me to overcome my wickedness." He has lived so far very exemplary, and the wicked have been compelled to acknowledge the hand of the Lord in it, and as the work of God. May it please the Lord to make him what he desired to be, "a worker in the vineyard of the Lord." There were several cases of thrilling interest, and the Lord laid his hand heavily on their abominations. There was one young man, who came forward to the anxious seat for prayers, wanted to be a Christian, and day after day he would come, but would not yield up all for God. What was in the way, I could not tell. One day he was on his knees trying to pray, but could not. He was told his sins must be confessed out, let them be what they were, if he died in the work. "I will," says he, "I will." He rose from his knees and said: "My friends, I did not intend to come to this meeting, but I could not stay away, and when I came, I was determined not to be found on the anxious seat, but I could not keep off. I thought I would be a Christian, but I could not. I was willing to do everything but one thing, and that I did not believe was necessary, but there I have stood, and can not live so. That one thing that kept me back, was a *beehive* full of honey. Every time that I would ask God to have mercy on me, the beehive would come up, and I said I cannot confess it." (An innocent man had been charged with it). "But I do now acknowledge that I took Mr. Bushnal's beehive. I have confessed it to him, and paid him for it, and I ask forgiveness of all in this house. I did not get stung at the time, but I have been *stung* ever since. It was sweet to my taste, but it has proved a *bitter pill* to me." He then, as we trust, found his heart willing to bow at the feet of the Lord, and endeavored to lead others to the Savior. It would have done your souls good to have seen parents and children, brothers and sisters, mingling their prayers, and tears, and confessions together. Parents weeping over the conversion of children, and children rejoicing over the conversion of parents. Oh, if there is joy in Heaven, why should not we have some little foretaste of what we shall in full by and by. There have been during this present year, about eighty hopefully converted to the Lord. But it should be hundreds, instead of tens. And relying on the promises of God, I expect to see it yet. "For the children of God shall be as numerous as the hosts of Heaven, and as the sand upon the sea shore, and when God's people shall take delight in the stones of Jerusalem, then will her light shine, and the glory of the Lord shall appear." Another meeting is expected here. Pray for me. I want the wisdom of God to direct me what to do.

Your Affectionate Son,

L. A. WICKES.

Antwerp, December 8, 1840, being the commencement of thirty-two years of the life of Lewis Alfred, eldest son of Jonas and Sarah B. Wickes, and who was born at Hyde Park, Dutchess County, New York State.

Most Affectionate and Kindest of Parents:

Another year has rolled into the eternal world, and is among those that have gone before it, and of which it may be said, "it *was*, and is gone." How different time is from eternity. It will there be said, that it *is*, but never that it *was*. When the Lord had created the sun, etc., He tells their use.—"To divide the day from the night, and let them be for signs, and for seasons, and for days, and for years." (Gen: 1: 14.) It is from these that we know of the flight of time. The sun has risen and set so many times, and the stars, like so many candles, have appeared as often, (though not always to be seen by us), and thus is known that a year has rolled round. But in eternity there is no sun, moon, or stars. (Rev. 21: 23). So we have no patterns to number the days, for there is no night (that is to the righteous), and no day for the abode of sorrow. But I suppose there will be a consciousness of the duration of joy and sorrow. How delightful the thought, that we may all meet there. Are our ranks to be broken, and who shall be the one? * * * Indeed, can you tell me when a child ceases to be a child, for Paul says, "when I was a child, I thought as a child, I spake as a child, but since I became a man" etc. Is it a sudden step from child to man, and from young man to—what kind of a man shall I call it, or is it a gradual process of little by little? But after all, what matters it. I am an immortal being, and so is my fellow, whether a child, a young man, a man in the meridian of life, or past the noon-time of life, and to all I have duties to do, according to my ability and opportunity, and may it please the Lord to grant me His grace to qualify me for them. In reviewing my life for the past year, I find so much of unfaithfulness in it, that it seems that I have nothing but a chapter of confessions on my part to record, and of God's unbounded forbearance on his part, for the more I see of myself, the more does the long suffering of Christ appear towards rebels, and compassion towards the chief of sinners. For truly the Lord is good, and his tender mercies are over all his works, and I find him to be good even to me, as vile as I am, and as unfaithful as I may have been. There is not anything peculiar in my history of the last year. I have seen some seventy or one hundred hopefully converted to Christ. This, to be sure, has caused the angels in Heaven to rejoice, and some have given glory to God on earth for the gift of his Holy Spirit. How cheerful it would be if all the converts could be counted by the 1,000 and 10,000 a day. May the Lord hasten the day. My labors have been more interrupted by ill health, than for ten or twelve years. But the Lord is now helping me, and I find that I have more strength given to me daily. Pray that I may use it for the honor and glory of God. May God crown your last days with joy, is the prayer of your affectionate son.

L. A. WICKES.

CHAPTER VI.

Beginning of Evangelistic Work.

In February, 1841, Mr. Wickes went to Richville and assisted Rev. Gorham Cross in a protracted meeting which was crowned with the blessing of the Lord. Also in the same month Mr. W. had business connected with the Black River Association, which called him down to Massena, St. Lawrence County. On his return he stopped at Rev. Mr. Taylor's, in Norfolk, and as his usual manner was to pray and converse with every member of the family on the subject of the soul's salvation, he found much tenderness of feeling on the subject. Brother Taylor requested him to come to Norfolk and hold a meeting; he replied, if his people would give their consent. Brother Taylor immediately wrote a letter to the church desiring it, for Christ's sake to consent to his coming to Norfolk and labor for the good of that people. The church were unanimous in letting him go for a short time. During this trip he writes as follows:

Richville, February 13th, 1841.

My Kind Affectionate and Dear Wife:

I have looked for a letter from you every mail to inform me of the welfare of my dear children and the rest of the family. Your letter almost unmanned me when you told me of the sickness of my youngest child, as well as the others and the care they must be. I felt that I could not stay away from home another hour, were it not for the greater good of the cause of Christ I often feel how pleasant it would be if I could spend my days and much of my time in the bosom of my dear family, and with them serve God, and with them meet around the domestic circle in serving the blessed Savior. How few there are that know the trials of a minister's family. The professional man, the merchant, the mechanic and the farmer, may enjoy the delightful time of spending the morning and evening in the pleasures of home and his dearest friend. But not so with the ambassadors of Jesus. But be still my treacherous heart, we shall one day meet where parting never comes. In the midst of all this, there is a sweet and pleasant thought that we may serve and honor God in his glorious cause and lead souls to Christ, for whom Christ died and Jesus bled. And let us make up of the suffering of Christ which are behind. I suppose you will want to know of the battle. The first Sabbath the Baptist house was thronged to overflowing, since that we have had a pretty fair congregation day and night. God's spirit has moved among the people; several backsliders have been reclaimed, and from fifteen to twenty, or perhaps more sinners have been converted, some of them very clear cases. There are from twenty to fifty on the anxious seat, and many who last winter were very violent in their opposition, now are quite serious. Some who state publicly that they were Universalists, have risen for, and some have come forward for prayers, and have been on their knees. There have been some converted from Gouverneur DeKalb and Hermon and the whole region seems to be under the moving of the

Holy Ghost. Brother DeKalb closed his school, his scholars nearly all left him. And such is the state of things here that I have felt that it was a plain case of duty for me to stay over the Sabbath, and it is thought by all of us that Brother Cook nor Cross can be spared, as the Sabbath will be an important day and we want an anxious meeting in one house and preaching in the other. I shall, therefore, send a messenger this morning to Bro. S. and request him to preach in Antwerp on the Sabbath. If he should come, you may have a part of this letter read to the church. Tell Bro. B. to come here and bring his family. The mail has come and I must stop. Dear wife if you can leave home, do come and help. Love to all.

As ever your husband,

L. A. WICKES.

RICHVILLE, Feb. 21st, 1841.

DEAR WIFE:

The stage has got the start of me. The state of things here are such that it is thought best to hold on over the Sabbath, and to make a little longer effort to save souls. The Lord is in our midst, to Him be all the glory and honor. Pray that our weak and almost exhausted strength, may be sustained through this conflict, we need all that we can command on the Sabbath. I have thought, therefore, that I should leave the church at A. destitute. I do very much regret to do so, but such seems to be the state of things that I cannot see how it can be otherwise. I wish there may be a sermon read from Dr. E. or C. G. F., and that the church keep up their meetings and have notice given that that the Lord's Supper will be administered in two weeks. We shall probably be home on Tuesday or Wednesday evening of next week. I have not time to write more. I will bring all the news when I come from the battle. Pray for us.

Your affectionate husband,
L. A. WICKES.

This was just before he commenced his labors as an Evangelist. This was the commencement of a most blessed work of the Holy Spirit throughout that favored region of country, particularly St. Lawrence County.

Returning, as he expected, he writes from his home to the pastor at Richville:

ANTWERP, March 4th, 1841.

DEAR BROTHER CROSS:

Before going to Norfolk. Providence permitting, I will be at your house on Tuesday evening to go on to Massena the next day, if the going is any way passable. I want you should be ready to go on that morning. Owing to my church affairs I shall not be able to start before four o'clock on Tuesday afternoon, so that I may not be able to get to your place before half-past six or seven o'clock. If you think best under these circumstances to appoint a meeting on that evening, you can, and Providence permitting I will be there. If, however, the going should break up so that it would be imprudent, our journey will be postponed until after the ground settles, and in that case you need not look for me. There has nothing special taken place since I saw you. I have preached two funeral sermons since I returned home from Massena, one on a child of nine months, and the other on Mrs. Blanchard, of Philadelphia. The last I preached on the Sabbath, and another funeral which I had to send Brother Cook to supply. How great the contrast between the salvation of the sinner and the burying of the dead. What a man of God a minister ought to be, to weep with those that weep and rejoice with those who do rejoice; one day to rejoice with friends over the repentance of a friend, and the next day to mourn with others over the loss of a friend. May God give grace and qualify us for all the great duties which are devolving upon us. Say to all, "Remember Lot's wife."

Love to Mrs. Cross.

In haste, your brother,

Rev. G. Cross.　　　　　　　　　L. A. WICKES.

The following letter explains how soon and where his next labors commenced:

NORFOLK, March 12th, 1841.

To the First Presbyterian Church in Antwerp, Greeting:

DEAR BRETHREN: In the providence of God we are disappointed in regard to the expected assistance of Rev. J. Burchard in making special efforts to revive religion among us. We had concluded to throw ourselves upon the Lord, and go forward trusting to him to furnish such assistance as he saw best. In this state of deep anxiety we had

[The first call to labor as an Evangelist in St. Lawrence Co.]

the happiness to greet Brother Wickes at our own door
It looked like a particular interposition of Providence. It
occasioned the springing up of relief and joy in our
bosom. I now write to beg you to permit him to come
and spend two or three weeks with us in a protracted
meeting. I have no doubt he will be the instrument of
the conversion of many souls here at this time. I am
asking you to make a sacrifice, dear brethren, but I think
I am asking it for the Lord's sake and for the sake of
souls. Will you not throw yourselves upon the promise,
" He that watereth shall be watered also himself," and let
your Minister come, and pray for the success of his labors
while here? I am confident that we shall not ask you to
make any pecuniary sacrifice. He is waiting and I have
time to say no more, only to beg you to hear our cry and
suffer your Minister to come over and help us.

With Christian affection,
A. TAYLOR.

NORFOLK, March 22d, 1841.

MY DEAR WIFE:

I have looked for a letter from you every day since last
Friday, and as yet I have not yet heard a word from you.
I have felt very anxious about the people on the Sabbath,
but heard nothing from you for which reason I did not
know what to do. I felt somehow as though you would
be supplied on the Sabbath, and here it was thought that
it would be impossible for any one to get there from here,
and indeed there was no one but Brother Taylor that I
could send, and the state of feeling was such that I
thought it was imprudent for him to leave. Though if I

had known that Brother Cook, or some other had not expected to be there in season, I would have made other arrangements. But it is past, and I wish you would write immediately and let me know whether the pulpit was supplied, and if you have heard from Brother Cook. Or if you know of any arrangements which will cause it to be supplied, I wish you to write immediately on the reception of this. Things are very interesting here. The whole community is on the move, there have been fifteen or more hopeful conversions; last evening there was a large number of persons rose for prayers. But the church do not move much, there are a few who do get hold a little, and the spirit of God seems to move all around. Brother Taylor's son and daughter are among the subjects of the work, and Brother Taylor's house seems to be a Bethel for the Lord to bless the souls of men. Some families are on the altar ready to work for God, yet others are standing back. If the church will only get out of the way I feel we shall have a work here, that I have not witnessed for years. Truly, the harvest is ripe and nothing to hinder. May God grant that it may be a work of his own glory and power. Do pray for us. There are some that feel for souls here, but I do believe it is Zion's praying in other places that does prevail in this great victory. It is time for meeting, I must close. Tell all to pray. My health is better than when I left home. Bless the Lord.

As ever, your husband and father,

L. A. WICKES.

NORFOLK, March 27th, 1841.

DEAR WIFE:

If I have one, for I most begin to think that something has taken place. I have been forgotten, at least, for I have looked for a letter from you for some days, or looked for you and seen nothing as yet. What is the matter? Do, I beg of you, write soon, for I feel very anxious to know whether Brother Cook has arrived at Antwerp, or whether there has been any preaching since I left. The state of things here is now quite interesting, and the whole community seems to be on the move. The cause of God seems to be gaining ground, and many begin to be taking hold; I cannot say now how many have obtained a hope as yet, but there have been some forty or fifty, among them are the old of sixty or seventy years down to the youth, some heads of families, and the Spirit of God seems to find way to the hardest hearts, and the mouths of scoffers seems to be stopped. And O, what a host of "old hopers" and "backsliders" have been dug out! We have two meetings in the morning, a prayer meeting and anxious meeting. There are four Evangelical denominations, and they *all unite* in the work to some extent. Last evening a Universalist wanted to come and help, but he was seated very soon. I do believe God has great blessings in store for Norfolk and the region around. Do pray for us. Tell the dear brethren of the church I will be home as soon as I can see it is duty and the will of God. God is hearing their prayers for this place. O may the Lord have mercy on Antwerp too. Gen. Blake has a good deal of feeling about his soul, pray for him, he has an interesting family. The Lord have mercy on him. I must close.

In haste, your affectionate,

L. A. WICKES.

P. S.—I have many *pressing invitations to hold meetings*. How much work to be done in the vineyard of the Lord, my dear, let us pray that God would direct. The harvest is great, the laborers few, the Lord prospers the obedient.

NORFOLK, April 5, 1841.

MY DEAR AND AFFECTIONATE WIFE:

It was with delight that I heard from you, I can assure you. But sorry that you had not concluded to come. I wish you could be here. Be careful of your own and the children's health, and do all of you pray much and lie low at the feet of Christ. Oh! how little I have tried to be like God and a minister of the Lord. I have but a moment to write, and I suppose you would like to know how the work is progressing.

To the Church I would say, that the work is the most powerful of anything that I have seen for years. It takes all, from the aged man of seventy down to the child of eight or ten years. I have not the most distant idea of the number of hopeful conversions—they are very numerous, indeed. Among the heads of families that have been converted is Major General Blake, and truly I never saw a more humble and devout convert; one of his aids, Col. Sackrider; Mr. B., the deputy sheriff; Mr. A., the supervisor of the town, and a host of others. Among the youth I know not how many. I counted yesterday in the choir of singers twenty-five who have given pleasing evidence of conversion since the meeting commenced, and scores of others. Every mouth seems to be closed, and a universal solemnity upon the whole community. Saturday evening there were more than one hundred and fifty forward for prayers, and more than sixty rose with a determination to serve the Lord. Amid the mud and bad roads we have a congregation of rising of four hundred every day, and the number seems to be increasing constantly, and new cases of conviction and conversion every day and evening, and some as interesting cases as I have ever known. Yesterday there was a congregation of between seven and eight hundred, at the least calculation. I asked for an expression of feeling and desire about having the meeting continued, with a pledge that they would do all in their power to help forward the work, as long as the providence of God should point out our duty to continue; and to attend when it was possible, and when it was not possible they would spend much time in prayer, and would work and do all they could, and there were as many as six hundred rose as one man, and did thus covenant. There are only about two thousand inhabitants in the town, and more than one quarter, if not one-third, have been under the movings of the Spirit of God. How could I do less than go on with the meeting? Truly, it was a call of God, and I have no doubt about its final results to thus obey God. A school of young gentlemen and ladies at Lower Norfolk has been suspended a few days. The feeling was so great, and some eight or ten have bowed to the sceptre of a Savior's love, and others are under very serious impressions. To God be the glory—to Him alone. " Bless the Lord, oh, my soul, for all His mighty deeds which He has wrought. He has overthrown the horse and his rider." And let everything that hath breath, praise the Lord. I ask, my dear family, wife and sisters, and my dear church, too, is it not evident that you did the will of God in letting me come. "Inasmuch as ye have done it unto the least of these, My brethren, ye have done it unto Me," is the language of our blessed Lord. How long I may continue here I cannot say. You may be led to ask, has our husband and minister lost all affection for his family and the people of his charge? No, no! never did my family and my dear church look so precious to me as at the present, when I see on what a slender point hung the destiny of so many souls (I mean the vote of the church in that upper room.) It makes them dearer and still dearer to my heart. When I have seen the members of the choir turning to God I have thought of those of the choir in my own dear church. Oh, remember them in prayer. May the Lord grant they may chant the praises of God in glory. They have been united on earth, may they be in glory, is the earnest prayer of their minister. I do still sincerely ask the church to keep their hearts right, and still pray for us here, for I have felt your prayers much. "Again I say, pray for us." In your letter to me you did not say whether Brother Cook would stay until I returned or not. I wish you would let me know all about it. I do earnestly request the church to stay up his hands and let his soul feel that the church are laboring *for* the cause and with him. And may I hear of the conversion of souls among you.

So much of this sheet as relates to the work of God here, I wish to be read to the church if I am not home before the next Sabbath.

My dear, pray much.

Your affectionate husband,
L. A. WICKES.

Brother Taylor's family all send love to you. Write me immediately, if you please.

TO EMMA AND ANNA:

Dear Sisters: I have felt very solicitous that you should live for God, as we entered into our mutual covenant around the domestic altar that we would. Do not have your minds taken up with the trash of earth. Oh! I wish you were here to help in this blessed work of God, but you are not and I suppose you cannot be. But get your hearts here, and by an eye of faith see us at the house of God. Our anxious meetings every morning are attended by some hundreds, Christians and all. Now, do spend much time in prayer that the Lord will bless for His name's sake. Do not be light and vain in all your intercourse with others, but do bear the marks of a Savior's love all the time. Oh, let us be like a family in heaven, all loving God and each other. Let us pray much for each other.

Your brother,

L. A. WICKES.

AUFELIA AND EMMA:

Your Pa thinks much about you and as we do not have any meeting this forenoon, while I wrote to your dear ma and aunts, I thought I would like to have you, one on one knee and the other on the other knee, and sing, "Salvation, O, the joyful sound." But you are not here, so I will just say a few words to you. There are a good many little girls and boys here that when they come to meeting they weep and cry because they have been such wicked children, as not to be thankful to God for all his kindness to them. Now, I want that my little daughters would love the Lord, and pray that Jesus would give them new hearts, indeed. Little Emma, do learn to read as fast as you can. When pa comes home he wants to come with the blessing of God, which he cannot do unless the Lord says, go home. When this work is done he will not stay long here, I can assure you. Be very good children, and make your ma as happy as you can. Your affectionate father,

L. A. WICKES.

NORFOLK, April 10th, 1841.

MY AFFECTIONATE WIFE:

I have but a moment to write, but will say a word. I was in hopes that you would have written so that I could have heard from you yesterday so that I could have had a little assistance from you to know what to do, for I know not what course to take or how to turn for the glory of God. That God does call here now I have not the least doubt. This week has been a week of favor. On Thursday afternoon I preached to converts, and there were one hundred and seventy that gave in their names to be admitted into some church, but very few children among them, mostly middle-age and aged. Quite a large number of heads of families. The evening after, there were some ten or fifteen more hopeful conversions. Yesterday several more of prominent cases, so that we can safely put the number rising of two hundred, who mean to serve God from this *day forth*. Truly, what has God wrought, to Him be all the glory. It is the Lord's doings and wondrous in our eyes. Notwithstanding the mud and "sap weather," we have a congregation of about four hundred every day. Last evening there were about fifty new cases on the anxious seat, most of them had not been there before. I can see no place to close the meeting. I have preached twice every day since I have been here, besides the anxious meeting in the morning and other labors. I feel somewhat exhausted, but the Lord is my strength. Several have been converted in Lower Norfolk. The church got together and voted they would do any thing to help forward the work if I would come there when I got through here, and about sixty impenitent rose and said they would attend the meeting and use all the means, if I would come, to get eternal life. What I shall do I cannot say until I hear from home. I I never had so much anxiety about my family and church before. But I do know if they will serve the Lord he will take care of them and bless them. I wish the church and society would pass a vote something like this: That so long as the Lord seemed to say so plainly it is my duty to labor here, they do cheerfully say "stay," and will continue praying. If they will send me a copy of it by the earliest mail from the clerk of the society, then I should feel to leave them in the hands of God longer. But I must close, may the Lord direct and bless you. Do continue to pray much for us.

Your affectionate husband,

L. A. WICKES.

I know not how long I may stay here, but I shall, God willing, be home on the first Sabbath in May, if not before, may the Lord direct. I do feel grateful that the

Extract from another letter. church were inclined to say, "stay there, and we will pray for you." I feel that God will bless them, and make His face to shine upon them. Since I last wrote you, the work has not abated at all. New cases of conviction and conversion every day. Some men have been brought to the Lord, who have not attended meeting before for ten or fifteen years. The infidels and the Universalists have been compelled to bow before the Lord. One man, a trustee in the Universalist Society in M. came out and advised all to forsake it, for he dare no longer build upon it, and would no longer stay from Christ; and another man, that was the leader of the Universalist Society in the same place, has come out and renounced his errors, and truly, he appears to be a regenerated man as well as a converted man. Both of them have been in my room and poured out their hearts to my Savior in prayer, and both set up the family altar. May God make them eminently useful to their deluded brethren in sin. I cannot say how many have been brought to Christ since my last, but I think I speak within bounds when I say one hundred. To-morrow I preach to the converts again, God willing. Truly, what hath God wrought! To Him be all the glory and honor. I can speak within bounds when I say there have been fifty, if not seventy-five family altars erected in this community since this meeting commenced. Last evening there were rising of fifty on the anxious seat, all new cases, some twenty of whom vowed to serve the Lord. The bell has called for meeting and I must close. Love to all.

Pray for your husband,
L. A. WICKES.

CHAPTER VII.

Revival meeting at Massena—Removal of family to Stow's Square.

MASSENA, April 22, 1841.

My Dear and Affectionate Wife:

YOU will perceive by this that I have removed my quarters a little farther North, so far as to get to brother Northrup's. I closed at Norfolk last Sabbath, and preached to those who had been converted; after I preached to the converts before, and there were seventy took their seats together, and there were something like fifty individuals that we knew of who where not present. There were, during that meeting, something over two hundred and forty that gave in their names to unite with the different churches. It was only by the earnest entreaty of saints and sinners that I came to this town. I have spent two days in the center of the town in closing up the meeting at Norfolk. Brother Northrup had been holding evening meetings, and at the close of the meeting yesterday there were forty-five expressed hope in the Lord Jesus. Things were very encouraging. I came here to the village last evening and preached my first sermon. I cannot say how long I shall be here; I think I shall be here but a few days. We have no place but a large school-house to hold the meetings in. The

Baptists, or rather the supporters of Kent, will not let us have the meeting-house here, and the school-house was almost full last evening. Nothing but the most plain and positive sense of duty will keep me away from home a single day. The work in Norfolk has affected this place very much, indeed, and the wicked are beginning to feel the importance of becoming Christians in a small degree. To-day I am left alone, as Bro. N. goes to preach a funeral sermon some six miles off. What to expect here I cannot say. I hope for the best. Christians are praying for this place in all directions around. I hope for a general breaking up and to have it a short work. May God hasten it. I think now I shall be home a week from next Sabbath, if the Lord will. But for fear I shall not, I think the Lord's Supper and the preparatory lecture had best be put off until the second Sabbath in May, when, the Lord willing, I will again meet the people in Antwerp. But the indications of the Spirit of God and His providence are such that I cannot for a moment say it is not my duty to spend a few days here. I have not time to write more now. Pray for us here, and especially for me. Let Brother Cook give the notice about the Lord's Supper. Pray much for me.

Your affectionate husband,
L. A. WICKES.

MASSENA, May 3, 1841,
In contemplation of May 3.

To AURELIA E. WICKES:

My Affectionate Daughter: This day you know is your birthday, and your papa has been for some weeks anticipating spending this day with you at home. But the providence of God is so ordered that he will be deprived of that privilege, so I thought I would talk with you on a piece of paper with my pen. You know that talking is telling one another every thought. And although I cannot make you hear my *voice*, yet I can write it on paper, and you and your dear ma can read it, and then you will know my thoughts just as well as if you heard my voice, and I had you on one knee and your sister Emma on the other. I have got this sheet of paper from Mr. Northrup to write this to you because I am a friend to the slave, and because my little daughter is also a friend to them, and so everybody says they *are friends*, too, but there are a good many that say they are friends that take and chain him, just as you see that man in the picture, because he wants to go where he can take care of his children. Now, do you think he can be a friend? And would you want such friends? Would you not think that person would be the the best friend who would cut off his chains and take him away from such a hard master? The stage has gone out and so I cannot send it now.

[The paper had a picture of a black man, Chains on his hands and feet, and the words "Am I not a man and a brother" printed around it.]

May 3.—To-day is your birthday. You are now *seven* years old. O, how fast time does go, and my daughter, I had another thought about slavery: and it is that all people are sinners and the slave master is the devil, and he was expecting to get them all in his own prison house of despair, and then to torment them forever. But the Savior came and died that we might be liberated from his iron grasp, and cut off the chains of sin and made us all free, and so no longer to be slaves. Now, when a

Saviour has done so much, should you not love him and be very good, and love to pray to him, and to get others to love him, too. You are now so old, my dear, that you must serve the Lord and obey Him. You have been taught to say your prayers by your dear mama; but that is not enough. You must feel in your heart to pray to that Saviour, and love to pray to him, for he is *only* the one you should love. I have seen a good many little boys and girls who have, I hope, given their hearts to God and are serving him, and I want when pa comes home that you will have the same good news to tell your dear father.

I am now on the Racket and Grass rivers; that is between and within two miles of the St. Lawrence river. (They call the St. Lawrence here "the big river.") There are some very pleasant places around here, and I have wished you were here with pa, too, and so also your mother and sister. But you cannot come until your pa comes after you, and he thinks now he will before next Sabbath, and see you all. I feel that it has been a great while since I saw you, and how should we feel if we never should meet again in this world. May the Lord grant that we may meet. But how much more deadful the thought if we should not meet in the world above, and may we so serve the Savior that we may *love* to meet that Redeemer in Heaven. See how good a girl you can be, and how happy make your mother and sister, and when you see everybody happy because you do good, then you will be happy yourself. I have found a little prayer here which I thought you would love to learn by heart:

"My father's gone away,
I wish he would come home,
I do not like to have him stay
Where I can't see him every day--
Ma, when will father come?

"He told me I must pray
To God, with love sincere;
But I do, I always say,
Please bring my father home to-day,
And keep him safely here."

But I cannot write any more now, I must bid you farewell for the present. Pray for yourself and for your dear father.

L. A. WICKES.

MASSENA, May 8th, 1841.

MY DEAR AND AFFECTIONATE WIFE:

You see I am here yet, when I had anticipated being with my dear family. But God's ways are not our ways, and our thoughts are not as *His* thoughts. As I said, on Wednesday I preached to the converts. When rising of one hundred and twenty, gave in their names to unite with some of the churches in this place. The people begged so hard for me to stay a few days longer, that I finally concluded to stay until after the Sabbath, when God willing, I shall start for Antwerp. I wrote to Brother Cross to go to A. and administer the Lord's Supper if I did not get to his house by noon on Saturday, and expecting he would do it, I felt it would be wrong for me to leave. Since Thursday, there have been some twenty or thirty hopeful conversions. The work is among all ranks, and classes. And God has got to

Himself a great and glorious name. Some of the wealthiest men and their families have been subjects of the work. I have not time to say more as I expect the mail every moment. I have many things to say when I see you. Still pray for your own dear husband. I shall, God willing, start for home on Monday or Tuesday. I have never felt more clear than I have since I left home that I am doing the will of God, and I feel to lay myself and family in the hands of God, and let Him do as He pleases, He will direct. In haste, but in love.

As ever, your affectionate husband,

L. A. WICKES.

Mr. W. from this time began to feel it his *duty to labor* as an *Evangelist*.

In June, 1841, Mr. Wickes, accompanied by his wife went to Potsdam and held a very successful meeting, at the close of which he received the following from the students of the academy:

Accompanied with the prayers of his Christian friends in the academy, Mr. Wickes will have the kindness to accept the enclosed; begging, at the same time, to be remembered as in his intercessions at the throne of grace, and especially that those of our number, whose hearts are not rich towards God, may never be forgotten.

Yours, dear sir, very respectfully,

STUDENTS.

Saturday, June 26th, 1841.

$20.00 was the enclosed.

The result of the meeting was given in a letter from Miss Lydia Raymond.

At Potsdam, June, 1841, a meeting was held, and very successful, after which sixty-eight united with the Presbyterians; fifty united with the Episcopalians; fifty united with the Methodists.

An extract from a letter, by Miss L. R., gives this result:

ANTWERP, July 2nd, 1841.

DEAR PARENTS AND FRIENDS:

You will perceive by this that we have returned to our home again in good health and strength as can be expected. I have but a moment to write, and should not say much. But the Lord willing, we shall see you face to face on Monday, and if you choose, and it is thought advisable, I will preach there in the afternoon, say half-past five or six o'clock. But if you think it not best, you need not give the notice. It may be perhaps, news to you and unexpected, when I tell you that we have concluded to occupy another field of labor for a while, I just mention it, that you may think about it some before we get to your place. I have invitations to hold meetings which will take at least six months, if not a year to comply with, and it is a most effectual door for doing good in the cause of God. I have a meeting to commence on Thursday, the 8th inst., at the village of Canton, the Shire Town of the county. It is a hard place, and I know a great responsibility rests upon me, and may I rely upon the Lord's strong and mighty hand. Now, we have thought a good many things about what to do with our affairs, and one thought which we have had, is to move them for the present, and wife and the children spend their time there while I may be off in St. Lawrence County. I just mention it, that you may think about it and be ready to give us your advice. When I see you I will tell you more about things.

Affectionately your son,

For Mr. and Mrs. J. Wilcox: L. A. WICKES.

During the months of June and August, 1841, Mr. Wickes held a meeting at Potsdam, which resulted in a glorious work of grace which was the occasion of the change in the above letter. Mrs. W. accompanied him to Potsdam.

CHAPTER VIII.

MEETING AT CANTON AND WADDINGTON.

CANTON, July 3d, 1841.

DEAR BROTHER:

YOUR church have concluded to hold a protracted meeting, provided they can obtain your assistance. There were some when the question was submitted to the church, who were in favor of having the meeting deferred until after the hurry of the season was over. It was, however, concluded on the whole to commence at once, as soon as the necessary assistance could be procurred. *All*, I believe, were in favor of having you come. I have just taken your letter from the post-office, and find that you have concluded to come and commence on Thursday, the 8th inst. The appointment will be made on that day for an evening service, and we shall expect you here. Opposition to this meeting is strong and powerful. There are many adversaries. I have given it all up into the hands of the Almighty, my only desire is to do right myself, and have the church do the same. " In the path of duty *is safety*." In undertaking this meeting at this season of the year, and in view of the hosts of the ungodly around. I feel that we need much of God's presence. We must have his powerful arm revealed or all is lost. May God's gracious Spirit descend with mighty power. Love to you and yours.

Your brother in Christ,
R. PETTIBONE.

NORFOLK, July 9th, 1841.

DEAR BROTHER WICKES:

It has become my painful duty to announce to you that our dear Brother Adolphus is gone to his rest, and a unanimous request of his friends is that you come and preach his funeral sermon to-morrow (Saturday,) at two o'clock P. M. Whether it is consistent with duty for you to come, we submit to you, and our brethren in Canton to decide, come if duty will permit. Otherwise it is our request that Brother Pettibone come and preach the sermon. Brother Pettibone is earnestly requested to attend the funeral at all events, and spend the Sabbath with us if he can.

Your brother in the gospel,
J. B. TAYLOR.

CANTON, July 11th, 1841.

MY DEAR AND AFFECTIONATE WIFE:

I have not had a moment's time since I have been here that I could get to write to you. I never left my family with so heavy a heart as when I parted from the Square. I found that if I stopped to say good-bye, I should only make you mourn and feel more and still more sorrowful. I therefore started off without ceremony or compliments. When I got to Antwerp, and then bid them farewell, I felt again a heavy load. When I saw the last articles put up for departure, I felt, indeed it was a heavy load. When I heard of W. setting his house on fire, and his leaving his family, and see how fast the steps of wickedness were rolling before that people, then again my spirit was oppressed. When Bro. L. came to leave me and start away with my horse and wagon, and think that all I had was now leaving me, I inquired for a room and there went and gave vent to my full heart. Ten thousand scenes of the future danced before my vision, and I could see you in all circumstances but that of happiness. But I found I was giving away to sorrow, that would lead me to murmur against the leadings of the Lord. I felt that God had made it my duty to take care of my family, and my family could not be with me, therefore it was my duty to be with them, and that I had decided wrong, and I should lament it when too late. The responsibility of this meeting rolled upon me, and I felt I was truly a vile and most sinful worm. But on Friday afternoon, I had a still heavier trial than all before. I received two letters from Norfolk, requesting me to preach the funeral sermon of our esteemed and dear Brother Taylor, the minister of that place. Yes, that dear brother is no more! I went and preached on Saturday afternoon at two o'clock, to a crowded house, and an afflicted family and church, but my feelings were such that I could not preach, though I tried to from Acts II. There were eleven ministers besides myself. Their large house could not hold the people that assembled. He died from the kick of a horse which happened about eight or ten days before his death. He had his reason until the last, and he bid all his friends farewell. Oh, how short and uncertain is life. There was a general mourning for him. The choir of singers were all dressed in mourning. The ladies with white dresses, black belts, and black scarfs about their necks. Truly, I began to believe what you told me, that I need not lean on Brother Taylor or any other, for we know not what the Lord would do with man. It is mysterious and dark! Sisters Taylor's feelings you can better imagine, than I can describe. They are afflicted in very deed, and so is also the whole county. May the Lord fill up his place, and his mantle fall upon some one. It is a lesson to me, to " be ye also ready," for in a day and in an hour, when I little think I may be called. Oh, may my work be done and well done. How God is kindly dealing with us as a family. May we remember the blessing, and acknowledge him in all our ways. What that dear people will do, the great Shepherd of Israel alone knows. By this circumstance there is a gloom over all the churches. As to the state of things here. On Thursday evening we had something of a little number out. I preached from " Search me, Oh, God," Ps. 109. And Friday morning there were quite a goodly number that were out, and some feeling, and so in the afternoon and the evening. Saturday morning there were some who professed to have given themselves to the Lord. Among them was the mother of the Misses E., whom you saw at Potsdam. Saturday afternoon and evening, Brother Pettibone

<small>Subjects of convicting sermons.</small> preached, while I was at Norfolk. Yesterday we had a crowded house, I gave them Abraham and Eli in the morning, in the afternoon, John 6:44, and in the evening, the Jailer and Felix. God's Spirit is evidently hovering over this place. Several of the lawyers were yesterday melted into tears. "But drops of tears can ne'er repay, the debt of love I owe." I pray God, they may be brought at the feet of Christ, and be men of usefulness and piety. The church has got a little started, and some of them get hold on the arm of the Lord. And I am of the opinion there will be more *moral* power here in the church, than was at Potsdam, and when they once get fully marshalled, the work of the Lord will move in earnest. I find many of the impenitent are seriously enquiring about the way to Zion. Oh, may I have wisdom to lead them to the Lamb of God. For which my dear wife, do pray. Observe the concert regularly, between seven and nine in the evening, for the descent of the Spirit of the living God. I wish you would have a season of prayer as often as you can in the family. Try to do good, all that is in your power, and to make the family holy and devoted. This evening, the church came out confessing their sins and promising a new life in the service of God, and there seemed to be a good degree of the Spirit of the Lord. Sinners are enquiring, and some from the most respectable parts of the community. O, for the faith that a minister of Jesus ought to have. The wicked are doing all they can to hinder the work of God. The Universalist minister advised his squad not to attend at all. For he said he "must acknowledge that some had been what they call converted," and therefore, their

safe way was to stay away entirely. But they are disobedient, and some of them do attend, and may God have mercy on them, and show them their sins and transgressions You may be surprised to hear Bro. B. from G. is here, to get me to hold a meeting in his church. What will not the good Lord do, if we will only trust in him. Brother Pettibone has been to-day, to preach the funeral sermon of a young woman who attended the meeting at Potsdam one day and refused to have Mrs. F. request prayers for her, saying she had no great anxiety about herself. She went out to bring in some cloth from the line in her usual health, and dropped instantly dead. She was to have been married in a few weeks. What a warning to all! But I must bring my letter to a close and lay me down to rest. How soon before I, with my Brother Taylor, must lay down not to rise again until the morning of the resurrection. It may be to-night. May my work be done, and well done, so that I may leave the world with joy. Remember me, especially to the children, and kiss them for me.

Yours affectionately,
L. A. WICKES.

CANTON, July, 1841.

TO MY DEAR DAUGHTERS A. AND E.

You may get the maps of the State of New York, (your atlas is in the bottom of the box that had my papers in,) and your ma will point out to you all the different places there is around Canton. The court house, the jail, academy, the Methodist, Presbyterian and

Episcopal churches, and the Universalist meeting house. I wish Emma would go to the front door and point to the East, West, North, South, so as to learn all about it. I want you to read much and not play all the time. I think you had best to get up in the morning before the sun rises, and see how sweet every thing looks, and how the birds sing. Pa wants you should get up early, not to lay until the cows are almost all milked. And then pray to your Heavenly Father that He would let you awake in the morning of the resurrection with delight and joy. And I want you to read your Bibles through, and tell pa all about what you read. I want that my dear children should love the Saviour, and pray with your dear mother every day and learn your Sabbath School lessons and be very good children. It is a very solemn thing to die, and I want that my children should love and serve the Lord, so they may be prepared for that certain hour. If you go to the grave yard, you will there see the graves of your mother's grand-father and mother, and your aunt Nancy. You never saw them when they were living, but if you want to see them, you must be good children, and do as the Savior commands you. You must be very kind to your dear mother and to your grand-pa and grand-ma, uncles and aunts. You may ask your ma to give you a pen and a writing book, and learn you to write so that you can write to me when I am far away. May the Lord bless you until we see each other. Your affectionate father,

L. A. WICKES.

CANTON, August 6th, 1841.

DEAR BROTHER CROSS:

You perceive by this that I am yet in Canton, as you

know it was the intention to close last Sabbath. I
preached to the converts, when about one hundred and
twenty took their seats together. At the close of which
the church took a vote to sustain the meeting until I
went to Waddington. So I could do nothing less than
to go forward, and the oaks began to bend. And we
went on until Wednesday evening, when they voted to
continue and sustain the meeting until next Sabbath.
And Christians begin to work now, there have been one
hundred and fifty forward for prayers at a time. But
what way God does take to forward his glorious cause.
The Lord laid his hand on Miram Johnson, and he began
to be anxious about his soul indeed, and as we hope,
became a Christian. But he is dead, and while I am
writing, the whole community are on the way to the
house to bury him. He left many warnings to the people,
his funeral sermon is to be preached this morning at
half-past ten o'clock. May God make both the living
and the dead to speak to-day. This is the second funeral
we have had in this house this week. There have been
several heads of families hopefully converted this week,
and the meeting is more interesting now than any time
before. I have wanted you here very much. But the
Lord has ordered otherwise. Do pray for us, the meeting will close on the Sabbath. And I shall, God willing,
be at Waddington on Tuesday of next week, the 10th
inst. Now, if you can come here on Monday, and go
down with me on Tuesday, I shall like it very much. Tell
your people to pray for Waddington. The wicked seem
to be tied up in a measure, and the ranks of Universalists

are broken in upon. Oh, let us be humble, and the victory shall turn on Zion's side.

In haste, your brother in the Gospel of Christ,

L. A. WICKES.

During a short vacation he wrote thus to his own friends, a record of some of his late experiences:

STOW'S SQUARE, Sept. 11th, 1841.

DEAR PARENTS, BROTHERS, SISTERS, &C.:

You perceive by this, that I am now at our friends in Lowville. I returned on Tuesday of this week, from St. Lawrence County, to spend only a few days and then return. I must plead guilty of not writing before, yet I have found it almost impossible to do it, for I have been in meeting every day from half-past nine in the morning, with but short intermissions until ten and eleven o'clock in the evening, besides persons calling for private conversation, so that I have often found it encroaching on my private devotions. Yet I do not forget you, though I do not write. The last I wrote you from Potsdam by my esteemed friend S. Raymond, Esq., since which I have spent about all the time in St. Lawrence County, holding protracted meetings. I returned from Potsdam about the time that Sister A. left for home. I did feel that God had work for me at another place than Antwerp, and accordingly told the people they must look for another minister. They felt very loth to have me leave them, and they would do nothing towards getting another until I sent away all my goods, and even then, it was hard to undertake it. But I felt that God called, and

I must obey, and thus, after getting my family all comfortably situated at S. S., started for Canton. This village is the Shire Town of the county, situated on the Grass River, about twenty miles from Ogdensburgh. It has Presbyterian, Methodist and Episcopal churches, and a Universalist and Baptist meeting house, academy, etc. The water privileges here are quite extensive. On the whole, it may be yet quite a pleasant village. The court and jail have a tendency to make the place grow and become populated. About a mile from the village is situated the county alms house, where there are miserable victims enough. This town was settled several years ago with New England Universalists, and they have kept the sway and awed down the professed followers of Christ, so that they supposed all was safe, locked up in universal apathy and danger. When it was known that a meeting was appointed, the Universalist preacher warned his congregation not to attend the meeting lest they should be converted, "for it is with sorrow," said he, "that I must acknowledge that some of those who we have been accustomed to call our people, have, by attending such meetings, been what they call 'converted.'" But this had a tendency to draw out the people. They then came out with a pamphlet to warn the people against evils of partialism, drawing a parallel with the temperance ox. But this only served to draw out the people more, to see how the ox would push with his horns, and so they got caught in their snares. Christians spent much time in prayer, and soon it was evident their labors were not in vain in the Lord. Many began to inquire what shall I do to be saved? The Spirit of the Lord did search out the hidden things, or works of darkness, and the sturdy oaks began to fall. The meeting lasted about four weeks and a half, and there were about two hundred and fifty who gave evidence of being the children of God. And many among them who had been very bold in sin before and had stood up for the defence of error, and some who had opposed their friends in attending the meeting, were themselves, made to bow at the foot of the cross. So that at the close of the meeting it was put to vote that the meeting be adjourned until I could go to Waddington and hold a meeting according to previous engagement, and then to be resumed again. Thus the Lord has shown His own power, and to His name be all the glory and the praise. How small is man before his Maker? Well would it be for him if he would only look at it and see how much we are indebted to Him. And then to serve Him as He should be served. The day after I closed at Canton, I commenced a meeting at Waddington. This village is situated on the St. Lawrence River, twenty miles below Ogdensburgh, has a population of over a thousand. It has a most beautiful location, with extensive water power. There is a large island containing seven hundred and eighty acres which lies some thirty or fifty rods from the main land. This island belongs to the United States. There is a crossing on this branch of the river, and below on butments stand a row of mills, etc., and the dam there is a canal or ditch, from which extended for more than half a mile, and from this, water is taken to supply several machines, and other shops, that may be carried by water power. In these are employed a large number of persons, who have never thought much upon the means of grace, or about their souls. The only public edifice is St. Paul's Church. The leading characters of that church are men almost dead with intemperance; they are real drunkards, and I was credibly informed that one-half of the male population were in the habit of getting intoxicated, and there are several cases of delirium tremens now, in that small village. The religion of the place has been in a great measure under the controlling influence of High Episcopacy, which is infinitely worse than no religion at all. There were, however, two or three of the female members of the church who came into the meeting and took quite an interest in it. There were a very few of Methodists, and they were perhaps not as bad, but nearly so. Their class leader right in the midst of the meeting went with wicked men to the bar and drank his gin. The Congregational was very little better. The whole church was composed of twelve members, five males and seven females Of the males, one was a gambling, dishonest, Sabbath-breaking, licentious man. Another was away nearly all the time, and when at home, did nothing to advance the cause. One did not maintain family worship. Another was very much engaged in parties, etc. The other had the form of godliness. Of the females, one was gone away, one was sick, one crazy poor woman has great trials, is sensible of her derangement, talks about it quite rational to all appearance, may the Lord be gracious unto her; another came forward and confessed that for years she was very sensible she was a hypocrite, one out of the three others was waiting for the consolation of Israel, the other two had never attended a prayer meeting for fear they should be called upon to pray. There was a minister of the Scotch Presbyterian Church which meets about three miles from the village, he resides in the village. As I called on him, he brought out his *decanter* of wine and brandy! Here you have the moral character, or power of that village and community, it is impossible to conceive of the desolations. There was no preaching of any kind, and had not been for a long time, except occasional Methodist preaching, and scarcely any attended on that. I obtained the use of the Episcopal Church to hold the meeting in, and entered the "Sanctum Sanctorum." The Lord blessed, I preached for about four weeks, and at the close, I had the pleasure of seeing about eighty hopeful converts, who professed to have given themselves to the Lord. Among them are the most wealthy and the most respectable part of the village. On the Sabbath, thirty united with the Congregational Society. I had but little help from any quarter except from above, without that, all other help would be useless and vain. Truly, how good the Lord is to those who will trust in Him, and serve Him with all the heart. Yet, I often feel my heart is far from God, and but little of the spirit of Jesus is found in my soul, yet I often feel to say, "O, for grace to love Thee more." Never have I felt the responsibility resting upon me as I have during the past season, while constantly engaged leading souls to Christ. But I need it still more than ever. Do pray for me, that I may be conformed to the image of my Savior God. I am now expecting to return on Monday or Tuesday to Canton, to resume that meeting again. How long I shall be absent from my family I cannot say. May the Lord prolong life and grant every needed blessing. The children are healthy and have grown much. My greatest anxiety is to see them praying children, walking in the fear of God. All other adornments I consider as useless, besides this in comparison, to be prepared for usefulness to glorify God, and enjoy Him forever.

But I must bring my letter to a close. I should like to hear from you all, and often as possible. I will endeavor to write oftener. Love to all, Pray much for me. As ever, your affectionate son,

L. A. WICKES.

P. S. I saw in a paper from Albany, a Mr. Wickes while lecturing on temperance, was pelted with rotten eggs. I should like to know whether it was father that had that high honor conferred upon him, and what he did in the midst of the salute; what a rotten heart the devil has got. At any rate, his fruit in that instance, was quite emblematic of his high and moral *worth*.

CANTON, August 21, 1841.

MR. WICKES:

I had just folded my paper to write a line to you, when Brothers Wood and Cross called, and gave me the cheering information of the good work of the Lord at Waddington. I had learned something of it by your very welcome letter, but more by them.

I pray God to renovate Waddington, and "create all things new there."

Our meetings here, and in all the neighborhoods about us, are very well attended, and the spirit of inquiry has gone forth throughout the town.

We held a prayer-meeting of the church yesterday, *all day*, commencing at half-past ten A. M. and closing a little past four P. M., with but half an hour's intermission. I think the spirit of prayer in the church now is more abundant than when you left here. The young converts as yet appear well and pray much. Mr. Baldwin and Baxter and Chamberlin appear *well*. Baldwin is a great help already in our religious meetings.

We design to resume the meeting again, according to our adjournment. We see, if possible, more cause for this than when we closed the meeting. Many persons are now disarmed of their prejudices, ready to converse on religion, and say if the meeting is resumed, they will attend it. I have no doubt but that many Universalists will attend the next meeting. I am of the honest opinion that another meeting of two or three weeks will accomplish more than has been done. *All the church* say, "resume the meeting," and so say *many men of the world*. The Universalists *rave* and *foam*. God has laid His hand upon them, and *they feel it*.

The bearer of this is *waiting*, or I would write more. I now mean to go to Waddington on Monday next, and stay one night, but must return home on Tuesday evening.

Mrs. P. sends love.

Your Brother,
R. PETTIBONE.

CANTON, Sept. 1, 1841.

DEAR BROTHER WICKES:

I received yours of the 31st, and I rejoice to hear of the good work. I advise you to encourage the young converts, and care for their future interest. If the church agrees to it, I would receive them into the fold before leaving them—*all* that are willing, and give good evidence of a saving change.

There is no abatement of interest here in religious concerns; at least, there is none on the subject of another meeting. I should like, myself, to have it begin a little sooner than the time you mention, but perhaps it is soon enough. The farming community will all be through with their harvests by that time, and in the meanwhile we will be doing all that we can. If you will return to Canton on Monday, and preach here on Monday evening, I will find you a conveyance over to De Kalb, and then by sending my own team, or by paying your passage in the stage. If you can do this, we should be much pleased, and I think it would do good. Should you conclude to come, please to send word by the bearer, Bro. C., and I will, on the Sabbath, give out an appointment for you on next Monday evening. I hope and pray that God will still continue to bless us here in Canton, and that He will go on with His own work until all St. Lawrence County is redeemed.

Yours affectionately,
R. PETTIBONE,
The Pastor of the church in Canton.

CANTON, Sept. 15, 1841.

MY DEAR AND AFFECTIONATE WIFE:

Last meeting at Canton. When I left you, on Monday, I did intend to reach Philadelphia the same evening, but was detained an hour at Deer River in getting my wagon mended. I staid at Br. Jackson's, in Champion. Had quite an interesting time in conversation and prayer. I started before sunrise; called at Br. Shattuck's; his wife feeble. Their meeting-house will soon be completed; it is thirty by fifty; will make a good house when finished. I arrived at Antwerp, and here I attended their church conference. But few attended, and they were quite disheartened. Br. R. said the dirty house was a testimony against them. Br. B. said their house was not half as dirty as their hearts were, and if they would only get new hearts, they would soon have a clean house, and so I thought. The church could not speak to me without weeping, and wanted to know when I would come back again. I gave no encouragement, if ever, unless it was the will of Heaven. I found immorality, like a tide, was rolling in upon the place. May the Lord lift up a standard, for "how soon the gold becomes dim, and the most fine gold is changed." After conversing with the friends, I went on and made several calls. Found Br. B. had made up his mind to leave Gouverneur; it was uncertain whether they would have a meeting. At Richville, the Baptist church had taken a *vote* to request Elder Clark to *leave*, for they could not stand the expense of attending the meeting, and paid him *two dollars*, and he left!! "O, Jerusalem, Jerusalem," etc. I reached this place just before evening. I preached this eve from 2 Sam., 5:24, "When thou hearest the sound of a going in the top of the mulberry trees," etc. Quite a goodly congregation was out, and the Spirit of God was evidently in the midst of us, and Sister Pettibone felt a good deal for souls.

Sept. 16, half-past ten in the evening.—At the

prayer-meeting in the morning, there were very few to attend—only about twenty, though there was a good degree of feeling with those who had come, tho' I was disappointed in not seeing more there. In the afternoon there was something of a number out to meeting. I preached from Eph. 6:15, "Put on the whole armor of God," etc.; and this eve, Matt., 12:30. And there was very good attention paid to the subject. O, may it be the beginning of better times for this place. Waggoner has gone to New York. I pray God to affect their hearts while he is gone, and reach him while he is there. I know God is able to conquer the stoutest heart, and reach him. To-day one young man has been turned away from home because he would attend on this meeting. It is the son of Dr. Noble, the inn-keeper, on the hill towards Potsdam. If the father does not yield to Christ, he will, in all probability, disinherit his son. The young man is twenty-three years of age, and a most faithful and industrious young man. How true is the language of the Savior, "A man's foes shall be they of his own household." That man cannot rest day or night. He says, "It is old Wickes and the Devil, and when I was away off in Lowville I was before his mind." Poor man! He ought to know that it is God's spirit that is pressing on his heart, and that his warfare is an unequal one. I do feel that the Lord will take care of that young man, and he shall have a hundred-fold more in this world, and in the world to come life everlasting. To have God for our friend is all that we can ask, and it is more than we deserve; yet we are His children, and He will regard His own followers, and protect those who will trust Him. "I will be a Father unto you, and ye shall be my sons and daughters, saith the Lord Almighty." Br. Pettibone has taken the young man into his house, and he will be a father to him. May the Lord let His blessing attend him.

17th, half-past eleven o'clock, evening.—This morning an anonymous letter, through the post-office, advising me to leave the town soon as possible, or I should be lynched or mobbed. O, how weak are the efforts of man against his God! Truly, God is more powerful than the arms of the wicked and the devices of the ungodly. The language of the Apostle is my trust: "If the Lord be for us, who can be against us?" To-day the meeting in the morning was pretty well attended, and some feeling among Christians. But few impenitent present. In the afternoon, preached to rather a thin house. The men stay at home, to keep the women at home. This evening, a large congregation, and very attentive. The Spirit of the Lord seemed to move upon the hearts of many. O, that the Lord will make bare His arm, and save this people from their sins. Brother Pettibone is confined to his house to-day on account of sickness; may it please the Lord to raise him up to bodily and spiritual health. I am sleepy and must close for to-night. Monday morning, Sept. 20th. Since I closed the other night, I have not had time to write a line at all. On Saturday the house was somewhat more filled than on the day previous, and some more feeling. The church took hold in prayer, and I do hope some have given their hearts to God. Brother Pettibone was taken sick on Friday, and he has not been able to be out since, and I have been almost alone in the labors, as far as to ministerial help, yet the Lord has sustained. On the Sabbath we had an overflowing congregation, and of course, a greater responsibility resting upon me. The Methodist and Baptist ministers were present, and took part in the exercises, and there was a universal expression of covenanting to take hold of the work and doing all they could, and it seemed to be a full and hearty covenant of the people, and I hope that our Heavenly Father will see it is His people's sincere consecration. Yesterday, there were people present from Canton, Potsdam, Norfolk, Massena, Waddington, Ogdensburgh, DeKalb, Hermon, Russel and Lisbon, and this being court week, we shall have representatives from all parts of county. Last evening there were some fifty or sixty rose for prayers, and after meeting, one of the first merchants tarried, and vowed to serve God, and opened his mouth in prayer, and also a young man from the academy, who was a backslider. I hope that institution may share more and more in the blessing of God, as the meeting advances in its time and interest. Do pray much for it, God has heard prayer in behalf of it. At the time of the death of Myron Johnson, the Principal elect of the academy, I prayed that God would grant that the trustees (the most of whom are Universalists,) might be inclined to obtain a teacher who would pray with those pupils, and the present preceptor is a talented young man, a member of the Presbyterian Church, of Middleburg, Vt. I do hope it will be the means of God visiting it with His Spirit. There are about forty young gentlemen in the academy, and the female department, I cannot say much about, only the instructress is an Episcopalian. This morning's mail brought me a letter from Rev. Mr. Barret, of Weston, Vt., wishing to get me to go and hold a meeting there, and to labor a few months in that State, among the Green Mountains. I think now that it is not my duty to go into another State, or to give him any encouragement of my coming at the present. And when I go into another State, I want my dear family with me, it is bad enough to be in another *county* from them. But be still my heart, I must not begin to talk thus, lest I begin to complain, and thus grieve my Savior. I find Satan is faithful in his temptations and trials on the mind, and they must not be pampered with at all. The wicked are raging like a mad bull in the net here, but the Lord, I hope, will tame them.

Monday, Sept. 27th. My dear wife, I do suppose by this time you will think I have forgotten you almost, and you are justifiable in thinking so, for I feel condemned in not finishing this before. But I have not had time to write at all, since last Monday. Brother Pettibone's health is so poor since he got better, that I have all the labor mostly to do, and I do not get to rest until about twelve o'clock at night. During the last week we have had all we could do till eleven o'clock at night in the church, and there was a real cry-out among the impenitent, and they could not leave the house until they gave up all to Christ, and fell at His feet. The meeting has not been in progress quite two weeks, and so far, it has been attended by the divine power, with a great deal more pungent feeling than the other, and there have been more conversions than there were at the same time in the previous meeting, but not as many as I did anticipate, and neither have the churches come up to the help of the Lord, nor attended as punctually and as generally as they did before. But you can conceive of nothing like the combination and alliance which the wicked have formed at this place. And the degree of rage which they seem to feel towards this meeting. Yet, nothing like violence has been offered at all, though it has been threatened. The Lord has a great hook for the jaws of the leviathan, and He can hold them in His hand. Oh, how I want to get them into the fold of my blessed Savior and Redeemer, where they may be made useful to build up His cause. I cannot say how many have turned to the Lord. God has taken some out of the families of the most strong and violent opposers in this place. What is puny little man, before the living God. But I will close and send this sheet without filling. I have hit upon Wednesday, the 6th of October, to go to Morristown and commence the meeting there. I shall aim to have it a short meeting, and get home before the 1st of November. I want you to write soon. I have more to say, but have not time. Say to all, love Jesus and serve Him. Pray much for me. Mrs. P. sends love to you. Give my love to all, tell them to pray much for me and for this place.

   I am as ever, your affectionate husband,

           L. A. WICKES.

MY DEAR LITTLE CHILDREN:

  I want you to be obedient, and kind to your dear mamma, and to your grandpa and grandma, and so to live and act, that they all will love you and esteem you.

Pa wants you to see what improvement you can make in working, reading and being good. There are a good many little girls who do pray here, and they love to pray, and why should not my little daughters too. Be careful not to have any unkind feelings towards each other, and if you have any, do not say a word, but get alone and pray our Heavenly Father to forgive you, and keep you from doing wrong. I must stop, people are coming to meeting.

Your affectionate father,

L. A. WICKES.

P. S.—I have not time to correct blunders, please overlook them, for there are many.

CANTON, 1841.

MR. WICKES—

DEAR SIR:

Anonymous letter written to Mr. W. while at Canton. I take this opportunity to inform you that the citizens of Canton have heard your preaching long enough, for you have divided every chord insunder that binds man and wife together, and parents and children; I need not tell you that, Joe Nobles has forbid his favorite from coming to his house on the account of you. This very son he had willed homestead farm to. But since you came back, the will has been altered, and he is cut off from home and property by your means. This is but one case out of fifty that I could mention, had I time, but serfice it say you can have this week to close your meeting. And I warn you as a friend if you stay any longer you will be delt with according to lynch law. Thirty of the best men in this town is this minite ready to put it into effect. I, therefore, as a friend, advise you to leave this place, for just so sure as you preach in this town next week, just so sure you will find trouble. I know this to be a fact, because I know there is metings every night to that efect, and if one excitement will take efect another will, I must close from a friend and well wisher.

Bye-and-bye you will hear my name, for I am not ashamed to own it before God and man.

CHAPTER IX.

REVIVAL MEETING AT MORRISTOWN.
BIRTHDAY LETTER OF 1841.

MORRISTOWN, Oct. 7th, 1841.

MY DEAR AND AFFECTIONATE WIFE:

YOU see I have finally reached this place. The meeting commenced on Wednesday evening, and but a small number out indeed, and it being an old school church, I found they were on the lookout for breakers and heresies, yet they seemed to move away from the house feeling that it was not so bad after all. It is a most desolate place as to morals. There are but two family altars in the village, a population of forty families, and one of those is Rev. Mr. W., the other is a Mr. P., a ferryman, who cannot attend meeting very frequently. There are, however, some sixty members in the church, and some fifteen or twenty females that reside in the village. I think from what I can judge, that good may be expected from the meeting. The other churches of the old school send in delegates to see how things move here, and spy out the land. I pray God they may see on what a barren soil they live, while God is pouring out His spirit on other churches, they are famishing for the bread of life, yet it may be, God has good in store for them. Let us pray for them. There have been one or two hopeful conversions, the first that was ever hopefully converted in the meeting-house, which has been built some three or four years. I pray God, it may not be the last. I find a young lady here that was converted at Antwerp, also M. M., the author of the book, "A New Order of Missionaries." I closed meeting at Canton, on Sabbath, the 3d of October, or rather, not until Monday morning, though we dismissed the congregation at about ten at night, yet sinners were calling for mercy, so that we did not disperse until after midnight, and there were some eight or ten we hope, gave themselves to the Savior, after the regular meeting closed. The whole number of conversions during the meeting, was something near sixty. The meeting lasted about two weeks and a half, and it was only by the power of Israel's God that anything was done, and to His name be all the glory, the praise and power. It is the hardest battle that I have had to fight, and the least help that I have had of human kind. When I came to this place, I went round by Waddington and preached there Monday evening, Tuesday P. M. and evening. Had a meeting for prayer and conversation in the morning, and in the mean time had church meeting, took six more into the church,* baptized one child, and there were some fourteen or sixteen souls hope-

---

* Speaking after the manner of men.—As practical, he acknowledged the great truth that to be genuinely converted, is to become a member of the General Assembly, the church of the first born.

fully converted to God. May the Lord keep them by
His almighty power. Also organized a society, appointed
trustees. They have got a subscription of some thirteen
hundred dollars for building a meeting house, and
the converts appear very well. They are the most active
of all the places where I have been. They have no minister,
and so have to work or die. I have not heard from
home since I left, but try to leave all in the hand of God.
Trust He will protect and bless us. Many friends send
love to you. I received a letter from Brother Whitford's
people at Watertown, requesting me to come and see
them as soon as possible, as their son and youngest
daughter were lying at the point of death, and were expecting
every day would be the last. How peculiar are
the dealings of God with man. Let us be prepared for
every exigency, and ready for all the trials of life. Aurelia
and Emma, be good children, love all, and be kind to
each other. Respects to all in haste.

As ever, your husband,
L. A. WICKES.

MORRISTOWN, Oct. 11th, 1841.

DEAR SISTER E.:

The sister was teaching at S. H.   You will perceive that I am on the banks
of the St. Lawrence, and the same waters which
you see at Sackett's Harbor, soon float down here too.
The village is on the river, and the steamers Oneida and
Telegraph, that touch at the harbor, call at the wharf
here; they arrive from twelve to three in the afternoon,

and if you can leave your school to come here, I will, God willing, carry you home. The meeting commenced last week, Wednesday evening. The religion was in a most deplorable condition among all. The church was very low, and still is, yet there are some who feel, and some that are willing to labor for the upbuilding of the cause of Christ. Yet they cannot come and plead for sinners with that earnestness, that I think Christians should, nor with that faith which they should exercise. Yet, this afternoon, we hope some eight or ten individuals have become hopeful heirs of immortal life. To God's name be all the glory, and the praise, and the power. The people are fast assembling for evening meeting. This house was never filled until yesterday, though it is a small one, and it was filled by His spirit too. We are in hopes to see great things here. "But let not him that putteth on the harness, boast himself as he that putteth it off." 12th. Last evening, the spirit of God was evidently visible in the congregation, a deep solemnity seemed to rest on the minds of the people. May the Lord send His spirit upon them, and bring them to bow at His feet. The meeting in Canton was a good one; I have preached there about eight weeks, and there were some three hundred hopeful conversions, and the work is still progressing, and souls are weekly coming to the Savior. But opposition to the cause of Christ was most powerful and strong. But the Lord has girdled the tree of infidelity, and it must die. May the Lord hasten it. At Waddington the meeting was glorious, and is an honor to the blessed Savior, who has so triumphantly worked. God is doing great things for this county. Hundreds are bowing to the scepter of Immanuel. Let us, dear sister, live more for Jesus, and nearer in prayer to God. The meeting will probably hold next week, or a part of the week. Pray for this place.

Your affectionate brother,

L. A. WICKES.

MORRISTOWN, Oct., 19th, 1841.

DEAR AND AFFECTIONATE WIFE:

I received yours, of the date unwritten, on the borders of mother's. The Lord is working here. There have been somewhere between seventy and one hundred that have expressed hope since the meeting commenced. They have never seen such a time here before, and do not know how to act now, sometimes they are all carried away with their extacy, and then all down in doubt, and hardly know where to look for help, or what to think, while others seem to feel they will look up to God at all times. There have been up to this date, some eight or ten family altars erected in the village, more praying families than was ever known here before. May the Lord increase the number still more and more, until every house shall be a praying house, and every heart a meet temple for the Lord to dwell in. I shall not be able to leave here before next Monday, (the 25th,) if then, and when I do leave, I wish to go directly to L. as soon as I can, with the Lord's help. I have been in hopes that I could get through what the Lord has for me to do here this week, and reach home before the Sabbath. But as the prospects now appear, I shall not be able to close before the Sabbath, and may be, not then. I feel that the Lord will do all things right, and let us trust in His hand for help, and He will be our support. The prayers of many Christian friends in this place are offered for us, and morning and evening, we are remembered here by the good family with whom I board. Be prayerful, write to me soon.

In haste, yours affectionately,
L. A. WICKES.

MORRISTOWN, Oct. 25th, 1841.

DEAR AND AFFECTIONATE WIFE:

You will perceive by this, that I am still on the borders of the United States, and shall probably be here a few days longer, it may be until next Sabbath. I feel anxious to be at home with my family. My first is to serve God in the salvation of souls, and the second, is my dear family. The work of the Lord is progressing here gloriously. There is scarce a day, but there are some new family altars erected here, and souls are turning to the Lord; 29th, I had only time to write the above, and was then called off so that I could not finish it before the stage went out, and it goes only every other day, and I have had one thing after another to give me no *time*. I do not get to rest until about twelve o'clock every night. I am willing to wear out, but I do feel solicitous about my family. Since I commenced this, the work has moved forward with unabating interest, yea, with an increasing interest. Opposition seems to be falling before the wheels of God's chariot. And the work among the heads of families is most like the work of Norfolk, of anything I have seen this season. Several openly avowed Universalists have been made to bow at the foot of the cross. The congregation is small, not much more than half as large as at either of the other places, though we have a meeting-house full, that is between three and four hundred, and of this number, one-third, if not more, is often forward for prayers, and the most have expressed hope in the Savior. To God, be all the glory, the praise and the power. Some who have been swearing mad, have been cut down in a moment. Nearly one-half of all the families of the village have altars erected in them, and some are rejoicing in hope in other houses. May the Lord still progress in the work of salvation. It seems as though the work has but just begun, and the whole region is on the move, and I have no doubt, if they will keep humble that they may see such a work here as has not been in the county for a long time. But yet, it seems that they hardly know what to do, and where to go, so long have they lived in sin, and backsliding, and now they have to be instructed in the first great principles of serving God with all the heart. Let us be grateful for what God has done, and show that we need not labor in vain, if we labor in the work of the Lord. I feel often that I am too ungrateful for all His favors, which He is showing us, and for what He is using me for, shall the saw boast itself against him that shaketh it? foolish indeed, can that be, and what am I, any more. I feel that I am indebted under God to the prayers of His people for all the blessings that have attended the truth that has been spoken. O, may I ever prove myself worthy of the prayers of the faithful and humble followers of the meek and lowly Jesus. I am very anxious to do what the will of the Lord is if I know my heart and then I can secure the blessing of God upon my whole family, and also my children's children, for I know that God will keep those who trust in him. "And he that honoreth God, God shall honor." We never can be safer than when under the hand of our Savior's direction, He never will leave us, and in our greatest trials He will uphold us, and do us all the good we need. I will still wrestle and pray for the descent of the blessing of God upon my dear family,

It is now meeting time and must I close. O, when will Christians, and ministers, too, get their eyes open, so as to see where they are, and learn to work as they should, for it behoves them to be workers with Christ, in the salvation of this dying world. Pray much for me. I shall be home as soon as is consistent to leave here, if the Lord will. Love to all.

In haste, yours affectionately,

L. A. WICKES.

MORRISTOWN, Nov. 2, 1841

MY DEAR AND AFFECTIONATE WIFE:

I preached to the converts on Sabbath afternoon, and there were something over one hundred and twenty-five who took their seats together and gave their names to unite with the different churches, which is a much larger number according to the number of those who attended, than any other meeting in the county; and according to the help which I have had, i. e., man's help, Morristown never saw such a day as this before. A large number

are heads of families, and many of the first men of the
town have been sharers in the work, and at this moment
there are some twelve or fifteen family altars in the village,
when there were only two at the commencement of the
meeting, and there are a large number in the town. There
are more old gentlemen brought into the fold of Jesus
here in proportion than at any other place. I expected
to close Sabbath afternoon, and as soon as I got through
the exercise a motion was made that they would lay aside
all their temporal affairs that were possible and attend
the meeting, so long as the providence of God seem to
indicate that it shall continue, if I would only stay longer,
and a very large part of the congregation rose and voted
for it, and a large number of impenitent among them, and
there have been some hard cases come to the Lord Jeuss
since the Sabbath, and how long I shall stay I cannot
say. But I do feel so that I cannot rest, yet I do feel
that I want to do what is right and for the honor and
glory of God, and then I know He will take care of us. I
must, however, seek His favor and His pleasure and leave
events in His hands. I have heard that the work is still
going on in Canton, and souls are every day bowing before the Lord. May it continue to ride on gloriously
over all. O, what a blessed and glorious privilege it is
for us to be permitted to be laborers in so glorious and
holy a cause. I am aware I do not value the work as I
should do, and the privilege as I should of seeing souls
bow at the foot of the cross and made heirs of immortal
glory. Truly, how unworthy I am and sinful, and how
vile a being I am; every day I see more and more cause
for me to humble myself at the foot of the cross, and to
cry unclean.

Nov. 4th. The stage went out before I had time to mail this, and so I have opened to say the work goes on most gloriously yet, though it has been the three days of election yet the spirit of God has been working among the inhabitants of the town and many more have bowed to Christ since I wrote above, and I have been all along making my calculation to close, at the farthest, to-day, yet there will be an uncertainty about that. For though the people have been at meeting for near a month, they are unwilling to stop yet. But when I do see the least indication that it would be the will of God that I should close, I shall not tarry long here. Every day there are new altars erected in the name of the Lord, and I must say that the work is the most genuine in its appearance of any that I have seen. Confessing their guilt and their opposition to the work and to God, and asking forgiveness of all. I do want to see the churches understanding their duty to God and to one another more, so they will be able to lead each other in the work of the Lord. They are often most unskillful. But still I have some hopes they will learn more and still more of the arts of war in this great battle field. Yesterday I had an invitation to go and hold a meeting in the Methodist church within about five miles of Ogdensburg, but I could give them no encouragement at all, for I have agreed to be at Parrishville on the 17th inst. unless they alter it, and the church in DeKalb are anxious I should get there as soon as possible, and the people in Madrid are rather expecting me to come there as soon as possible, yet this last place I have some doubt about. Wherever the Lord sends me I am ready to go, for he will go before

Morristown, Nov. 2, 1841.

me, and I shall find Him a help in all times of need. Do pray much for me and for this place.

Yours affectionately.

L. A. WICKES.

To My Little Daughters:

I want you to become good children. Be very kind to your dear mother and to all. Learn as fast as possible. I wish you were here with me to see this river. The St. Lawrence in some places is three miles wide, probably the largest river in the world, though not as wide. The prospect is beautiful. But I must close. Give my love to all. I hope to see you soon.

Your affectionate father,

L. A. WICKES.

MORRISTOWN, Nov. 2, 1841.

Dear Brother Cross:

To Mr Cross to come to Morristown. I have but a moment to say a word. God is at work in this place, and I am almost worn out, yet salvation is flowing like a deluge, and the work is the most like the work of Norfolk of any that I have seen this season according to numbers of the population. Last Sabbath I preached to the converts, and there were 125 took their seats together, and the feeling was such that there was a voluntary vote that they would lay aside every temporal work that was possible, and attend the meeting as long as the providence of God should point out duty. Now, my brother, I want your help, come here to-morrow evening, with the calculation to stay over the Sabbath if possible. The meeting will not hold longer than that probably. You shall not be the loser in anything. Your church surely cannot say no. My Brother, do come, I pray you. Start as soon as you get this.

In haste your Brother in Christ,
L. A. WICKES.

P. S.—Call at Brother Taylor's at DeKalb as you come and see if he has got my pocket Bible, and bring it with you, when you come. Enquire for Rev. Mr. Williams who lives opposite the Episcopal church.

L. A. W.

STOWS SQUARE, Nov. 11th, 1841.

DEAR AND AFFECTIONATE PARENTS:

I sent you a letter by Mr. M. from Morristown on the eve of my departure, from that place home. I arrived at this place on Tuesday, the 9th inst., being absent nearly two months. I found all in comfortable health. I found C. down stairs with a babe in her arms two weeks old, (a little daughter), both doing finely. Thus you see the Lord has smiled upon us again and showed us his favors. Truly, God evinces His care for those who put their trust in Him, and will sustain those who will obey and trust in Him, and may we ever show ourselves worthy, through Jesus, of the favors God does bestow upon us. Why God has dealt with us as He has for the last year we do not pretend to say, or even desire that the future should be open to us; it is enough for us to know, that our present course is pleasing to God, and secures His blessing. You seem rather in your letter to think that it would be better for us to settle in some place if we could find any. There are some seven or eight churches where I could find a permanent place, but God has ordered different for us. I have now preached in two different churches for nine years, and all the time I have felt that I wanted to get out into the more laborious life of the evangelist, tho' I do think that the experience of the pastor's life has been one of the greatest blessings to me, to prepare me for this work, and I do most sincerely believe that the place which I have now been called into, is one that God has placed me in, and shall I play Jonah and run away from him? I am afraid I never should come off as well as Jonah did. While I love my friends and my family, and should be pleased to have them with me as well as any one could, but I love the cause of Christ more, and the providence of God has ordered it that we should be separated for a short season. I have ever felt this prevailing principle in my bosom since my hopeful conversion to God. "Lord direct me into the path of usefulness."

Does my dear mother recollect the conversation which she had with me in Elbow Street while I was living in sin? It was this. I was sitting in the front room, and on a Sabbath towards evening she came and sat down on a little stool and leaned upon my knee and began to talk with me about my soul, and among other things, she said, "My *dear son if you become* a *Christian*, you may be useful in the world." This one idea had more influence on my mind than anything that had been said to me about being a Christian, to turn my mind to be favorable towards the Christian life, and after my conversion, it was my constant reflection, and while a student, while my fellows were expressing themselves of a desire to be great and learned, my mind and my greatest wish was to be useful in leading souls to Christ, and since I have been in the ministry, I have endeavored to keep this before me. Though I find I have been of but little service in the church during my life; yea, comparatively nothing have I done for Him who has done so much for me, I feel that I only wish to honor and glorify God in all my course, and God will be our help and support.

How long I shall continue to occupy the post that I am now in, I cannot say. I may another year, or part of the year At any rate I wish to obey the Lord in everything, and I do earnestly ask you to pray that God will direct me. Since I wrote to you before, I have been to Canton and spent three weeks besides the other four weeks which I spent there in the summer, and there were some 60 or 70 conversions, and the work still moves forward and every week more or less are hopefully converted to the Lord. I left there for Morristown and went around by Waddington, about 20 miles out of my way, and spent one day there and held meeting one day with them and there were some 16 hopefully converted to God. And in the evening there were some six or eight avowed connection with the church who had been hopefully converted during the protacted meeting there, and the society was organized and some fourteen or fifteen hundred dollars raised toward building a church edifice. The Lord has done great things for that place and to His name be all the glory and the power, for He, alone, is worthy to be praised. The ride from Waddington to Morristown is on the banks of the St. Lawrence river, and it is most delightful to see the wonder of the Lord in uniting so many drops of water and with such force as in some places it sweeps forth with majesty and power.

The banks of the river above the water are not high; in some places they are quite bold. The river is interspersed with one thousand islands Some are covered with forests while others are nearly barren. The appearance of the opposite side of the river is very delightful. The crops look very fine. The full grain had gained a beautiful appearance from the hand of Him who nourishes every spear. The foliage had just begun to fall from the trees and change their hue, and warned me of the approach of my dissolving nature. The distance from Waddington to Morristown is thirty miles, and passes through the village of Ogdensburgh. On the opposite side of the river about once in four or five miles there is a church erected of some kind, and occasionally along there will be a round wind mill for grinding grain. It was in one of these that the self-styled patriots took refuge in the late broils and from which they were carried as prisoners to Fort Henry; it stands a little below Prescott, which village is opposite Ogdensburgh. Prescott has quite a large fort and considerable of a village. Ogdensburgh is the largest village in the county and is a business place. They have two steamboats a day arrive, and depots for water privileges are very great. The Indian River empties into the Oswegatchie, and this breaks over something of a fall of 100 or 150 rods above the mouth where it empties into the St. Lawrence and from the dam above the falls there is a very swift race way, and on this are situated a large number of mills and machine shops. At present the moral aspect of this place is rather lonely and sad. There are churches there of the four evangelical denominations and all equally asleep. I pray God they may be aroused from their apathy. When I arrived at M— I felt very sad indeed. There were in the village forty families, and only two where the family altar had been erected in the fear of the Lord, and it was given to sin of almost every name, yet the Lord had a blessing in store for that people. It was evident soon that the Lord was moving among the people, and soon many sinners began to enquire what they should do to be saved, and enquiry came from many: "What do these things mean?" The church belongs to the old school assembly though a large part of the church are bitterly opposed to it. Yet they would watch very closely to see what would be said and done and look out for heresy. They soon found they had enough to do to look after their own hearts, and to watch their own evil ways and doings, and began to feel they must work for souls and do all they could to save sinners. And the impenitent were now trembling. At the commencement there was only one professor of religion in the choir, and that a female. The choir consisted of about thirty, and at the close every person, with the exception of one, professed hope in the dear Redeemer and in the village there were rising of twenty family altars erected, and in the town something like fifty. In most cases both parents were brought in the work and hopefully made anew in Christ Jesus. Some who had been the bitterest opposers to the work of the Lord had been made to bow at the foot of the cross, and the whole work seemed to be characterized by an humble confession of their great sins and numerous faults, and there seemed to be a child-like spirit in the whole and many seemed to have the greatest desire to get low before God and abase themselves in the deepest dust. The congregation was small to what have attended in other places. Their house would seat only about three hundred, though we crowded more than five hundred into it. There were something like one hundred and seventy or more who professed to give themselves to the Savior. Truly, the Lord shall be praised for all His wonders which He hath wrought in that place. The meeting lasted thirty-two days (a little over a month), and the interest continued to increase more and more until the last amen was pronounced, and it seemed only to give the work a new impulse. The whole region is truly on the move and may it be thus and more so, until every soul is brought to bow at the feet of the Savior. Why is it that we have so little dependence on God, or in the use of means to accomplish the end? O! may God forgive the unbelief, and awaken His people to their privilege.

Hope you will write soon, and give our love to all.

Your affectionate son,

L. A. WICKES.

CHAPTER X.

MEETING AT PARRISHVILLE.

PARRISHVILLE, Nov. 27th, 1841.

DEAR AND AFFECTIONATE WIFE:

AFTER leaving you on Monday the 22d, I reached Mr. Jackson's in C. soon after dark, and tarried with them all night. I found their children quite serious, and inclined to listen to the things that make for their everlasting peace. May the Lord have mercy on them. I took breakfast and fed my horse at the Bend, and then had a most muddy ride to A. Had an interesting interview with a number of our friends. I started for Richville where I arrived between seven and eight in the evening. On my way I called on Brother Stevens. The Lord is at F. neighborhood. Several have been hopefully converted, and there seemed to be a moving among the "dry bones."

When I arrived at Potsdam my horse and I were both tired out, and Mr. Parker, the teacher in the academy, came and brought me up here in his buggy. Kind man may the Lord reward him. I did not arrive here until after the meeting closed on Wednesday evening and found myself very tired and weary. There was no meeting appointed on Thursday morning. In the P. M.

I found some twenty or thirty persons there, and some little freedom in prayer, some little confession of sin, but there is much to be done. In the evening I preached from "Search me, oh God," etc. There were quite a goodly number out, three hundred persons or more. They were mostly attentive, though some whispering and running out. The house is a comfortable stone building, with a gallery for the singers over the porch. The building will comfortably seat from three to five hundred persons. The pulpit is at the further end of the house, is easy to speak in. There is a small bell on the church, a basement, not finished. Village is not large. It is situated on the St. Regis river. Parrish has a large distillery here, and manufactures a great deal of the *poison*. Between three and four thousand inhabitants in town and many hard hearts. This morning the prayer meeting was very thinly attended, and resembled the commencement of the meeting in Massena. I find there is much to be done here, and but a few to do it. Last evening there was no singing at all in the church. I am one hundred miles away from you on the field of battle. The people are not prepared for the meeting. I hope you will pray much for me and for this place. I must close and go to church.

Yours in haste,
L. A. WICKES.

A Birthday letter.

PARRISHVILLE, Lawrence Co., Dec. 8, 1841.

Being the commencement of the 34th year of the life of Lewis A. Wickes, eldest son of Jonas and Sarah B.

Wickes, and 66th year of the American Independence, also the tenth year of my gospel ministry, and eighth year of my married life and seventh of being a father.

Dear and most Affectionate Parents:

You will perceive that this is dated away from my home and that is the reason why I cannot write you as fully as I have been accustomed to, on the occasion of the same in other years, for I am in the midst of a protracted meeting and cannot have the day to myself as I have devoted for the last fourteen years of my life. I do, however, suppose that you will expect from me a few lines, and you shall have them by the blessing of the Lord, and one question I do wish here to ask. Have you another child who gives you their yearly history? or even a synopsis of it? This, however, has been one of peculiar providence with me and mine. A year ago now, my health was such that I had almost concluded to give up preaching entirely, and follow some other occupation of life. My health was good with the exception of my talking machinery which I was told must not be used, and for about two of the first months of the past year I did not labor much, though I preached three or four times every week. I felt I could not drag out a life so useless and so barren, and feeling the pain from my lungs remove, I engaged to hold a meeting of days with the church in Richville. Before the time came I was attacked with a severe cough. Being able to ride I went on the day appointed to tell them I was not able, but yet to do what I could to advance the cause of the Lord, and expecting if I went forward that I should go to my grave. I commenced the meeting amidst a hoarse cough and shortness of breath, and would preach and cough and cough and preach, and during the first sermon I suppose near one-quarter of the time was spent in coughing and raising. But my cough soon began to give way and I to feel more encouraged I preached three times every day for three weeks in succession and my cough was all gone. In the mean time I made use of the lung tube and Dr. Jane's India Expectorant, and from that time you have had something of a clue to my engagements and how I have spent my time. Suffice it to say that only by grace I am what I am, and it is the Lord that has been my help and my strength, and by His power I have done what I have. And yet I feel that much more might have been done. I have during the year preached about five hundred and twenty-five sermons, besides a large part of the other exercises connected with it. Also, I have held rising of two hundred and fifty prayer and inquiry meetings in which I have done more labor than to preach a sermon of common length. In these I have witnessed the hopeful conversions of between fourteen and fifteen hundred souls to the Savior. Of these between four and five hundred were heads of families, and quite a number were over seventy years of age. To the Lord be all the glory; to Him I will ascribe thanksgiving, and honor, and glory, and all that is within me. I will call upon to give to Him glory and praise for all His wonderful acts to vile and sinful man! Oh, how unworthy am I for all that He has done with me. Shall the saw boast himself

A remarkable number of aged and heads of family brought to Christ.

over *him* that shaketh it? Surely not. "He that honoreth Me him will I honor." During the same time I have traveled rising of nine hundred miles besides the walking to and from meetings, and now I feel fully as well, if not better than I did last year when I commenced and have grown corpulent all the time. I have been confined to my room *two days!* under the care of a physician during the year. Truly, I can say, "Oh, to grace how great a debtor daily I'm constrained to be." And what an account I must give at the last for the non-improvement of the blessings God has conferred upon me. Oh, for a heart more devoted to the service of God and to advance the cause of the blessed Savior. During the year, too, I have left the people of my charge in Antwerp in opposition to their most earnest request. What the result may be I cannot say, but hope it may be for the good of souls. So far, I think I have done what is right and pleasing to God, in regard to that. This year I have also refused to accept an invitation from the church in N. to become their pastor and what the consequence may be, I do not know, but hope for the best, both to them and also to myself and family. This year I have organized a church; the first that I have ever organized and assisted to one other. This year I have assisted in organizing a Congregational society and the foundation for a meeting house to be built at W. I have broken up keeping house for the present. This year, too, I have become the father of the third child, a sweet little daughter. Thus we feel that heaven has smiled upon us and been our protector and support. If the Lord spares her life, I hope she may be an ornament in the cause of Christ, and that she may early be taught the knowledge of God.

This year, too, I have by the blessing of God, arrived at that post when I can say I owe no man anything but love, (i. e.) I have the means as soon as I can attend to it, for which I am thankful to my blessed Savior, for I have long been perplexed with debt, and when can I be thankful enough for all His kindness to me? Eternity itself will only be long enough. And as a family, we feel we have much to do to honor Him, and we want greater love to do it. Since I wrote you I have traveled one hundred miles on horseback to this place, and commenced a meeting. There seems to be some good feeling and a great deal of bad. The church is in a most wretched condition. They have been by the ears for some eight or ten years, and, also an unholy feeling between different denominations, and seems like bringing great rocks together and neither want to give way, and both must. It has been so far a heavy lift indeed, but many have turned to the Lord and the whole community have seemed to be more or less affected by the Spirit of God, and almost Christians. I pray God they may be inclined to turn to him and that, too, with all the heart. There have been several protracted meetings held here, and some good has been done. But the impenitent have become very hard, and there is a *Death Pit* in the midst of the Village, (*Distillery*), and this poisons all that is lovely or may be useful. There is one tavern, three or four stores and groceries, and two school houses, two churches and some few shops of the various mechanics, etc., etc. There is rather a low state of morals and a most vile set of young people, though there is rather a better set among them. There is but little refinement among any, and yet they have souls to save or to lose, and they are just as much worth saving as anybody's, and I do pray the Lord they may be brought at the foot of the cross.

In view of the dealings of God with me I feel that it becomes me to renew my consecration to the service of God, and to promote the cause of Christ on earth. I feel anxious to hear from you all to know how they are growing in the Divine life. I must close. I do hope when you have a nearness to the throne you will remember me. Do pray much for me, that I may live at the foot of the cross. Remember me to all the dear brothers and sisters, and ever praying that I may be an ornament to your gray hairs, I subscribe myself to you,

Your affectionate son,
LEWIS A. WICKES.

CHAPTER XI.

REVIVAL IN DE KALB.

DE KALB, January 7, 1842.

MY DEAR, AFFECTIONATE WIFE:

YOU see by this that I have finally got to the region of rocks, and have commenced the meeting here. Things are very forbidding and very unpleasant as yet, and it is very doubtful how long the meeting may continue. Should have been home this week had it not been judged best to continue this meeting, or rather, to commence it. The most of the members of this Presbyterian church that have attended the meeting at any one time is SIX!!! And since I have got here I have learned that not more than one third of them will be able to come to the meeting at all. They either are at such a distance they cannot come, or they are sick, or else superannuated, or have a disease about the heart, which is very prevalent in cold regions. I have given this day to decide the case whether or not they will go forward with all their might and power. I will let you know in a few days again if the prospects are more favorable. I knew not how long I should be at Parrishville, for the meeting held about two weeks longer than I expected it would; but the Lord came off with a glorious victory. There were something like 130 to 150 hopeful conversions. To God be all the glory and the praise and the power, for He alone is worthy. The field of labor was one of the most forbidding of any that I was ever acquainted with. The churches were in a most miserable, wicked state, and it took a long time to kill all the corruption, and now it may come to life again. But may the Lord forbid, and cause His spirit to flow upon them yet. The meeting closed on the evening of the 2d day of January, 1842. On Monday I came to Potsdam and preached in the afternoon to a few who had assembled for the day of fasting and prayer for the world's conversion. I called at our friend's, Mr. Raymond's, and there is a great vacancy in that dear family by death. It is our friend Mrs. Raymond herself. She died on the last Monday of December. She was taken on Friday, on Saturday she called for medical aid, and on Monday eve she fell asleep in Jesus

DeKalb, 1842. and was buried on the last Wednesday of the year. It was a great loss to all, and especially to the family. Mr. Raymond feels it very sensibly. She rests from her labors. How God has protected us whilst others have gone to inherit the promises. May we so spend our lives as to advance the cause of our blessed Redeemer. In the evening I came to Canton and there preached to a large congregation. Found things there quite interesting, and many souls in this place were inquiring what they should do to be saved. Found one individual trying to take shelter under the doctrine of universal salvation without confessing her sins. Oh, what a delusion! But the Lord, we trust, has saved her from so fatal a fall. What debtors to grace we are! Debtors daily. Oh, how great His loving smiles have been over us! Truly, by "grace are we saved through faith, and that not of ourselves; it is the gift of God." I do really want to see my family. The people live so scattered over this town that if it was consistent I would have them with me wherever I go. But the will of the Lord be done; and may we ever seek His honor. Kiss all the little ones for me. Write soon as possible and let me know how all are.

In haste, your husband,

L. A. WICKES.

HERMON, February 1, 1842.

MY AFFECTIONATE AND DEAR WIFE:

You have no doubt looked for me ere this, as I expected to be at home during the month of January to pay a visit to our friends at Watertown. I did expect to close the meeting in DeKalb a week ago last Sabbath, but the state of things was such that I found it would be difficult to close and it was continued another week and closed on the last Sabbath in January. There were something like seventy or eighty hopeful conversions to God, and to His name be all the glory and the power. In some respects it was as forbidding as I ever had before me. The state of the church; the distance from the meeting-house (I boarded a mile), the prejudices against each other, together with the unprepared state of the Christian community, were barriers that were great to be overcome. But the Lord has kindly overlooked and has been the faithful God to forgive their transgressions when they humbled themselves. There were quite a large number of those who expressed hope in this town (Hermon),

<small>Hermon, Feb. 1, 1842.</small>

and the state of feeling in this place was such that we thought it best to spend a few days in this place—some five or six days—and I do not know but all is right. I felt it, perhaps, duty to come here a few days.

February 2d. When I arrived here, there was a severe rain, and supposed the house would be rather *thinly* filled, but it was literally crammed. They have nothing but a *large school house* to meet in, and it cannot be had only in the evening. The Lord opened a door of hope by bringing an excommunicated member from the Presbyterian church back, and he opened his house for day meetings and the whole community turned out and made seats for the accommodation of some 150 persons, and the house is thronged. This is the second day of the meeting and there were six or seven hopeful conversions and backsliders reclaimed, and there seems to be a sound of an abundance of rain, and some conversions of men seventy years old. I feel this whole region may be shaken, and hundreds may be brought at the foot of the cross. May the Lord grant it for his name's sake. Some three or four Universalists have been brought to bow at the foot of the cross, and it is shaking the whole region. There are only five family altars in the place. May the Lord have mercy on the people, and pour out His spirit upon them. My abode is with a Mrs. Green, a member of Brother Taylor's church in DeKalb. Her husband and hired girl have both been hopefully converted during the meeting here. She appears a good sister in Christ, and a woman of prayer.*

* Since deceased.

I have now some half-a-dozen urgent requests to hold meetings and they each want me to come first, and what to do I hardly know; which way I can scarcely say, but I do think duty calls me home before going to either place. Still I may be mistaken. I do desire to do what is right. How the Lord does bless us, and what debtors we are and shall always be to Him. Now, how does my little family do. I feel so great a desire to see them that I could forego almost any other privilege for their company, except it may be the salvation of souls and the glory of God.

I must close. I cannot tell when this will reach you, or when it will be mailed. Kiss the dear children for me. I wish you all to be like the whole family in heaven.

Remember me to all. A short adieu.

Your husband,
L. A. WICKES.

At Hermon, sick, Feb'y 11, 1842.

HERMON, Feb'y 11, 1842.

MY DEAR AND AFFECTIONATE WIFE:

Being bolstered up in my sick bed at the kind and hospitable abode of Mr. O. Green, in the village of Hermon, I drop you a line. I have not strength enough to write but a line. I had packed up my valise to start for home last Wednesday morning, but the morning came, and with it a sick morning. I had an engagement to preach a funeral sermon at DeKalb, but in a few hours I was under the doctor's care. My disease is "*Bilious Pneumonia*," with a very bilious state of the whole system. The doctor thinks that with care, I may be able to leave my bed and room in a week. I have the kindest of care from Mr. and Mrs. G. The people here are also very kind in doing all in their power to make me comfortable; truly the Lord has prepared for me a home among strangers. How good and how kind is my Heavenly Father to one so unworthy. But I must be short as I am very much exhausted. I wish brother Lewis would take my wagon and start for this place, *but not on the Sabbath*, and if you are able, bring the babe and come with him; I should be glad to have you come. My horse is here and we can all be accommodated on the return home. I leave this entirely with yourself. It may be I shall not be able to return, but my hope is in the Lord. But, I must stop for I am so exhausted. My labors must be suspended, at least, for a season. Pray for me that I may do all the Lord's will in life or in death. Love to all.

I am as ever your affectionate husband,

L. A. WICKES.

Feb. 23d.

DEAR PARENTS:

I have an opportunity this morning of sending a line to P. O., for I know you will feel anxious how Mr. W.'s health is. He is very weak, yet, we think gradually gaining. Monday he sat up over two hours; yesterday a little longer. Hope he will be able to have his clothes on soon. It is about a fortnight since he was able to be dressed. Begins to have a little appetite. The Lord is very kind to us; He has surrounded us with His mercies, in sickness and in health, and among strangers. We have reason to bless His holy name. How soon we shall see you, Providence must determine.

Yours affectionately,
C. WICKES.

STOWS SQUARE, March 11th, 1842.

MY DEAR AND AFFECTIONATE PARENTS:

After his sickness, March 11, 1842. Stows Square.

Your letter of the 6th inst. to Capt. Wilcox came to hand yesterday, in which you express the desire that some of them will write to you every time they hear from Lewis. I thought perhaps it would not be entirely unwelcome if L. should answer it himself. Though I am so weak my penmanship is very poor, yet mother can decipher the almost *hieroglyphics*. You may be astonished to see that I have got home with my dear family; but just as soon as I was able to sit long enough to ride eight or ten miles I started and was about two and a half days coming home, a distance of sixty miles, and the last day I found it very muddy and slow traveling. My disease was inflammation of the lungs together with a high degree of a bilious state of the whole system, produced by excessive labor in crowded houses where the atmosphere was very much confined, and taking cold after leaving the house. I preached Tuesday evening and was expecting to preach a funeral sermon, and then start for home. But before Wednesday evening I was not able to sit up a single moment. My life was despaired of one day only, though dangerous for several days. But by the blessing of God I do feel much better and am better but extremely weak, as of course, I must expect to be. And now with all our little ones by the blessing of our Savior, we are permitted to be together in our room. I have some trials in my mind; there are so many places that are now ripe for the harvest and begging for me to come and help, and so eager were they, that hearing that I had got able to sit up a little, they came with carriages to carry me off. If it was only for sitting in my room and counseling them what course to take, and many doors are open to me. O, for humility to meet them and strength to sustain me in the work. How long before I can resume the labors I cannot say, but if it is the Lord's will I hope it may be soon, yet I am reconciled to His providence, and wait for His leadings. I find it has been good for me to be afflicted. I have felt to review the past of my life; to examine the motives which have led me to the ministry, and the truths which I have presented to mankind. I find there is much wrong in my heart. How little of the spirit of Jesus have I possessed in comparison with what I ought to possess as a professed minister of the Lord Jesus Christ. Though I have tried to keep my heart somewhere near right, yet I have found much to regret. Never have I viewed the immense responsibility of my station as I have during my short sickness. O, how few of the professed ministers of Christ feel the responsibility of the station they hold. An ambassador of the *Court* of *Heaven*! A minister in the stead of Jesus Christ! That he speaks not himself but the order of the *Great I Am*. How little do many expect their words shall have any lasting and permanent effect. May the Lord have mercy upon them. O, how awful to have garments spotted with the blood of souls, for not being the faithful ambassador of Jesus. O, may I not be found there, for His great name's sake.

March 12th. I cannot write long at a time on account of weakness and headache, though I feel some better this morning, for which I will adore and thank my heavenly Father. How little is this world worth. How short a time we need it. Truly "man wants but little here below, nor wants that little long." While we consider heaven as being the place of the greatest delight, why should we not labor to be more like the heaven which we hope to be our final resting place? How strange it is that we tell what is our high expectation of final glory and then live as though this earth was to be our long home, or as if heaven was a place of sensual delight. I do desire to see more of Christ in my soul, and to have stronger confidence in His precious promises. For this I hope my dear parents will ever pray.

13th. Sabbath afternoon. To-day is the first time I have been to the house of God in five weeks. I have attended church twice a day. It made my heart ache to have the word of God take so little effect on the hearts of the hearers, and a servant of Christ should not act as a gentleman of Christ, to sit in the parlor to be served and waited upon, but a laborer in the vineyard of our Lord. Oh, it is good to wear the yoke of the Savior, whose yoke is easy and whose burden is light. (Matt. 11: 29, 30.) Much of the world have just religion enough to make them miserable; they know they ought to live for God, and yet have not grace enough to be anything but a slave to themselves, to the devil and to the world.

* * I hope my dear parents are ripening for that heaven where they hope their children shall meet them, in that glorious rest that remains for the people of God. Love to all.

I am your son.

L. A. WICKES.

STOW'S SQUARE, March 31, 1842.

DEAR BROTHER CROSS:

Extract from Letter to Rev. G. Cross. By the good hand of the Lord I am still in the land of the living. And what a debtor to grace I am for all His kindness and care over me, and yet how often do I forget the Lord I love! O, this treacherous heart of mine! How much it needs to be under the control of the Spirit of God. But I find I have scarce any control at all over myself. Though raised from the verge of the grave, yet how soon I lose the image! Why is it so soon that we forget how we stand on the verge of the tomb constantly? Why is it that we do not all the time do as the psalmist said he would: "Walk before the Lord in the land of the living"? How much of our lives would be changed if we kept the Lord always before us! What lives of devotion would we live! and how the image of the Lord would constantly be seen in our place, and standing on our post. I do not know, my dear brother, as you have such a polluted heart to deal with, but it does seem to me that I must sometimes be conquered by sin, the devil, and give up my hold on my Savior. And I verily think I should were it not for the thought which rushes into my mind that it is the Savior has hold of me, and in His blood there is perfect safety. But there is much to be done in the Savior's cause, and I do desire in some little measure to advance the cause. It has been a cross to me to think of what is needed to be done in the cause of the Lord and yet have my tongue tied up. But I broke away night before last and made a short temperance address, and felt no very great inconvenience from it. To God be all the glory! Now, dear brother, there is no time to be idle. Death is crawling on very fast, and we have but a little time to do a great work, and souls are fast going to the chambers of death and how can we sleep or be idle? O! may we ever be found on our post as faithful watchmen who watch for souls, as those that must give an account. I have just received a letter from Huvelton, and they say they are all waiting for me to come, the Spirit of God evidently is moving among the people. My heart aches to get once more into the field and work. What I wish to say is this, my strength I do not think is sufficient to perform my accustomed labor. But if I should be able in the course of two or three weeks to go there will you go there with me and do all you can? It does seem as though it was the time to strike for that place. I will also write to Brother P-- and he will come also. How much I can do I cannot say, but I can try, and I will be the stool-pigeon to call them together and you spring the net. I do not

G. Cross,
March 31, 1842.

think it would be prudent for me to venture alone in the conflict.

Now, I wish you would write and let me know what you will do, and I will write you soon again. We are all enjoying a good degree of health, and bless God for it. Pray for me and mine.

In haste, your Brother in Christ,
L. A. WICKES.

CHAPTER XII.

STOWS SQUARE, April 8, 1842.

MY DEAR PARENTS:

YOURS was received the day after it was mailed, and I was rejoiced to hear from home once more. Since I wrote to you I have been gaining strength, so that I have delivered a short temperance address, and last Sabbath I preached to the dear people of this place, and assisted in a communion season. My chief medicine has been the axe and the saw, and eat what I wanted. This course, by the blessing of our kind Heavenly Father, has done me good. I shall probably start soon for St. Lawrence County, N. Y., where by the blessing of the Lord I may spend the year, making short excursions home. The field is already white for the harvest, and the laborers are few. May the Lord of the harvest send forth laborers into His harvest.

Remember me affectionately to all. All join in love. Pray for me.

L. A. WICKES.

OGDENSBURG, April 12, 1842.

DEAR BROTHER CROSS;

In the name of our Blessed Lord, whose we are, I do earnestly ask you to hasten here to this place. The people have agreed to do all that the Lord commands them, and now we want to see you here with the whole armor on, and, leave your family as the soldier leaves to go into war. You are aware of the great work before us, and now see what it is that God would have you to do.

In haste. Pray for this place, and for your

Brother in Christ,
L. A. WICKES.

OGDENSBURG, May 20, 1842.

MY DEAR AND AFFECTIONATE WIFE:

Letter from Ogdensburg.

I have finally arrived here in the chief place of course, and where the cause of the Redeemer has been almost looked out of countenance, and where many have sold themselves to work deeds of darkness, but where, too, the cause of the Savior has had some most strong and endearing friends. I arrived here last evening just before sundown and came unexpectedly to all. The news, however, was trumpeted, and a pretty large congregation assembled. I preached to them from Ps. 139: 23—"Search me, O God," etc. There was quite good attention and nothing unfavorable as to appearance, but yet I do not feel exactly what is duty. The Baptist meeting held in one shape and another for eight weeks, and forty-one have been baptized by them as the fruits of the work, and some few more hopefully been brought into the fold of God. May the Lord increase their number and add to His cause. What can be done here I know not. I called last evening before preaching on Rev. Mr. S. He appeared quite *gentlemanly* and kind, but does not like the system of evangelist. As to the course which I take, he had no objection, if I was a pastor, or only a stated minister, and had come to help a brother, and then all would be well. We cannot expect much help from that quarter. The Baptist church will, and their minister will co-operate some, and pretty heartily. *But, my dear*, it is with many misgivings that I do undertake this work, both as to body and to soul. I feel unprepared for the responsible work before me. O, that God may *direct* for His glory and for His honor. I came by *the Bend* on my way here, and did not stop until I got there. I called a short time at Philadelphia; their meeting house is on the advance. It will be quite comfortable and neat when it shall be finished. I arrived at A. about sunset, and was cheerfully received by all. Heard Brother W. preach in the morning; his text, Deut. 32: 9. In the afternoon at five o'clock, I stood once more in the place where my voice had so often been heard, where old associations were weighty. I found I had not so much as lost *one jot of affection for them*. The congregation is about as when we were there. I visited a few families. I had hard work to get away on Tuesday, in the evening, I preached at Richville; not a great many out. Brother Cross came on with me.

May 20. Visited our friends at Hermon; preached in the evening to quite a goodly number. We came to Brother Cleghorn's and Brother Cross left and took my horse back so as to have conveyance here next week; Brother Cross brought me down here. The people were very anxious to have me come, or rather, stop at Huvelton. I had some misgivings to know what duty is, but on the whole have got here, and may God direct, for His own glory, what shall be done. As to my health, I feel rather poorly this morning. I have taken some cold and feel very sleepy; some pain in my head and ear. If I find I cannot endure the fatigue I shall stop. But the Lord's will be done. They are all afraid that there is no house sufficiently large, which will hold the people, and O! what a responsibility, truly, rests on so vile a worm as I. May God be my strength, my portion and my guide. I feel the need of more prayer, and of being more broken-hearted and wearing the image of my Savior more. Do pray much for me. This afternoon we have a prayer-meeting; may the Lord be with us! And what wilt thou have me to do, Oh Lord? A minister at D— tells me that within nine months he has attended fifty-two funerals, among them three drunkards, and drunk at the time of their death. How the Lord does spare us!

Affectionately your husband,

L. A. WICKES.

TO MY DAUGHTER:

To-day, if you are alive, is birthday of your sixth year, and I am seated in an upper room in the house of

May 20, 1842. Little daugher Emma.

Rev. I— S—, at O —, St Lawrence County. I feel quite lonesome while I do think of you on this day. If it was the Lord's will, O, how pleasant it would be to have the privilege of being with you to-day! Your Pa has thought a good deal about you since he left home, and he has sometimes thought he should not see you again, but if it will please the Lord I hope we shall meet once more. I have thought how you are spending this day, and how long you have been thinking about having your birthday come and then what you was going to do. You are to-day six years old, just about this time of day (four o'clock), and when this gets to you, you will be in your seventh year, and you cannot grow any younger, and you are six years nearer the end of your life; six years less to live in this world; six years less before you must go where there are no more prayers, no more asking for the Savior's smiles. And then, if time is so precious, and once gone cannot be called back, how you should love the Savior and spend your time as you will love to meet it at the end of the year. Perhaps you will never see the end of the seven years of life. Then you will want a friend that will go down into the grave with you. That friend is the Savior. Now you must begin to be a little woman. You may play some; you may read some; you may take care of your little sister some and you may work some, but in all that you do you must be kind. The other day when I was coming I saw two little girls about as large as A— and you, and they were walking to school hand in hand and they made a very pretty curtesy, and they made me think of my little daughters, and I thought it looked very pretty indeed, and while I have been writing

I looked out of the window and saw two other little girls just about as large as you, too. They had a doll carrying in their hands between them and I thought it was another little girl (for it was about as large as little S— was when she was born), but they soon began to call each other "black niggers" and "you are ugly" and I thought how unkind and how unpleasant such little girls do look! Do you think it was very pretty, and which of these two companies would you choose to look and act like? I saw little lambs playing and birds singing, and then I thought my dear little Emma will do as the birds rather than follow the example of the wicked children.

Ogdensburg, May 20, 1842. Birthday to little Emma. I think more about you than I ever did before when I have left you. The Lord has raised you from a bed of sickness and do, my dear child, love Him for all His kindness to you. He is worthy of your love. Be very kind to your sister and affectionately obedient to your ma. I want you should write to pa a letter and tell how you do. Love to all, pray and read the Bible, and be a good girl, is the prayer of,

Your affectionate father,
L. A. WICKES.

Mr. W— invariably kept a memorandum of text, time and a remark or incident connected, of which the following specimens copied from his note book may prove a pleasant and profitable reminder, especially to those who once listened to him:

TEXT.	TIME.	PLACE.	REMARKS.
Ex. xix: 5–8	May 1, 1842.	Martinsburg,	
Josh. vi: 44.	" 1, "	"	
John xv: 3.	" 1, "	Brick school-house in Lowville.	
Address.	" 8 "	Stows Square.	Maternal Association.
Ex. xix: 5–8.	" 15, "	Antwerp.	
And being made perfect.	" 15, "	"	
Ex. xix: 5–8.	" 17, "	Richville.	
Isa. lii: 9.	" 18, "	Hermon.	
Ps. cxxxix: 19.	" 19, "	Ogdensburg	Commencement of protracted meeting in the Methodist house.
Gen. xviii: 32	" 20, "	"	
Deut. xxxii: 31.	" 21, "	"	
Gen. xxviii: 19 and I Sam. iii: 13–14.	" 22, "	"	
Jud. v: 23.	" 22, "	"	The house this evening was crowded to overflowing. The Lord has helped me to preach to-day. To His name be all the glory.
Jno. vi: 4.	" 22. "	"	
Acts, xvi: 30 and 24–25.	" 23, "	"	
Amos vi: 1.	" 24, "	"	
Neh. ii: 17.	" 24, "	"	Some little feeling. A storm, and house not full.
2 Chron. vii: 14	" 25, "	"	The church confession and a large number out.
Isa. lii: 1.	" 25, "	"	Things more encouraging.
Rev. vi: 17.	" 26, "	"	
Heb. xi: 30.	" 27, "	"	
Job 35: 30.	" 27, "	"	
Eph. iv: 14.	" 28, "	"	Some more feeling, and all day

TEXT.	TIME.	PLACE.	REMARKS.
Eph. ii: 8.	May 29, 1842.	Ogdensburg.	
Isa. xxviii: 16.	" 29,	"	
" " "	" 29,	"	
" vi: 2.	" 29,	"	
" xlv: 22.	" 30,	"	
Gen. xxxii: 26.	" 31,	"	
Matt. vi: 20.	" 31,	"	A most miserable time of preaching. God forgive!
Luke xii: 20.	June 2,	"	
Ps. xlix: 8.	" 2,	"	
Ex. vi: 12.	" 3,	"	
Isa. ix: 2.	" 3,	"	
Matt. v: 20.	" 3,	"	
Luke xiv: 23.	" 4,	"	This in afternoon.
" xxiv: 26.	" 5,	"	To-day the people renewed their covenant.
Neh. vi: 3.	" 5,	"	
Ps. cxix: 9.	" 5,	"	This was by request, and notice to young people
Ps. lxvi: 13–14.	" 6,	"	
Ps. xciv: 14.	" 8,	"	
Ps. cxix: 8–9.	" 8,	"	
Isa. lxii: 2.	" 7,	"	
Prov. viii: 36.	" 7,	"	
Jud. vii: 26.	" 9,	"	
Rom. vi: 23.	" 9,	"	God's truth took hold, etc.
Rev. ii: 21.	" 10,	"	
Isa. lv: 3.	" 11,	"	Talked in the afternoon.
Job xvii: 15.	" 11,	"	
John i: 29.	" 12,	"	
Ex. xix: 5–8.	" 12,	"	A covenant for the people, nearly unanimous.
Matt. xxiii: 37.	" 12,	"	Mr. Smart here
Gen. iv: 9.	" 13,	"	To-day the aspects more favorable. The Lord save!
Heb. xi: 35.	" 14,	"	

TEXT.	TIME.		PLACE.	REMARKS.
Josh. xxiv : 15.	June 15,	1842.	Ogdensburg.	
Luke xxiii : 39, 43.	"	16, "	"	
John xii : 43.	"	16, "	"	
James v : 16.	"	17, "	"	
My son, give, etc.	"	17, "	"	
Rom. i : 16.	"	18, "	"	
Talked.	"	18, "	"	
Heb. v : 9.	"	19, "	"	
Josh. xxiv : 22.	"	19, "	"	A new vote for the continuation of meeting.
Luke xiv : 22.	"	19, "	"	
Deut. xxxii : 29.	"	20, "	"	
Matt. xii : 30.	"	21, "	"	
Eccl. xi : 19.	"	21, "	"	To-day the young.
Matt. xxi : 28.	"	22, "	"	
Isa. lx : 8.	"	22, "	"	
Heb. iv : 11.	"	23, "	"	
Rom. x : 21.	"	23, "	"	
Isa. v : 7.	"	24, "	"	Eve. Bro. Layer—half-a-doz.
Rev. iii : 20.	"	24, "	"	
Jer. xiii : 21.	"	25, "	"	The girl that could not rest, etc.
John iii : 3.	"	26, "	"	
Rev. ii : 11.	"	26, "	"	130 names and
John vii : 37.	"	26, "	"	Twelve o'clock closed.

OGDENSBURG, June 1st, 1842.

MY DEAR, AFFECTIONATE LOVE:

I suppose by this time you are having a thousand conjectures as to the reason why I have not written, yet, you know enough about my engagements to know that

I have not been at play, and that I have as much as I can do to attend to my work. Since I wrote you the Lord has been with us; there have been quite a number of hopeful conversions of the aged and the young, and many of those who have been very careless and hard, yet the great s*ink* of sin is not by any means destroyed. There are many who are *almost* convinced they are wrong, yet are pursuing the wrong course. Still we work in hope. There have been somewhere between seventy and one hundred who profess to have given themselves to the service of God. To God be all the glory and the praise, for He, alone, is worthy to be praised. I think that when I wrote you before, that I mentioned about Rev. Mr. S. not being willing to come in. He has not stepped into the house since I have been here, and the wicked are saying they will not go to meeting if Mr. S. won't. So they are screening themselves behind him. O, fearful responsibility! Yet they have been compelled to say the Lord is in our midst, and have as a church agreed to spend the hour of six in the morning to pray for the success of the meeting. How much their prayers may avail in accordance with their works, I know not, but I am afraid it is dead faith, or, at least, faith without works. And yet I hope it may be like Paddy shooting the squirrel—they get the wrong end of the gun. O, how cruel they are to the souls of the impenitent; and they will see it when it may be too late. Some of the churches come in and take hold. There have been some five or six conversions of those among the Episcopal church. O, what a winding sheet of death that is; may the Lord have mercy on them. The meeting they had here last winter left things in a most unpleasant state, so that the whole community is very much prejudiced against these efforts. I intended to close up the meeing yesterday, but through the urgent entreaties of all, I have concluded to stay a few days longer. How long, I am not able to say, but there is very much to be done here, and the *Lord's power* is only sufficient for the great work to be done. It is hard to bring them up to the work, yet I am in hopes there will yet be a pretty general display of His power here. I intended to have closed the meeting here yesterday, but the people voluntarily said they would do all that the Lord commanded them, and they would do everything which was consistent for them to do to establish the work of God, and so I have concluded to stay. As I before said, if I close on the next Sabbath, I think I shall take a little respite and attend the Association before commencing at Huvelton.

Love to all.

L. A. WICKES.

CHAPTER XIII.

MEETINGS AT HUVELTON AND DePUYSTER.

HUVELTON, July 2, 1842.

MY DEAR AND AFFECTIONATE WIFE:

I arrived here about half past six o'clock and went directly to the church and preached to about sixty or seventy persons. A female took the lead of singing. The Lord helped me preach, though I was very tired and had the headache. God's spirit is here and the impenitent are enquiring about their soul's salvation. May God shower down His salvation as the rain is descending from the clouds upon the roof above my head, for this place needs it very much and for a long time. I am now seated in an upper room; may it be a room where my Savior may meet with me. This morning I have to preach a funeral sermon for a young woman whom they hope has gone to the bosom of *love*. How long before I may have mine preached by others I know not. O, may I be prepared for that hour. Let us love God in sincerity and in truth. I must now go to the prayer meeting. I shall have, I expect, but little ministerial help here, though I am in hopes to see some of my dear brethren here, but above all, I do want to see my Savior here and follow close to Him. Monday morning, 4th of July. Funeral sermon of Saturday had a blessed effect on many. My text, "Set your affections on things above, not on things on the earth." Col. 3: 2. To God be all the praise, honor, and the glory. God's word will have the desired effect when it is spoken and heard with *faith*. Saturday evening the Lord was in our midst and some felt, who had ever been hardened and obstinate. Yesterday there was a large gathering from all places, and much of the spirit of Heaven seemed to be in the congregation This morning the Lord has been with us in our family devotion, and one soul, a young woman of about fifteen years, we hope has given her heart up to God and made herself a willing servant of the Lord through the agency of the Holy Spirit. May it be the commencement of a better state of things, and of salvation flowing to this entire community. To-day I have exercises, as on other days so as to help people at home, and to exert a happy and blessed influence over them. Afternoon:—We had a very interesting meeting this morning; some seven or eight rose for prayers—some fathers and mothers, and some say they will serve the Lord. May the Lord seal their hearts. This afternoon I had a good congregation and gave the national sermon, Jer. 18: 4-10.—"Blessed be the name of the Lord he was in our midst." Some impenitent were led to give vent to their feelings in sighs. Oh, that they may give their hearts to God and not their tears merely. Just as

I left the church, I found a large party of young people from R. and D., come from Ogd., and called at the tavern and had a short talk with them. Oh, how important to be ready for every exigency where the Lord may call us. God's spirit will be our help if we will only trust Him. Several friends were out to-day from Ogdensburg. May God bless them in all their duty. 6th. Yesterday I could find no time to write a word scarcely. My 4th of July sermon was blessed of God, and many souls were brought to see, in some measure, their situation. The Lord did appear in His glory; several were brought to bow at the foot of the cross. One strong champion of Universalism was brought to acknowledge his error and bow at the feet of Immanuel; and one man who swore that his wife should not go to the meeting, but weed out the garden. She went into the garden, but the Lord got hold of him, and he called his wife and both started for the meeting. He was quite hard when I first commenced talking with him, but before he left the house he was on his feet asking for prayers, confessing and begging for mercy, and confessing to all, and gave up his heart to God, and some eight or ten others. To God be all the glory. And there have been pretty hearty confessions from some who have been long the professed friends of God, and parents begin to look at their children with a deep feeling of heart. They go about with sorrow depicted on their countenances. Universalism begins to tremble here and the strongholds of sin to totter. Oh, may it please the Lord to destroy all the influence of such vile and miserable stuff from the minds of this community. I feel that this state of things places me under great responsibility, and I feel that I am called upon to take the shoes from off the feet, for the ground on which I stand is holy ground, and yet, I am vile and sinful indeed, and need much of the spirit of the Lord under all circumstances. Evening:—It is meeting time this very moment and I suppose I should go, but I must write a few words before I go and mail this. To-day has been a most glorious day to many souls; several cases of hopeful conversions. The Spirit of God is weighing on the hearts of all this community. There are many that seem to be much affected and they come from a distance. I have no help as yet of ministerial kind, except Bro. C. His body is here and his mind at home half of the time, yet he does get hold on the Lord's arm most gloriously and the Spirit of God does seem to be speaking great things for him and all. But I must close and hasten for the meeting. I board half a mile, or nearly, from the church. My health is pretty good. Kiss the children for me. Love to all the friends In haste.

Your affectionate husband,

L. A. WICKES.

HUVELTON, July 20, 1842.

MY DEAR WIFE:

Yours was received yesterday morning and I was much rejoiced to hear from home, but it makes me feel some solicitude about my little family as to health, yet do feel that God will do all things well and for His own glory. I think the meeting here will close on Sabbath, if not before. The meeting is not attended now as it was the first week, though every day new cases of conversions are taking place, and the feeling is spreading over this whole region. Last Sabbath the congregation was very great; hundreds were there. *I had to make my pulpit in the window of the church* and preach to those out of the house and in it, and there was considerable feeling for the souls of men. May it increase more and still more. There have been hard, and openly wicked and vile persons who have been brought to bow at the foot of the cross. To His name be all the glory. Bro. L. intimated something about a visit to Albany. It will be very doubtful, although it would be very pleasing if the Lord will, but we must ask counsel of God, that we may walk before Him in that manner that will be pleasing to Him, and for His glory. I am anxious to do what will best promote the cause of our blessed Lord. The prospect is that I shall have enough to do as long as God will strengthen me, and as I shall have a heart to work. I have received a request from Copenhagen to hold a meeting in that place. As my engagements now are, I could not comply at present. I do ask counsel of God that I may do my whole duty according to His will. I must close as it is time to commence meeting. Pray much for this place, and for me. I have been much of the time alone as to ministerial help. In haste.

Yours affectionately,
L. A. WICKES.

Closed at Huvelton, July 31st. Sabbath, administered Lord's supper, organized and received into membership sixty-two. Dismissed congregation at half past twelve o'clock.

DePuyster, August 13, 1842.

Dear Children:

As I have a moment to write, I will just tell you of our coming here. We had a pleasant journey on the whole. When I got to Wilna we found that there had been a heavy hail storm the day before we started from home. Some of them were as large as butternuts and some as large as walnuts. They broke windows and broke down the corn and potatoes. There were about seventy lights broken out in the "checkered house." So we see how great and powerful is the army the Lord has got to teach men their dependence on Him, and if the Lord be for us who can be against us? We came to A: took dinner with Miss F—. While here they had quite a heavy shower of rain, but we were in a house and thus, again, we were very kindly watched over by our heavenly Father. We started about five o'clock, tarried all night at Mr. Temple's, in G—. We found some mud a part of the way. There was a heavy shower of rain accompanied by much heavy lightning and thunder, but did not reach us, so God did again protect us. O, how thankful we ought to be, and I trust we are in some measure. We spent about two hours at Major Sargent's and started for this place. The bell soon rang to let the people know I had come, and we went to the church. I preached from Luke, xvi: 2, middle clause. Quite a goodly number out. We board at Mr. B—s. They have a large family. Some of them are Christians. May they all be brought to the fold of the dear Redeemer.

August 11, commenced a meeting in DePuyster.

To-day, 15th, prospects of the meeting appear encouraging. The class leader confessed he had not maintained family devotion for a long time. The eldest appears like a Christian; is the chorister in this place. I think he will do much good in the meeting. The second has just come out on the Lord's side. The congregation yesterday could not near all get into the meeting-house, which is a very snug stone building, with a bell. The evening meetings are full and attentive, which makes it easy preaching. There was not a family altar in the place except the Methodist preacher, and he tried in vain to establish a weekly prayer meeting. Among this people, until the meeting in Huvelton, this whole vicinity was one unbroken moral desolation. But, thanks be to God, the wilderness begins to bud. It is refreshing to the Christian soul to be here now. May the Lord give complete success to the efforts now in progress. The people are in the midst of their harvest. It is more forward here than in L.— county. Some are threshing new wheat. And the spiritual harvest is white already to harvest. Pray the Lord of the harvest to raise up and send forth laborers into the gospel field. Hope the children will be kind to each other, and pray the Savior to give them new hearts. Love to all. Aunt E— will please to read this to the little daughters.

With much affection, yours,
L. A. WICKES.

DePuyster, August 28, 1842.

My Daughters:

You see by this that your dear pa and ma and little sister are yet in the place to which we first came. We have all enjoyed a pretty good degree of health. There have been three deaths in this place since we came here, but our lives have been spared. The people here to-day decided that the meeting should continue some days longer, so I can not tell you when we shall leave this place. The Lord is doing a great work here. A great many have been converted and a great many are enquiring what they shall do to be saved. Many family altars have been erected and we hope many more will be. A great number assembled at the meeting-house to-day that could not get in. Some came from Ogdensburg, Lisbon, Canton, DeKalb, McCombe, Huvelton and I don't know how many more, but I spoke with persons from all those places. Tell grandpa a Mr. S. P., brother of Mrs. A. and Mrs. B., in the village, has become a new man, he thinks, and we hope so, too. He came over to see your ma yesterday after meeting closed, where he thought he gave his heart to the Lord, and he appeared very different from what he did about a week ago when one evening I invited him to go forward to the anxious seat, but he was then a hardened Universalist and forbid his family coming to meeting; but to-day they could all come together. They had a good meeting last night; probably more than a hundred forward for prayers. There is a great interest felt all over this region. Two gentlemen from Lisbon were here yesterday urging your dear pa to come and hold a meeting in that town. There are above three hundred inhabitants in that place, and the fields are white already to harvest, morally as well as temporally. Your dear pa wants to do the will of the Lord. Therefore we must pray much and watch the

Letter from Mrs. W——.

leadings of providence; a few days more will determine. But I must close.

Love to all, Your Mother.
C. WICKES.

At the close of this interesting and successful meeting Mr. W—, with wife and infant, returned home and made a visit to his parents, in Albany, N. Y., performed the marriage ceremony of his eldest sister, and returned to St. Lawrence early in October, and commenced a meeting at Lisbon.

He was strongly urged by his friends to settle down as a pastor, and many churches were offered for his services, but he could not feel it duty to give up evangelistic labors, although sorely tempted by his affection for his home.

CHAPTER XIV.

MEETING IN LISBON AND BIRTHDAY LETTER 1842.

LISBON, St. Lawrence Co., Sept. 30th, 1842

MY DEAR AND AFFECTIONATE WIFE:

A solitary and lonely one, I feel I am, on the banks of the St. Lawrence, in a room eight by twelve, in a log house, with a bed, a table, a cupboard. A clock, two chairs, my trunk, etc., in the family of Mr. D., half a mile from the church, I now sit and talk with my bosom friend. I have been brought into the hardest place that I have been in since we were married. It is leaving my dear family. I have been almost overpowered and my heart swelled and my throat choked up much, yet I tried very much to keep myself in command. But when I arrived at our room in Stows Square I was not saluted by joyful embrace of my little ones, nor the welcoming smiles of my dear wife. All solitary and lonely, I could not refrain my self any longer and gave

Mrs. W. and children staid in Albany for a visit of months.

vent to my feelings. When I sat down at the table your place was filled by another. And I about to make the breach eighty miles longer. My heart swelled greatly I can assure you until I became almost like a child. I thought of your trust or care, of the health of each child, of the dangers of temptations into which they would be placed, and for the moment I felt it was wrong for husband and wife to be separated, and was almost a good mind to start for A. and go and settle down once more. But yet feeling must not be my guide. The Lord forbid. Let me do the will of my heavenly Father. We have covenanted and let us not go back, so long as God opens the way before us let us all and each follow on. And may God protect and direct. On my way here I made several calls till I reached Bro. C's., as my horse was tired Bro. C. kindly put his horse to the wagon and brought me through, making the day's ride sixty-five miles. When I found a goodly number come together and waiting for the minister to come, and I tried to preach from "Search me O God" etc. though I found myself very much exhausted. But there was an ungainly and wicked set of people, and an opportunity to do much good. There were perhaps two hundred or two hundred and fifty present the first evening. To day but a little handful to the prayer meeting, and a small number at the preaching in the afternoon. To night a large congregation out and the spirit of God is evidently moving upon many hearts. But there are a vast variety of folks here. There are Seceders, Covenanters two kinds of Baptists, two kinds of Methodists, Presbyterians, Congregationlists and Episcopalians, Mormons, Christians, and Universalists. So you can see what a motley mess there is, and they are made up of Dutch, Scotch, English, Irish, French, Canadian and Yankees and each with their prejudices and predilections and nothing but the wisdom and power of God will accomplish any thing here. Thus to "become all things to all men" is a vast and great work and one which I feel entirely inadequate for the task. But I do know that God will guide me, and keep me if I will only lean upon His almighty arm. I found that the Episcopal clergyman had been rather forestalling the minds of some of the people and had intimated they were all weak minded and ignorant ones who were converted in their meeting. But weak as they are, they are the very ones he has tried most faithfully to get into his church. I pray God he may find mercy by repenting. The work still goes on in DePuyster. At Huvelton they have hired the meeting-house to get ready for the other house so that they will have a year to repair the old house in. Truly what has God wrought. To His name be all the glory and the honor. I am at the close of my sheet. Do pray for me, Write soon. Love to all. Kiss the children for me. In haste, etc.

Your husband,
L. A. WICKES.

LISBON, Oct. 6, 1842.

DEAR SISTER A.

I arrived at the old forsaken church after the people had all got together, and a pretty large congregation. But of all the heterogeneous parcels that I ever saw, this is the climax! But the Lord is truly in the midst of us. There have been some few hopeful conversions, and the work seems to be spreading around and deepening. There was one man converted that was an active captain in the late war; was in several engagements and been a magistrate for twenty-four years here. He talks most nobly, and confessed with much frankness and sincerity. May the Lord carry forward the work in His own way! To His name be all the glory! I board about half a mile from the church, on the bank of the river, with Canada shore in view. The going and the weather is delightful. May the Lord smile on us all! Love to all.

Your Brother,
L. A. WICKES.

LISBON, St. Lawrence Co., Oct. 11, 1842.

MY DEAR AND AFFECTIONATE WIFE:

I commence this morning filling my large sheet not knowing when I shall finish it. Since I wrote the Lord has appeared for our help and prejudice begins to vanish away, and the people begin to inquire what do these things mean? There was considerable preparation made by the people externally, for the old house had stood unoccupied for some six or eight years, except used for the young people's gambling house. The windows were so much broken it took over half a box of glass to mend them. The floors had broken down and the sway of Lord Tobacco had been so awful that his marks had been deeply stamped on all his steps and piled like heaps of pollution, and thoroughly dried in; and the spiders, worms and bats had seemed to have had a war to see who should claim the house as theirs. But the people had made war with all these and removed them, so that the shell seemed to be a little decent for intelligent beings to occupy. Some seemed to feel very anxious to have the Lord's work revive here, but yet there was a great amount of incredulity in the final good of the meeting. The Episcopal minister had been putting people on their guard against being excited, for none but persons of *weak minds* and *inferior intellect* were affected by such meetings. One of the plain men of the place answered him by saying that if this was the case then the two great political parties of the day were great fools, for they had made choice of "*two* of Wickes's converts (B—, Whig, and Readington Law), to represent them in the State Legislature and *all that knew them knew they were men of no ordinary minds*. But such arguments men do not think anything of. The Lord, however, will have all the glory and the honor of His own work. There have been some twenty or thirty hopeful conversions since the meeting commenced. One man, Captain L—, a reformed inebriate, has been hopefully brought to bow at the foot of the cross. He was an officer in the late war, and in several actions, and had become a very hardened, wicked and profane man. Once, in a drunken frolic, he had sold a pew in the church for a glass of ardent spirits. His mind was so affected while sitting in it before he bowed to the Lord, that he could not stay in the house, "But went out to get rid of them," as he said. That, he felt, was wrong, so he returned and, we hope, became a praying man. He has for twenty-four or five years filled the office of magistrate in this

Lisbon,
Oct. 11, 1842.

town. They are driving the temperance reform here, and there is great need of it for it has been a most drunken hole, and the proverb is, or has been, that it was "Satan's gate to hell. And it has been, indeed, the very case. We have reason to fear too many souls have gone to the eternal world unprepared. Last Saturday, being the time of their monthly meeting, I gave them a short address of an hour and twenty minutes. Last Sabbath was a very rainy day and the congregation were late in getting in to meeting, so we concluded as it rained so hard we would have only one sermon. I preached from Isa. xxviii: 16; the spirit of God was in our midst. One young lady became a Christian, as we hope, during the exercise. To God be all the glory and the honor! He will make His word effectual when we will not cripple it by our unbelief and unfaithfulness. One man, the other evening, went away from church mad, cursing, and swearing he would never come to meeting again. But the Lord was too strong for him. On Sabbath evening, we hope, he became the heir of immortal glory. O, what a forgiving God is our Redeemer! The meetings are not very well attended in the day time, but evenings the house is thronged. I find my own heart is very hard, amd unprepared for so great and so responsible a work. What a deceitful heart mine is! And how much I do need God's constant care and His subduing grace to keep me anywhere near the bounds of truth and love to God; and how ungrateful I am for all the favors which he is conferring upon me! O, for the meekness of Christ to fill my heart! Yesterday, on getting to church, I was greeted by Captain L— saying: "There was a scene in my house yesterday that was never there before; there was father, mother, grandparents and children and grand children, all on their knees together, each calling on the name of the Lord. It melted my hard heart before the Lord. Oh, I never knew what happiness was before! I used to think when I could get some half dozen or more of my old comrades together and get about half dead drunk, that I was really happy; and being a great politician, put a little flag on a broom and stuck it on the counter and then gave three cheers; then I was completely happy. O, how wicked and what a fool I have been! I am now determined, by God's help, to be as faithful for God as I have been for the devil." And while he talked the soldier's tears flowed in streams. Last evening one of his sons among some forty others, hopefully gave themselves to the Lord in an everlasting covenant. Why, how good the Lord is to such vile and sinful worms as we are! The meeting-house, which will seat some four hundred or more comfortably, is crowded every evening, and some come a distance of five, six and eight miles; but in the day time the meeting is small—so small that I told them last evening that I would allow them to-day to see whether they will turn out to meeting, and if they cannot I should close this evening; yet I felt it would be an awful step for some of this community. But the Lord's cause must be promoted in every place. People begin to be afraid the meeting will close, and begin to pray some.

Lisbon, Oct, 11, 1842.

Yesterday I received a pattern for a coat from an old blackleg (gambler) that was hopefully converted to God during the meeting in H—. He lives up country in Canada, and is trying to get me there. Thus God supplies our wants; but soon we shall leave our earthly abode with all its wants. O, that we may ever be prepared for such an event!

13th. We had a very good congregation and there was a good deal of feeling among all classes. Several we hope gave themselves to the Lord in an everlasting covenant not to be broken. Some cases of interest, one man by the name of McCrea, he is a nephew to Miss McCrea who was taken and murdered by the two parties of Indians in their anxiety to convey her to the British officer who was intending to marry her. He has been a miserable toper, a man of good education and an excellent natural ability. He has been sometime a Washingtonian and now we hope a Christian. To God be the glory. There were several others yesterday whom in charity we hope bowed to the Savior and backsliders were coming back to the Lord. How strange it is that any heart should or would ever forsake a God of so infinite love and kindness, and where true and lasting joy may be found, yea truly, enjoyed, is yet strange, as it is we are prone to wander from the God we love. Husbands and wives, parents and children do now begin to pour out the soul for each other and begin to feel that there is something to do for each other more than they have ever done. And when God's people do thus feel and then pour out their prayers they will not labor in vain. But greater ignorance upon the subject of religion among a professed enlightened people I never saw than I find here, moral obligation seems not to have any weight upon them. But the Lord can teach them. One of the prominent men of the town, an active justice of the peace, told me he had never thought of abstaining

Lisbon, October 11, 1842.

from wrong because it was sin against God!! He is secretary of the Washingtonian Society and yet he did not engage in the cause because intemperance was a sin against the Lord. This is about the character of a large portion of these people. It is no wonder that man has gone on in sin. Nor that they do forsake the Lord when these principles are the only ones which would govern them. Truly how great is the blessing which we have had. No principles as weighty as eternity, and to have God's eternal truth press upon our hearts, to keep us within bounds of God's mercy. How different was Joseph when he was tempted by Potiphar's wife. "How can I do this great wickedness and sin against God." Here is a fortification which I ever wish my dear children to be fortified with in all things; this principle will stand when all the others will be banished away, and when the eye of earthly parents are not present to superintend the actions of their children, let it be stamped deeply upon ours whether we survive them or they us. The other day a lady came to me with a bitter moan and felt heart broken. Her daughter had after evening meeting gone with a young man to the justice's office and had been married unbeknown to her parents. "I have brought up my children very tender and kind and to have my eldest daughter begin in this way it is more then I can endure." I asked her if she had taught her daughter the Bible principles of obedience. She confessed she had not, but had brought her up very tenderly, and here we have an evidence of the necessity of Bible training, and to act from right principles. To look at wrong as being sin against God. How much wisdom we need. But, my dear, the Lord is with us here. Yesterday He was with us and His mighty power was gloriously displayed. I can not say how many have become hopefully disciples of Jesus. Among them one of the physicans, two justices of the peace, the supervisor of the town, the former supervisors, some five or six men of grey hairs and a goodly number of youth and middle aged persons. Blessed be the name of the Lord for all His kindness and the favors He has shown unto us. I can truly bless the Lord. Oh my soul, and all that is within me bless His holy name. Truly if we will only be humble before our God he will be entreated of us. How great, how large are the favors which heaven bestows, to spend our lives in His cause. And yet how comparatively useless are the days of our life to what they should be. I sometimes feel that earth has but little hold on me. But when I think of the dear family in Albany, I find I yet am a social being and have an attachment for my earthly friends. But, Oh, how I do want to be heavenly minded and full of the love of God. There are brethren who do come in and labor for souls. This day thus far has been a very good time, some have bowed to the sceptre of the Savior's love. Truly what has the Lord wrought. How blessed a Savior He is. How glorious and how great. Man is a most ungrateful being who will not serve and obey him! Those who yesterday professed to give themselves to the Lord came forward and took part in the morning meeting, and there was a feeling for the welfare of others that there has not been, apparently, since the meeting commenced. When the meeting commenced they used to bring in requests for

Lisbon, Oct. 1, 1842.

the prisoners of Van Diemen's Land, the persecuted Christians in Germany, God's ancient people, the Jews, the inmates of the poor house. But they begin to find others are poor, oppressed by the devil and prisoners. While those were laudable objects of prayer yet they were only a form. Now they work. Last evening I stayed at the house of one of the young converts, where we had a house full of them, and a glorious time we had of it too. To day the Lord has been with us, three or four fathers among others have been led to believe on the Lord Jesus, and some mothers, also some young people. The Lord's work moves forward and has a good effect on the town, and especially upon the first men of the town. To His name be all the glory and the honor for all that He has done. Oh, let us magnify His great name that we can have the privilege of working for Him. Tell the dear children to be kind to each other, and to all. Let the greatest pains be taken to teach them the fear of the Lord. Let them daily read God's word. If you are in want let me know. Love to all.

Your affectionate Husband.

L. A. WICKES.

LISBON, Oct. 25, 1842.

DEAR BROTHER CROSS:

I have been very much disappointed in not seeing you at this place before this. I think if you had known how much you were needed here, you would have come.

The Lord truly is in the midst of us. Now I wish, Bro., if it is possible, you would come down here that you may finish up the work here after I leave. The work has got among the first class of the town; nearly all the town officers have become subjects of the work. To God be all the glory given! O, how good and how glorious it is for men to serve God! May the Lord bless you, my dear Brother, and you be the honored instrument of great good yet in His glorious cause!

Remember me to all, especially to Mrs. C—. Do not fail to come if possible. Do not let a little storm prevent you. Pray much for

Your unworthy Brother,

L. A. WICKES.

LISBON, Oct., 28th 1842.

MY DEAR AND AFFECTIONATE WIFE:

Your letter was received not until the 17th inst., when it was a welcome messenger I can assure you. The postmaster handed it in at my room before day with a candle, and I lost no time in perusing it. I have felt all the time that the Lord would take care of you and would be your support. Friendship is too weak a term for me to express the feeling which I have for my dear family, and love is a lame expression in comparison. I have sometimes thought that I was almost verging on to the borders of idolatry when I see what are the emotions of my bosom. Yet the Lord does truly say, " Husbands, love your wives." * * * Since I wrote you the Lord has been among us. Many have bowed at the foot of the cross and subscribed unto the Lord with their own hand. To God be all the glory!

November 1st. I have not found time since I wrote the above to scarce put my pen on paper for a moment. Last Sabbath I intended to close the meeting with my farewell address to the converts. There were one hundred and ten who took their seats together, and a goodly number that were absent from the place. We entered the church at nine in the morning for prayers, had about three-fourths of an hour's intermission, and closed the meeting *after sundown*. Commenced meeting at seven and closed at half past eleven o'clock. At the close there was a resolution passed requesting me to stay longer, and they would turn out and attend the meeting so long as there are evident tokens of the will of God that the meetings should go forward. Now they have gone and prepared the other old shell of a forsaken church and are earnestly begging me to come there. It is about three miles back from the river. A wicked man who keeps a tavern close by says he will stop selling liquor while the meeting lasts if I will come, and will give me the best his house can afford. I finally have postponed going to Woodville for a week longer. Next Friday to Sabbath I shall spend at Huvelton, to administer the communion to the church, and shall probably return to this town on Monday. Such a state of things as was never before seen in this town exists now. And all that has been done by God's people is to lay low before God and do their duty, and scores of souls fly to God. I feel that I hardly know what duty is, yet I am inclined to believe that the providence of God says, stay here for the present. There is much land to be possessed in this whole region and may the Lord send up His people to possess it! Many of the converts are very strong and work very well, but a great deal of ignorance in regard to the things of religion has prevailed. Now there is but little heard here but temperance and religion; the cause is prospering. The house has been so crowded that the only way I could get into the house myself has been to get through the window and then have to climb over the heads of many.

<small>Lisbon, Nov. 3, 1842.</small>

<small>Unusual Interest.</small>

November 3d. Last evening there were about a hundred and forty or fifty forward for prayers, and the most of them are expressing hope in a Savior's love and pardon. There have been some of the vilest of characters that have been led to the foot of the cross. You would think it almost incredible if I were to attempt to describe the scenes that have been exposed on the banks of the St. Lawrence. H— in its abominations can scarcely be compared to it. One French girl that God laid His hands upon so powerfully, came and wanted help. Her confessions to God and to man were awful! She walked some ten or twelve miles to confess to persons she had abused. I sometimes hardly know what to do with many. O, for wisdom! I need to be "Wise as a serpent and harmless as a dove." And some of them would make the cheeks of hell to blush; and that, too, among those who have supposed they were in the first ranks of society. In short, the first ranks of society and the dregs of society are, as a general thing, the two classes that will meet in hell together. May the Lord show them their abominations! Many who have been members of

the church, yet have to learn, their way is very perverse before the Lord. Last evening my little room was crammed and jammed in with men and women crying for mercy; some of the hardest cases in all the town. To God be all the glory given! Let us pray and give thanks, and continue to labor. Miss L— P— is at this place. You will remember her decided piety. She has now the privilege of having four brothers hopefully serving God. This she has long prayed for. She is known as a faithful and an esteemed Christian by all who know her. She and others wish to be remembered to you. Pray much for this place. As to the children going to school, you must do as you think best. But to none but a pious teacher who does their duty as a Christian. Love to all. Kiss the little ones for me.

Your affectionate husband,

L. A. WICKES.

LISBON, Nov. 12, 1842.

MY DEAR AND AFFECTIONATE WIFE:

You perceive by this, I am yet in the North, on the border town. Since I wrote you the Lord has been in our midst. I think I finished my last after I had preached to the converts, when there were some over a hundred and twenty together. After that, the meeting continued until Thursday evening, and there were some thirty-five more who professed hope in Christ. I then left to spend the Friday to Sabbath in H.; preached there in the afternoon and evening, and church meeting, and all day Saturday. On Sabbath, the Lord was with us, twelve were added to the church and we had a heavenly sitting together. I do not know, my dear, as I have ever felt more the sweet delight in the service of the Lord than I have of late, such close communion with my Lord. It is delight, it is joy and peace. I have felt that it was because I have been more willing to deny myself and forego privileges than I have at any time of my life, since I have been in the ministry, and I do feel that God has heard and answered prayer. We can do each other good when we are far away from each other, and can in faith oft unite. The converts at H. are very faithful and grow in grace. It does my soul good to hear them pour out their supplications to the Lord. The church in H. now numbers seventy-six. There is altogether a different state of society here, than there was a few months ago. They are very solicitous for me to stay with them, but let the Lord direct, and we will follow in the path of duty. On Tuesday I returned to the centre of the town of Lisbon. Here I board with the innkeeper who has closed the bar as long as I shall stay here. The meeting-house was a wretched miserable shell, been used for town-meetings, elections, sheep, cats and gambler's home. "The swallows had made their nests there," but the people had gone to work and cleaned it out, so that there was a little appearance of boards and a floor. The house is, indeed, an unpleasantly contrived one. Doors on three sides of the house, ten slips in the centre and then surrounded with square pews, the pulpit on the side of the house. But the Lord has kindly condescended to grace it with His holy presence and his forgiving power. There are many of the most powerful prejudices to be overcome among some of the old South Presbyterian Church here, but may they have a refreshing from the presence of the Lord, which will melt down all unholiness and bring sinners to the acknowledging of the truth as it is in Jesus Christ. The Lord was with us yesterday and some souls were brought to the fold of Jesus. To His name be all the glory. The prejudices of the people are very peculiar. They are the old Scotch. They want to sing the Psalms of David in metre, but get no rhyme or even metre at all. They want one to stand under the pulpit and present it out line by line. They wish it to be sung by all, yet not to have a bass-viol, nor the flute, nor any other instrument. Last evening there were about one hundred forward for prayers. The most of them were young men, and quite a number, we hope, gave themselves to the Lord, but still there is much to be done yet. Here are hundreds in this town that are without hope in the Lord; may the Lord have mercy on them. This morning I have been called to visit a man in the last hours of life. His hope is strong in the Lord, and his prospects of heaven are apparently bright. He could say but a word or two, but it was full of grace and the spirit of God. He leaves a large family nearly all grown up, a part of them are rejoicing in hope. How sweet it is to have our friends, if they are taken from us, sleep in Jesus. I have just returned from the funeral of the man that I mentioned to you on the 14th. He died in an hour or two after I left in the triumph of hope. Bro. Wing of the Methodist Church, preached the sermon, John 14: 12, by the request of the dying man. There is a work

Lisbon, Nov. 12, 1842.

16th

for somebody to do to save this vast waste. Every day there is some one who, we hope, comes to the Lord. They are of various grades, but all most wicked and sinful. How long I shall stay, I cannot say, probably not very long, may the Lord direct. The other day, while preaching, I referred to the bones on Brier hill, at Sackett's Harbor, in illustrating the vision of dry bones by Ezekiel. There was present Capt. Lytle, whom I mentioned in my former letter. He was one who helped deposit them there, and when I mentioned them he could scarcely contain his emotions, he said he could see nothing but dry bones all the evening and all night. He is truly now a soldier of Jesus, and trying to do all in his power to advance the cause of the Lord. Brother Hotchkiss, from Potsdam, is here, The mortality in that place has been very great; in less than six months one hundred and fifty deaths, but scarce none of them members of his church. The Universalists buried nearly one-half. There were some few dear lambs of the flock that were brought to the trying point and crossed the line Oh, how great is the care of them; perhaps they were taken from the evil to come. J. C. the person, our dear friend, Mrs. R. took such interest in his behalf, is dead. He died rather indulging hope before he went thence. We have heard that there is much need of moral reform efforts, for there are alarming reports of the violation of the seventh commandment in this region. Something should be done for the safety for the people, especially the young of our land, or it may become a nation of blood, if not already ripe for destruction. But may God graciously save us from the jaws of death. Little did I think,

Lisbon, Nov. 1842.

when I was in A., and our friend Miss L. P. used to request prayer for Lisbon, that I should be sent to this place to prophecy over these dry bones, but so it is the will of the Lord toward us. I have had some of the most delightful soul communions in drawing near to God, an enrapture of soul at the feet of Jesus, yet I find it is one thing to be in such a frame and then to be full of the longing of soul for our Redeemer's cause. I do want that constant feeling for souls that Paul speaks of, " I say the truth in Christ." It is a privilege that we may have to draw near to God and feel that he draws near to us. I hope you are cultivating a spirit of earnest devotion. How much does your faith take hold on the promises of God? I hope you will lean much on the arm of the Lord. The family are daily remembered. It is a comfort to my heart that we have the prayers of Christian friends. * * * I have but little time to write, and now my room is full. There have been four of the family hopefully converted. The head of the family is almost persuaded to be a Christian, but there he seems to stand. May the Lord have mercy on him. I must hasten to a close. Love to all. May it please the Lord to let His blessing descend on you, is the prayer of your affectionate husband.

L. A. WICKES.

An extract, Dec. 1st, 1842. Last Friday, Saturday and Sabbath, I organized the Congregational Church at Lisbon, with sixty-five members, baptized twenty-eight adults and two children, and administered the Lord's supper. A crowded house of all denominations of Christians, a scene which was never before known in that town. Many of them are the first men of the town. But what they will do for a minister I cannot divine. They need one very much immediately, and one of the right feeling, views, and a *workman.* " Pray the Lord of the harvest to send forth laborers into the harvest, it is great and the laborers are few.' There were quite a goodly number united with the Methodists, and many will go to other churches. Truly, what hath God wrought for poor despised Lisbon. To God be all the glory! I left on Monday with many tears and kind greetings and adieus. Arrived home 2d December.

L. A WICKES.

STOW'S SQUARE, Dec. 8, 1842.

MY DEAR AND AFFECTIONATE PARENTS:

You will perceive by this that I have reached another anniversary of my life. Truly, how rapid time has rolled her wheels around! As the poet says, "My days, my weeks, my months, my years, fly rapid as the whirling spheres." And neither the sun nor the moon have stood still for me to accomplish any of the duties of the year. O, how sweet the reflection that we may live so as to give some good account for every moment at the last. But such, I find, is not my life. O, for that heavenly character of my blessed Lord, who went about doing good! I find it the most difficult thing to keep my heart just right; and especially in making my yearly returns to my parents. If I have done but little I feel ashamed, and almost would look for some excuse. And if I have been the means of doing any good, pride shows his deformed head, and I almost feel as Moses is said to have felt when he smote the rocks and said: " You rebels! Shall *I* bring water out of this rock for you? If Moses was, for the sin at those waters, forbidden to enter the promised land, why may not I expect that God will be grieved for the pride of my heart? Oh, how subtle is Satan! How vain and how pretendedly humble! How devoted and how zealous, too! How affectionate and yet how hateful! O, my Heavenly Father, prepare me to stand against every wile of the deceiver!! While I look over the past year, may I have my heart right in the sight of the Lord. During the past year the hand of the Lord has been over me. I have preached about 450 sermons; attended about 250 prayer and inquiry meetings. Here is responsibility! How much good the Lord has done through my instrumentality, He only, knows, and His name shall have all the glory and the honor. And how much injury I may have done, eternity may unfold a vast amount. O, may the Lord pardon! How heavenly minded I should be with all these privileges, and yet how little of the love of God do I possess in my soul! God will certainly require more of me than many others if my indebtedness will be according to the privileges which He

1842.   does give me. I do feel that I am far from that heavenly state where the Christian should be; and especially the Christian minister, who stands to point souls to the port of rest. O, for a new baptism of the Holy Ghost! During the year I have seen the hopeful conversion of about 900 souls! To God be all the glory! Yea, " Bless the Lord, Oh my soul, and all that is within, bless His holy name!" Heaven has rejoiced, and so will I mingle my joys. But how many of these may yet be living in sin, and may be deceived, I know not. O, may the kind Lord undeceive any that may be thus! Possibly some were. If I only knew who they were I would warn them. And those who have been brought to the true fold of Jesus, precious souls, my heart feels for them! O, the snares which will be laid for their feet! Great Shepherd of Israel, keep Thou them! I have organized two churches one of sixty-two and the other sixty-five members; ordained four deacons by laying on of hands; baptized about fifty adults; administered the Lord's supper four times. Some have gone to the grave from among those who have given evidence of their turning to the Lord, and they have gone in the triumphs of faith. For which, may the Lord accept my humble thanks! O, I love to see or hear of their leaving earth with the prospect of heaven in full view; to range the blessed field on the side of the river, and sing hallelujah for ever and ever! Oh, the Christian's work is only begun when he enters upon his immortal spiritual life. Who would not love Jesus? Who would not be a follower of the Lamb? What an honor conferred on mortals of a sinful race! Cold and sordid must be that heart that can behold no beauties in the Savior. When all heaven does adore Him, and all hell stands trembling at His power! O, for more faith in Jesus—to see greater things than these. Why shall I limit my blessed Lord? May heaven forbid and forgive! I have traveled during the year about 1,300 miles. Truly the Lord is my helper!

And this year, too, has been signal with the afflictive hand of God upon me. For a few days He brought me to the sides of the tomb. For four months, nearly, I did not perform any ministerial labor of consequence. My affliction was good for me; I adore His hand for it. It has taught me many precious lessons. It was truly a testing spot. Then I saw truly more than ever the beauty of my Savior's love. For a little moment I did feel that I must be the first to be taken from your circle, but the Lord otherwise decreed. It was then He brought me to see the need of being more faithful in the cause of Jesus. Then I renewedly consecrated all the powers to this service which He will give me. Yet how poorly have I fulfilled what I did vow! I can truly say: "Prone to wander, Lord, I feel it; prone to leave the God I love." Yet pray the Lord to place His seal on this heart of mine. The clock has struck twelve of the midnight hour and I must close. This day of public thanksgiving, I feel, should have thanks from one so greatly blessed as I have been. Adieu for the night.

Friday morning, 9th. The Lord has been very kind to me another night, and His tender mercies are over me again. "O, to grace a debtor, daily I am constrained to be!" Every day brings new mercies and lays me under renewed obligations to God for all His kindness. While the Lord has not taken me away, and thus broken the family circle, yet that circle has been broken by another —yes, she has gone! Dear sister! the Lord has called her away. That voice that so sweetly used to make the circle delighted with her sweet anthems is now hushed upon earth. But, blessed be God, I hope it is not closed in the courts above. Let not the heart murmur, my dear parents. We have always known that we must be broken as a family. While the heart may weep (and it would be unnatural not to), yet feel all is well. I know that all our hopes must hang on Jesus, who can bind up the broken heart and say to all sorrow depart, and it shall obey Him. I have looked every day for a letter from some of you, giving the particulars of her death, but as yet have looked in vain. I hope such a letter I may soon receive. I have sometimes felt it was too much to be separated from my family as I have been since the month of September; and yet I feel that the Lord has called me to this very place. I wish to do the will of my heavenly Father, and all the self-denial which I can possibly practice is nothing to be compared to the self-denial of my Savior. I want the family all to hear the voice of Providence in the death of our dear sister C—, saying: "Be ye also ready!" and all serve the Lord faithfully. All send love. Remember me affectionately to all, and ever pray for

       Your son,
        L. A. WICKES.

CHAPTER XV.

MEETINGS AT WOODVILLE, COPENHAGEN AND RODMAN.

My Dear Affectionate Wife:

WOODVILLE, Dec. 12, 1842.

I REACHED this place on Saturday evening about eight o'clock, and found a few gathered together for a prayer-meeting and there seemed to be some feeling among them. On Sabbath, Bro. Pond went to Belleville and left me alone to preach to his people. The church is small, and will not hold to exceed two hundred and fifty or thereabouts. The congregation on yesterday was only about one hundred and thirty. A small number, indeed. Responsibility is diminished as numbers diminish, yet it looks rather dark. It is true there have been several protracted meetings here, and they have been burnt over by all kinds of fire, holy fire, wild fire, and Satan's fire. They have two churches, Congregationalist and Baptist.

Here are some scattering Methodists, and there is almost everything else here. The village contains about twenty families, no tavern, one distillery (the devil's teapot) that keeps a constant groaning in its machinery resembling very, very faintly the groaning of those who shall be destroyed by their works. O, that God would break down their iniquities. What the Lord may order about these things here and in this county, I cannot say. It truly is a desolation. Bro. B. wants me to labor with him, and Bro. S. wants me to come to Rodman. But what duty is, I cannot say. I think I shall not, however, make any positive engagement in this region for the present. But let us cultivate much of the spirit of our heavenly Father. There is a joy that the child of God may possess in the life of the Christian. I do feel that we may have a more glorious view of heavenly realities, and the worth of souls, the infinite sacrifice that has been made to purchase our eternal redemption from sin, and I do feel that I want that love of the Savior to dwell in me that the life which I live "I may live by faith in the son of God." O! that God would help my unbelief. Do pray for me that I may possess more of the Spirit of the Lord, whose I am and whom I serve. Remember me affectionately to all the friends in Albany and in Troy. May my little girls be the best in A. until I come, and do every thing to please the Lord and then you will be loved by all. * * * I have just heard from Lisbon. The work of the Lord is still going on in that place.

Your affectionate Husband and Father.

L. A. WICKES.

WOODVILLE, JAN. 2, 1843.

DEAR SISTER E.:

I received your line by Mr. C. yesterday. I intended to close the meeting yesterday but some felt they could not consent to have it closed. Though it is very thinly attended indeed, and it promises to be extensive from the fact that the people in the vicinity around do not attend much. Nearly every person who has attended in the day time has been hopefully converted, how many I can not say. But there is an unpleasant feeling between some members of the churches. Though in this church there is now pretty good state of feeling. Backsliders have been reclaimed by the scores. There is a large circle of young people, who have been brought back to the fold of Christ, among them are two sisters of Mr. C. To God be all the glory. The meeting I now think will hold but a few days. May the Lord direct. The people in Belleville are very anxious to hold a meeting there. But I know not whether I shall. So also Bro. Spears has been here, to have me go to Rodman. But I now think that my first business will be to go after my family when I close here. Pray much dear sister. Live at the feet of the Saviour. Love to all.

Your brother in haste.

L. A. WICKES.

Soon after he brought home his family from Albany and commenced a meeting at Copenhagen which resulted in much good.

*COPENHAGEN, FEB. 11th. 1843.

MY DEAR BRO. CROSS:

To Mr. Cross. You will perceive by the date of this that I am still in the land of the living. Though it is just a year to day since God laid his hand on me in H. and I came near to the grave. I am a great debtor to the Lord for all his kindness to me. And I should have gone to the tomb long ere this I do believe if it had not been for the prayers of God's dear people. "I was brought low, and he helped me." To His name be all the glory and the honor—I have endured much more labor the year past than I ever thought I should be able to perform. And my health is now quite good. Since I parted with you my dear Bro., I have had many conflicts in my own feelings I can asure you. I have never had so heavy weight on my heart as I have had for the dear friends in St. L. County. My very heart has been borne down with a longing for the dear people of God. I did not know how much I did love that people. Truly my heart was knit to them and I feel they are like parents and children to me. May God preserve them. I have had many feelings of whether

---

*In a sermon preached, while holding a meeting at Copenhagen, he related an incident respecting a young man putting up a barn. He had prepared his timbers, got his bents all placed ready to raise, called his neighbors to help raise it. It began to rain, his neighbors thought it dangerous to raise such heavy timbers when wet. He took an oath and said it should be raised if he "went to hell"!! They all attempted to raise the first bent, when about half way up it slipped and fell, and caught his head, and smashed his brains, scattering them in every direction. A man in the congregation immediately arose, and said it was a fact for he saw it. It produced a striking effect.

it is duty to remain in this region. Yet there is an appearance of a great door being open in this community. The meeting at W. was rather poorly attended. Much of the weather was very unfavorable and the obstacles in the way were most mighty and great, yet the Lord got himself a name there. There were somewhere between sixty and eighty hopefully converted and reclaimed from their backslidings. Our Baptist brethren did not come in as a church. Though some took hold with all their might. I have been here a little over three weeks. God's spirit is among us though the whole community are on the move yet Christians are not where they should be. I wish I had you here to help. No. I do not either. For I want you to go to L. if it is duty. And I do think it is for the present. I received a letter from there a day or two since in which they say they could have got you there, if you had not thought it would have interfered with me. Now my Bro. you need not be afraid of such at all. And I do think you cannot serve the cause of Christ better than to go there, and at W. or H. I had thought about the time I left you that I should locate. But the providence of God seems to forbid my doing it. Calls multiply above measure. I have calls from Rodman, Belleville, Brownville, Smithville, Mansville, Sackett's Harbor, etc., etc., so that I do not know where there is a stopping place. I do think brother that you can do a good work in L. And if they send for you, do go, if it is only for a year. I have written to them accordingly. May God direct you. Put on your fisher's coat and bound into the great deep of the fishes' abode, and God will help you. I feel dear brother you would be the means of saving that church in its infancy. May God direct and bless you. Write soon and let me know all about things. Tell Dea. W. to pray God to direct me. Love to him and all the dear brethren. Remember me to Mrs. C.

In haste your Bro. in Christ.

L. A. WICKES.

RODMAN, Feb. 27, 1843.

MY DEAR AND AFFECTIONATE WIFE:

My ride to this place was very cold and tedious. I called a little while at Bro. A--'s. Met there a Bro. S-- and wife, from over in Greig, whom I had not seen since I left there, when holding a meeting there. They informed me that prospects were more favorable than they had been. Called at Dea. D--'s, about four miles from this place, who is a deacon of this church and one of the most efficient members, and found him very sick, and still is so. Reached here while people were assembling for meeting. Bro. Spears was reading the Scriptures, introductory to a prayer-meeting. There were something like a hundred present and many of them were real loungers, as though some of them had come to meeting to make it a place of rest. Got hold of the feelings of some. Friday morning but little done; only a few there, and that few very cold. The state of feeling has gone back for a week or two, so that I did not have a just idea of it. In the afternoon a few out in comparison to the whole number. In the evening a pretty good attendance and some feeling. Saturday, some few out, but not much increase as to feeling or numbers. Sabbath we had a houseful, which will hold about four hundred, and the Lord has made His truth effectual during the day. The characters of Abraham and Eli had a most powerful effect on all the congregation. May God, by His spirit, carry it home to the conscience, and sanctify it to many souls. In the evening I did not feel well, and did not preach much. I felt ashamed to think I should cripple the word of the Lord so much. Last evening went to meeting much as the ox goeth to the slaughter; felt unable to preach. But the Lord helped me very much, thanks to His holy name! Why should I be so distrustful, and question the promises of God so much, and be so unwilling to leave all in His hands? O, that this heart of stone were subdued! The forenoon meeting was quite interesting; some considerable feeling. This afternoon the Lord was in our midst. One lady to-day, a married lady, hoped she gave all to Christ, though very weak and feeble. Some of our friends here from Woodville. The Lord is still there, though no conversions since I left there. It is a subject that I think I must devote some thought upon: Why there are no more conversions after the meetings close, and the remedy for that evil? I have coughed so much that I feel some sore across my lungs, but the Lord may strengthen me yet. To-day is the last day of winter. How quick time has fled and gone, and yet how replete with deep interest! How much good or evil the Lord only knows, has been done. O, how I should live at the foot of the cross, where I may have the aid and direction of my heavenly Father! One year ago

Rodman,
Feb. 28, 1843.

now we were in Hermon and in other circumstances than now. How kind the Lord has been to us! O, may we be humble, and ever adore the grace that God has given to us! What may be the result of another year we know not; let us act accordingly, and live more like pilgrims on the earth. There is more need of our living humble than, perhaps, almost any others, for we are liable to temptations which others are not, or may not have from the very places in which we are placed in. Thus, we have commenced the months of spring. O, may it prove to us a putting forth of new and strong desires for the salvation and good of souls, and a new life of obedience to God! On the last day of winter we called forward the whole of the church in public confession and humiliation, when a large number came forward and renewed their covenant vows to God; and the day following they unbosomed themselves in full, so that the impenitent felt they were left without one excuse. Yesterday I called for prayers in the morning meeting and there were about thirty came forward, and, we hope, some seven or eight gave themselves to the Lord, and the work seems to be deepening quite fast. Bro. S—'s family I have some hope for. May they come to Jesus and live devoted lives! O, what a thought to bring up children for sin and woe! The more I think of it the more I see the importance of placing children under the influence of piety and humble devotedness to God. And what a responsibility is resting upon us! May the Lord direct us in the path of light. At the closing up of the meeting on the last evening, about one hundred expressed an interest in the love of a Savior. Pray much for me, and for this place. Love to all. Your affectionate husband,

L. A. WICKES.

RODMAN, March 18, 1843.

DEAR AND AFFECTIONATE WIFE:

On account of snow we have had no mail from the east for a week, but we have not had enough snow to prevent our having meetings, until this evening I thought it not best to have any meeting, for it snows and blows very much and the prospects are very gloomy as to getting out a congregation. The roads are very much blocked up, and it is doubtful whether there will be any getting out to-morrow. "But sufficient to the day is the evil thereof." Since I wrote you the Lord has been with us here, and quite a number have bowed to the sceptre of love. A much greater proportion are females than the other sex.

21st. Since dating this I have not had time to write any more until this morning. I preached on Sabbath two and three-fourths hours in one sermon, on account of the storm, which has been very severe here. The roads have been completely blocked up, so that it has been about impossible to get out, yet we have had a number out and almost daily some have come to the Lord; yet things drag much. I said nothing though I was at meeting, except in personal conversation, and last evening stayed at my room and tried to cure my cough, which has followed me up all the time and is now accompanied by a pain on my lung, something as when at H—. But I am in hopes to throw it off; perhaps I cannot. May the Lord direct me what to do! Elder C— has gone on with the meeting at B—, and I think it very doubtful whether I shall go there at all. The people of Adams

are quite anxious, and are making arrangements for me
to come there, I will if possible. I have not given them
much encouragement as yet, and I doubt very much
whether it will be duty for me while I have such a constant cough. Yet there is appearance of good for that
place. Some from there have been brought to bow at
the foot of the cross. Since I wrote you Bro. N— has
sent from Hopkinton to get me to come there. I have
answered in the negative. So there has
been a delegation here from Gouverneur, to
have me come and hold a meeting with the new church
organized there, by the St. Lawrence Consociation.
But I do not see the way clear, for the present, to go
there Also I have had a pressing request from the
church in Rome, Oneida County, under the pastoral care
of the Rev. C. Jones. To this, for the present, I have
returned a negative answer. What God has for me to
do I cannot say; or whether it is to come to the grave
I know not, but let me be prepared for any and every
place where the Lord may call me. I have no positive
engagement after this meeting, though quite a number of
applications. Let us pray much for the guidance of His
spirit in this time of anxiety. The churches here were in
a wretched and broken condition and no piety that
showed itself among the people, except in a very few
cases. But some of the brethren have got hold on the
arm of the Lord. And the young converts do work
nobly. Yet it is difficult to please all, and it is a hard
matter to keep things in that path where they may all
feel to work. The Methodists want more noise; some
of this church do not want any noise at all. One thinks
that no one can be converted without crying out loud;

Rodman, March, 1843.

another, none can be savingly converted because there is now and then an "amen" through the house, so that unbelief is on all sides; yet the Lord will honor Himself in the salvation of souls. Mr. Spears feels very deeply for his sons, and prays very much for them. May all the family feel an equal responsibility and act in the fear of God, praying without ceasing. Pray much for me and for this place. Bro. Spears has just been in and advised me not to go out this morning, but I think I must. Tell the dear children to be good and love their ma and all, and especially their Savior, who is their best friend. Kiss little Sarah for me. Sweet child—she hardly knows what *father* means. She is almost like a fatherless one. May the Lord smile upon her! Let us study to be more of a heavenly temperament, and our little ones learn to become like Christ, our glorified Savior. I must close. Love to all. In haste,

Your husband,
L. A. WICKES.

CHAPTER XVI.

FROM MRS. WICKES, TO HER SISTER. MEETINGS AT BELLEVILLE, AND ADAMS.

BELLEVILLE, March 31st, 1843.

DEAR SISTER:

BY this time you will begin to look for a letter as you see we have not turned our course towards home. After getting to Rodman through untrod roads, snow-drifts, and storm, I concluded it was the will of Providence that I should remain until husband had determined what his duty was in regard to his engagements in this place. He had an appointment at Belleville, on Wed. eve. He commenced the meeting Monday and closed up on Tuesday eve., but at the earnest solitations of the people of R. they constrained him to stay another day still. Wednesday morning the meeting continued, and in the afternoon messengers came from Belleville to see if he was going to come and commence here in the evening, as every arrangement had been made, and all were expecting him. He sent them word he would be here Thursday eve., putting them off one day. When the meeting closed Wed. night about seventy rose that thought they had been converted since last Sabbath. Bro. H's house was thronged until noon yesterday when we left and came to this place. There was a large congregation out last eve. The results of this meeting are yet to be seen. I hope the Lord will overrule all to His own glory. If the Lord has a work for us to do in B. I trust He will strengthen us to do it. The Presbyterian church is in a very low state though they are quite united with the Methodists who are considerably engaged in sustaining this meeting. The prospects have been very favorable to-day. Sat., April 1st. Last night the churches consecrated themselves to this work publicly. I trust the Lord will do great things for this people. Husband works on without stopping to think about his cold. We are in the family of Dr. H. They have five children. Youngest is a pleasant little girl between eleven and twelve; the oldest daughter is hoping. All appear attentive, the two sons especially thoughtful. Their own mother died about three or four years since, a devoted Christian. Hope we shall see all the children choosing God for their portion. I trust the Lord will make you all His care while we aim to labor in His blessed cause. Pray for us.

Your affectionate sister,
C. WICKES.

BELLEVILLE, April 1, 1843.

An Extract.—Have just returned from meeting this evening. A large congregation out; and it was very solemn and attentive, and indeed, in all the exercises of the day the spirit of the Lord has seemed to overshadow the sanctuary. Humble confessions, with many tears, have been poured forth from professing Christians. At the close of the sermon to-night quite a number rose to be prayed for. May we not expect glorious things at the hand of our God? There is a large body of snow on the ground; sleighs come loaded to meeting with people from every direction, which seems very singular at this season of the year, but our "God that rules on high, and thunders when He please," he rolls the seasons round and will overrule all things right.

Tuesday evening, 11th. I know not when the Lord will permit us to return home. There is a great work to be done here. The meeting is increasingly interesting; there have been conversions daily, and to-day quite a goodly number have come out on the Lord's side, for which we thank God. Elder C. closed his meeting last Sabbath. The work is moving on here. People come to meeting on wheels and sleighs also. The meeting with the children has been very interesting every day since it began. The people in Adams are waiting impatiently for pa to commence there. Their minister was after him yesterday, wishing to commence immediately. Hope the Lord will direct in all the way. The meeting continues here; the work, however, moves slowly. The churches were in a different state than what was supposed—many hindrances and obstacles in the way to impede the progress of this blessed work. There has been no open opposition from the wicked, but rather a disposition to linger around and listen. The lack has been altogether on the part of Zion, and a general backsliding equal to any place of our acquaintance, and an inclination to cover it up and smother it, rather than confess and forsake it, such as never was seen in any

other locality. This has been one great hindrance. If
they could only come as impenitent sinners they would
be willing, but to confess any former pretensions to religion—then be called backsliders!—it was so humiliating
and vexing that many detested the thought of it; even
some members of the church yet remain in the same
plight. Another great hindrance, and which ever gives
the death blow to the work of God. For about ten days
before the Baptists closed their meeting there was but
little else done but to urge individuals into the water;
consequently it would be the prevailing talk, and so the
spirit of God was awfully grieved away.
This has happily subsided, in some meas-
ure at least. When will men learn not to pursue such a
course of wrong?

April 20.
Belleville.

Some interest manifested in meeting to-day, and many
professors of religion just begin to think that God is
going to do a great work in B—. Now, "God is the
same yesterday, to-day and forever." He is always ready
to pour out His rich blessings, and He would never withhold it if His people were always ready to receive it, and
just in proportion as they open the avenues to receive,
so He pours in the blessing. What a striking providence
in the death of Brother A—— S——. May it be overruled
for the good of the Zion of God in S. S. Truly the
church is called upon loudly to "work while the day
lasts." May not some mercy drops fall on that place
yet, while the genial showers of divine grace are visiting
multitudes of other places all around. The meeting in
Belleville closed Sabbath night or rather Monday morning;
considering all things it was a very profitable season.
If it could have continued two or three weeks longer,

obstacles would have continued to be removed, and the results would have been many more conversions. About eighty took their seats and gave their names as subjects of the work. On acount of the badness of the roads, quite a number of the converts were not present. Dr. H's family shared in the work. Left the kind and dear family that afternoon and came to Adams, Tuesday evening; preached to a very large audience Wednesday.

Adams, April 26. Not as many out during the day. Fri., prospects yesterday more encouraging. Many are expecting to see great things; should their expectations be founded on a right source, no doubt they will realize their anticipations, especially if they act accordingly. No meeting at the church this morning, but we have had an interesting prayer meeting around the family altar, at the house of Mr. D. Here a young woman commenced a praying life, and a young man came out last night and prayed with us at the family devotions. The work is moving on in this place. Some fears of relaxation of responsibility on the part of some, while others are coming in more readily. There is a great work to be done here, and unforeseen obstacles do, and will appear. But God is able and willing to accomplish and triumph over all. Yesterday was a Sabbath of much interest. People from Rutland, Rodman, Belleville, and Woodville, here at meeting. We do not forget our dear children and friends at home, but morning and night commit them to our heavenly Father's care. Shall write soon again. Love to all.

May 1st.

Yours affectionately,
L. A. AND C. WICKES.

ADAMS, May 9, 1843.

An extract. Sabbath afternoon, the people voted to have the meeting continued and all say he must not leave now. There are conversions, some very interesting cases, among the first class of young gentlemen and ladies. The Lord is evidently with his Holy Spirit like a cloud of mercy hovering over this place. But the season of the year among farmers especially, and other reasons, occasion the movement of this work to be gradual. The work of the Lord has taken a new impulse and it has been remarked by individuals that this place has not seen such a time since the revival when the Rev. Mr. Finney and Mr. Parker were converted. Religion is the general topic of conversation throughout the community. Yesterday there was a full, attentive and a solemn congregation, and a unanimous vote by all to have the meeting still go on. Many express the conviction that seems to be deeply impressed on their minds that this is the last call they shall ever have, and truly it does appear to be a time of momentous interest to many, not to say of awful consequences for time and eternity. A young lady from Washingtonville who was converted last week called this morning to say farewell; she returns home to-day, and another from Western. A young man from Henderson has become hopefully pious. Some friends from Rodman and Belleville have been here considerably. There are three or four churches in Ellisburg destitute of any minister and they are trying to unite all their energies to see if they cannot get help and a protracted effort. The church in North Adams have sent a special request to have a meeting commence there next week or as soon as possible. Thus calls for labor continually multiply.

May the Lord teach what duty is and give a willing mind to perform it in the fear of the Lord in all meekness, trusting Him as to results, so that these "trials" may work patience, and patience experience, experience hope, and hope maketh not ashamed because the love of God is shed abroad in the heart by the Holy Ghost given, and may it be abundant, especially at this time. At a season of prayer before preaching, the Lord appeared by His Holy Spirit and it has been a precious season. One old man melted down like a little child and prayed, another a young man who had passed through a glorious work at Lockport, the account of which was published in the Evangelist, arose and begged for prayer, bowed down and prayed. After the season of prayer he arose and told his determination to serve God. Other cases might be mentioned. Soon the bell rang for preaching; there was then a deep and fixed attention followed by earnest prayer which is always followed with glorious results.

Pray much for this place. As ever yours. C.

STOWS SQUARE, June 2, 1843.

DEAR PARENTS:—After an absence of four months I am once more seated with my little family in our own hired rooms, and enjoying comparatively good health. You will recollect the village of Adams (the first village you came to on the second day of your visit with Uncle to our house.) A pleasant village. I spent rising of four weeks there after the close of the meetings at Belleville. The Lord has been with us and His mercy has been over us. Many have bowed to the sceptre of His love, and the church has been brought to consecrate themselves to the service of God anew. I cannot say how many became the subjects of renewed grace, but somewhere over one hundred and fifty hopeful conversions. The aged and the young of all classes were among the subjects of the work. Especially among the youth of the first class work was most effectual, while there were several persons of seventy years old. To God be all the glory and the honor. For to Him it is due. "Shall the saw boast itself above him that shaketh it?" The meeting at Belleville was owned and blessed of the Lord. The more I see of my own vile heart the more I feel that it is only the abounding grace of God that does attend the efforts of one so vile. I shall probably leave in a few more days again for Jefferson county. I want the Lord to guide me in the path of rectitude. My greatest desire is to see my children serving the Lord in their early days, and to be encircled in His arms when parents shall be no more. They have no preaching now on the Square. There is rather an unpleasant state of feeling in the church about the choir, all of it I feel is the production of backsliding from God. He has said such shall be filled with their own ways. Remember us to all and all join in love to all. Let us lay aside every weight that may impede our progress in the divine life. Pray much for me, especially that the Lord will direct my path. In haste.

Your Affectionate Son,
L. A. WICKES.

CHAPTER XVII.

MEETING AT MANSVILLE.

MANSVILLE, Oct. 3, 1843.

MY DEAR AND AFFECTIONATE WIFE:—

YOU will perceive by the date of this that I have at last reached the destined place for which I left you. There was nothing particular took place on my journey. I did not make any call until I reached Dea. Dodge's, at Sandy Creek, a few miles above Rodman, where I found him enjoying much of the presence of God. And praying that God would guide me, I called at Rodman, and found most of the friends very well. Some had gone to eternity. One of the young converts, a hopeful subject of the work of grace, had lived a consistent and devoted Christian, was drowned; the other was not a Christian (oh, sad end!) Another man who had become a Christian during the meeting had gone to the grave. He died in the triumph of faith. He was an Englishman who came to mill during the meeting and was attracted to the house by the throng and had not heard preaching before for a long time, and on the spot, he hopefully gave all to Christ, and had lived faithfully and his end was triumphant. To God be all the glory. Another had also gone to the tomb. He also died in the Lord. I arrived at Adams about 4 o'clock, p. m. Received a hearty welcome from many. After considerable consultation concluded to stay over the Sabbath. I visited most of the day with Br. Kirk, the pastor. Preached on Saturday evening and twice on the Sabbath and assisted in administering the Lord's supper; four united with the church. One young man by the name of H., who attended the meeting and who had been the subject of prayer, but who resisted all that could be done, was killed by a pitch-fork falling from a load of hay and penetrating the heart. An affliction to a widowed mother and a warning to others. They were very anxious I should tarry with them, and if not, to return and spend a few weeks there. The prospect of things is quite favorable in this place. I arrived in M. about 5 o'clock last evening, and was welcomed by Dea. Man to his hospitable mansion. The state of things is such that it is doubtful whether I shall stay here and hold a meeting. To hear the members of the church talk last evening, as I visited a few, I felt a mingled emotion of pity and diversion. They were so afraid of what would be the consequence of the meeting, etc., etc., but friends are quite anxious I should make a stop here all around. May the Lord's will be done is my greatest desire. I feel the need of much prayer that God will direct me in the path of duty. I must go out and visit the church. Nov. 17th. Thus far I wrote some three weeks ago and I have not had time to write any more. I have been alone nearly all the time as to ministerial help. I do not get to rest until twelve and one o'clock at night. The prospects are very favorable now, though of all the places which I have been in this exceeds all. You cannot describe or form any idea of the extent of the wickedness.

There are a very few families that are very fine people, but the state of society around is very peculiar. They have exerted themselves (the wicked) to the utmost to grieve away the Lord. They have tried to keep up balls in the place every week or nearly so since I came here. They ransacked the whole region from Pulaski to Sacketts Harbor a distance of 40 miles or more, and they get a very large company together and they act as much like the devil as possible. At one ball they wrote a notice of my being here, styling me as the authorized agent of the Hell Fire Insurance Company, and put the accompanying notice upon the church.

"HELL FIRE INSURANCE OFFICE!

"Mr. Wicks wood inform the ladis and children of Mannsville and vasinity that he will insure soles agains the fires of hell as chep as any other Pope or Pries. He holds his office at the meeting hous in sd place whare thos who wish to be insureed must attend and obey his mandates and suc down all he ses, say all he doos is wright he will say with us six or eight weks if he is well fed and paid and you spend your hull time in hearing his slang and expoits but is you do net he will leave you and you may go to hell and bedamd."

But God has turned it upon their own heads. It only had the effect to bring out more. Several of the ball characters have been brought to bow at the Savior's feet. To God be all the glory given. But God has been insulted by the vile. The language which has been used by some persons here to drive out the work of God from this place I will not repeat. But one man called upon God to damn his soul if he did not put a stop to this meeting. He has labored as hard as he could together with some other of kindred spirits. Night before last while I was preaching I got about half through when the cry of fire! fire! was heard, and the church was soon emptied and we were all found trying to save property from being destroyed. It was a wagon maker's shop in which the wicked wretch worked who was going to break up the meeting and by the sad accident he was turned out of the place. May God have mercy on him and show him his vile course and bring him to repentance.

Among all the other difficulties, we have been nearly broken up four times in meeting by the cry of fire. And in each time it was the work of an incendiary. Once they set the church on fire where the Millerites worship, but it was extinguished after burning the stairs down. There has been the alarm of fire five times since I have been here. You can scarce form any idea of the awful wickedness of this place. It is a real nest of backsliders and old hopers. I know God will appear for His own glory and honor.

And also, I find my heart needs to be guarded in order to keep from rejoicing in the overthrow of the wicked and their plans. I want to lie humble at Jesus' feet and cause His blessing to flow over my soul. To-night, God willing, I finish what was left of the sermon on Universalism which I did not finish at the time of the fire. And may God direct me in the path of love and wisdom. I must now stop; my room begins to be thronged again. 11 o'clock, after meeting. Some good has been done to-day, and I hope the Lord is on the giving hand. Oh, for more of His spirit to reign in my soul. There have been some fifteen or twenty family altars erected and a host of backsliders have been reclaimed. Some cases of conversions that have astonished the most incredulous, and the work seems to have only begun. To-day one man sixty-five years old was hopefully converted. To God be all the glory given. Friends and some individuals who were interested in this place from A. have been here at different times, made confession to the church and entered into the work and gone home with joyful hearts. As there is no pastor in this church the people here are very anxious I should remain here. Four men have made large offers and they think a remunerative amount will be made if I would only say the word. But as yet I do not see my way clear. The Lord has led us in a way we know not. I desire to be obedient to His will, but let us ask and obey His answer. What He means to do with us is not for us to know. May we trust His promises and pray for His hand to lead. What debtors to grace we have been? And through *riches* of *free grace* may we triumph. How does your soul prosper? Does your faith look up to God so as to feel God will still work in this place? Hold on upon the Lord's arm. I cannot say when I shall be home but I now think in a few days. If the Lord will, a week from next Tuesday. My health is better than I expected it would have been when I left home, though quite hoarse, yet not as hoarse as before I closed at Adams. Kiss the children for me and pray for

Your affectionate husband,

L. A. WICKES.

MANSVILLE, Oct. 10, 1843.

MY DEAR AND AFFECTIONATE WIFE:

Your kind letter came to hand. It did my heart good to see the marks of your pen. Since I wrote I have visited nearly all the members of the church in this place and you can scarcely make any calculation about the state of the church. As to individual or social duties as Christians, secret, family and social,—yes political duties are very much neglected. I have been here a little over a week and have heard only two females open their mouth in prayer. There are some who feel quite deeply, but cannot say anything for God. They have a great deal of —what shall I call it? *Modesty!!* Shame would be much more appropriate. To-day is the first day I have had meeting in the day time; some out, and some feeling, I never felt in my life as though I was staying where I was not wanted as I do here, and yet feel as though it was duty not to leave. But what the final issue will be, I cannot say. There is some moving on the waters. They seem to be afraid that I shall leave them, which they cannot bear to think of, yet seem to be sorry that I came when I did; but the Lord means it for good.

October 11th. Yesterday my leisure moments were so much occupied with reading "Luther at the Diet of Worms," that I did not take time to write any. There was a funeral here; the daughter of a widow woman, member of the Baptist church. Sermon by the Baptist Elder from, "Cast thy burden on the Lord and He will sustain thee:" He talked very well. At the close of the exercise the widow rose and addressed the congregation herself, in a feeling manner, and confessing her sin in not doing her duty, and warning parents against pursuing the same course of neglect. I hope and pray it may have some effect. Last evening I preached from 2 Chron. 7: 14. "If My people which are called by My name shall humble themselves and pray and seek My face, and turn from their wicked ways; then will I hear from heaven, and will forgive their sins and will heal their land." And I should think something like thirty or forty persons came forward for prayers, and humbly bowed together, confessing their sins, and entering into a covenant with their God and one another to return to duty and serve the Lord. There was something of a melting time. After returning to my boarding place (Dr. K.), in the same house with Deacon M., we had another. The Doctor went the rounds, confessing to all; and a good deal of real feeling and brokenness of heart. I do pray God it may be a blessing to all—that from this hour there may be a consecration to God as there never was in this place. Yesterday afternoon there was some feeling; more than there has hitherto been. Some females got their mouths open in confession that never before were heard to say a word in meeting, and last evening a pretty good congregation out. I preached on "Jericho walls falling," and after meeting I was told that the great Dr. K., of H— Seminary, was present, and I felt that it was rather poor food for such a man: But after all I did not come here to preach to him; though I believe if I had known he had been present, I should have given him a portion. But perhaps the Lord will give him what is much better. Last Friday I went to Woodville to preach the funeral sermon of Miss L. B. She hopefully experienced religion at the meeting in W. last winter.

She left a pleasing evidence that she had gone to rest in the bosom of love. Thus the Lord is taking away one and another of those who, in connection with my labors have bowed at the feet of the Lord. Yet it is a source of solemn reflection to me, that they have gone to test the grounds of their hope in Christ, lest I should have given them any reason to trust to a false hope. May the Lord forbid I ever should, and keep me from doing so great evil! O! what responsibility is attached to the gospel ministry. The more I reflect on it, the more I feel unfit for it. You spoke of converting the children, etc.; I hope God will enable you to do it, and bless your labors; and that they may be (are) the true children of God. It is the great desire of my heart to have them love and honor God. I have just this moment had a call from Dr. K., and had a pleasant interview. He is affable, affectionate and agreeable in his manners, making himself at home, and those with whom he converses to feel at home with him. His topics of conversation are familiar and easy—none of that distance and ostentation which is often found in persons looked up to as a great one. I felt conscious of being in the presence of my superior and yet he made me feel at home. Thus may we feel when we come into the presence of our heavenly Father who cares for us. The Doctor is a tall man, like Mr. D. long favored, hair gray and braided over a bald spot on the top of his head. Nothing very remarkable as to his phrenological developments. People look at great men with much curiosity, but after all they are nothing but, flesh and bones, with an accountable soul like all others. I must hasten to a close. I board in Dr. Kinney's family. There are five children. A daughter Julia makes me think of sister J.; another, Sarah, which reminds me of my little daughter S. It is a fine family. They read the Bible with their father at family devotion, and are very attentive. May the Lord bless them and my own little family, is the prayer of,

Your husband,
L. A. WICKES.

CHAPTER XVIII.

MEETINGS AT HUVELTON, WEST POTS-DAM, MADRID AND WADDINGTON.

HUVELTON, Jan. 15, 1844.

MY DEAR AND AFFECTIONATE WIFE;

YOU will perceive by this that I am now in H. I arrived here on Wednesday eve., and on Thursday I preached the dedication sermon to a house full, from Micah. 4: 2–3; and not much of a sermon it was, either. But we had a real pleasant time of it, and the Lord was in the midst of us. They have a very good man, and one who does take delight in doing good, and I think will be a blessing to the people. At the close of the exercise they plead with me to stay and preach in the evening. I finally consented, and they begged I would stay till after the Sabbath, as it was communion with them, and hold meetings Friday and Saturday. On the Sabbath they put the vote to request me to stay a few days, when there was a unanimous vote by the whole congregation, to have me stay. The house was literally crammed full, and many loaded teams were unable to get in. But what duty is, I cannot say. There seems to be an appearance of good here. There have been one or two conversions already—Mrs. G.'s mother one. Nine united with the church on Sabbath; two old men rising of seventy years. I shall determine in a day or two what duty is and act accordingly. The day I left I saw the people in Denmark, and left an appointment for a meeting to commence next week, on Tuesday eve. if the Lord will. When I arrived at Antwerp they were just relating over the scenes of Mrs. Church's funeral, which had just taken place that day. She died in the triumph of faith: " Precious in the sight of the Lord is the death of His saints!" But let us be humble, and show to the world that God can and will dwell with us as long as we will dwell with Him. I feel for the church of God in S. S. O! that God will dwell in the hearts of men and cause them to see where they are.

I have but a short time to write a few lines to let you know where I am. The church and people hold on to me very strong, and the Lord is truly in the midst of us. The word of the Lord has got among the old country people, and a goodly number have hopefully given themselves to the Lord. There have been somewhere between twenty and thirty hopeful conversions, and some quite interesting cases. To God be all the glory and the honor! Most of them are heads of families, and some are advanced in life. And such is the state of things here that I wrote to Denmark to have them postpone their meeting for a few days; and since writing them I have been earnestly requested to go to West Potsdam. The state of society and the feeling is such that I have written again to Denmark to say whether they will give way for that object; *i. e.*, for me to go to

Huvelton,
Jan. 24, 1844.

Potsdam first. If they consent to that I shall go; if not, I think I shall be at Denmark next week I hardly know what duty is.

O! that I might do what will be pleasing to Him. The vineyard is all one, and though it may be in the different portions of God's vineyard, yet it is all His, and all for His glory and His cause. Keep humble, and live low at the foot of the cross. Pray for me.

Yours,
L. A. WICKES.

HUVELTON, Jan. 29, 1844.

DEAR AND AFFECTIONATE WIFE:

Since I wrote you, I have seen the salvation of the Lord. Several have, as we trust, bowed at the foot of the cross. Mostly among the old country people. Those who, when I was here before, were standing aloof, have many of them been brought to see their need of a Saviour, and we trust have given themselves to the Lord. And the work seems to be spreading and deepening. I did intend to close up my labors here yesterday, but by the earnest solicitude of friends I stay a few days longer, how long I cannot say. I have written to Denmark to postpone that meeting until after I go to West Potsdam. I think that it will be best to go there before returning home, if my health and comfort of my family will allow. I have taken a severe cold and my voice is becoming as it was at Rodman, last winter, though not as hard a cough as then, yet I think prudence is becoming me. If I find that it increases on me I shall stop at once. May the Lord direct. I have received pressing calls from Madrid and Lorain. In both cases they want me immediately, and so I shall not think of going to either of them until after I have been to the other places. As the people of Madrid waited so long before they concluded to have a meeting, I do not at *present* think I can go. But in this let us ask counsel of the Lord. The Lord is still in the midst of this people though things drag some and there are many obstacles in the way, yet there is still a slow move and nearly every day souls are coming to Christ. The work has been among the old country people while some others have bowed at the foot of the cross. To God be all the glory and the honor. Half past eleven, P. M. I have just returned from meeting. The Lord was in the midst of us. Text, Mal. 3:18. "Then shall ye return and discern between the righteous and the wicked, between him that serveth God and him that serveth Him not." Some fifty forward for prayer. Some of the first ones of the place. Many professed to have given themselves to the Lord, and I do hope that God will draw the hearts of *all* to Him. But, oh! how little faith there is in the promises of God. Why is it that God's people have no more of the love for souls in them? If they would only go to the fountain head they would get their hope in the Lord strengthened, and then might exercise more confidence in his promises, and hence, as a matter of course, they would see more abundantly the displays of His power. I feel daily the need of more faith in the Lord, and I sometimes have felt that I could hardly say that I had any faith in the Lord, yet I cannot say so, because I do believe that as unworthy as I am, God has heard my prayer, and I will give Him glory and honor. And Oh, that I might ever so live as to feel that Christ would ever hear me.

Feb. 1. The stage is coming, I must mail this. Write next week to Potsdam.

Love to all.

L. A. WICKES.

WEST POTSDAM, February 1, 1844.

MY DEAR WIFE:

You will perceive by this where I am. I closed the series of meetings at Huvelton on the Sabbath (4th), and the Lord was in the midst of us. The house was so jammed that we could not get the converts together. I cannot say with any accuracy what the numbers of conversions have been, but I should think not to exceed some fifty or sixty; and a large number of these were among the old country people. To God be all the glory given! I find many of our friends passing away; and so we are all fast going to the Lord: Well, welcome the hour! But let us be on the watch whenever our Lord shall come. I have, of late, had much delight in reading the 21st and 22d of Rev., especially the sixth and seventh verses of the 21st chapter. These are promises which are so glorious and blessed! "I will give unto him that is athirst," etc. Let but our souls take hold of that promise, and all is well; and what He gives us will be for the glory of God. Freely He will bestow upon us the waters from the fountain of life, which is Christ, Himself, purchased by His own blood and at His own suffering. Such love—how great! Such blessing—how dearly purchased! O, that such love may be enough to draw our hearts to Him! "All things." Oh, how rich are the children of God; made so by the benevolence of the Lord of glory. And am I one that the Lord has bestowed such great favors upon? May I live at the feet of my excellent Lord! So also the description of the abode of the blessed, who are made partakers of His grace, from the 9th verse of the same chapter. No wonder that Paul said it would not be lawful to speak of it. O, what joy! May my own little family have a mansion there?

I arrived here last evening. They have rather a small house, and it was pretty well filled. There is evidently some feeling on the subject of religion; there have been a few souls hopefully born into the kingdom of Christ, and some are quite serious; and the church have some little feeling on the subject. I have visited among their neighbors, and I am in hopes that something may be done which will tell on the annals of eternity. The name of their preacher is Rowley; a young man, but I think a devoted, pious man, and a laborious and faithful minister, or rather licentiate. He will do them good. The Methodist minister is a brother of Bro. K., and a pretty good man, and they have a Freewill Baptist minister here that they say will lie; and so, of course, they are unwilling to have him do anything in the meeting. O, that ministers would ever live before their God as becometh the ambassadors of the Lord Jesus Christ! May the Lord bring all things right! The meeting this afternoon was pretty well attended, and some feeling. May the Lord increase it more and more, and may God help, to-night, by overshadowing this place with His cloud of mercy, and may the presence of His spirit visit every heart, and an altar be erected in every house, for His name's sake. Pray much for me.

As ever, yours,

L. A. WICKES.

Here the churches unanimously adopted the following confession:

* We, the members of the different evangelical churches in West Potsdam, feel called upon to testify before our impenitent friends here present, the solemn dealings of God with us during the day now past.

We have set apart this day to mourn, and fast, and pray, and search our own hearts, and inquire why so little blessing attends our present labors for the souls of our dear, impenitent friends. We trust it has not been in vain, but that the Holy Spirit has shown us that great wickedness still remains in our hearts and in our churches. Many of the members of these churches have voluntarily come forward and confessed in the public assembly their personal difficulties with other members, especially such as have involved unhappy feeling between different denominations. We believe that the Lord Jesus has but one Bride, and that there is but one household of the faith, and that every action, every word, and even every thought which tends to alienate the brotherhood and produce denominational

Feb. 1844. The confession of all the evangelical churches. A revival followed.

---

* Members from all the churches came forward and knelt in the aisle of the church while the consecrating prayer was being made.

dissensions, is wounding the body of the Savior. We do not expect the work of salvation to go forward while we remain liable to the imputation of loving our party names better than we love the one glorious cause of the Lord Jesus.

This day has shown to us deep and awful sins against the law of brotherly love, far exceeding anything we were before aware of, and we have together mourned over them, and, we trust, repented of them, and confessed them to one another, and on our bended knees, confess them before God.

Brothers and sisters who have mutually indulged hard, acrimonious feelings, have obtained from each other full pardon, and united their petitions for pardon from on high. Members of the different churches have extended to each other the hand and heart of love, and we hope that some of the scandalous obstacles which have impeded the cause of salvation will now be removed, and a way be cast up over which the chariot of the Holy Ghost may roll in triumph.

<small>Confession.
February, 1844.</small>

But we have yet one more duty to perform, and we now come forward in this solemn and public manner and humble ourselves before our impenitent neighbors and friends.

Although we do not find that each of our number is guilty of all the sins which have been named, yet, as a congregation of believers, we come mournfully before you and confess our sins. O! it is the most bitter part of our remorse to reflect that our obstinate attachment to our own *self will* and *party feelings* has stood between our souls and salvation. We confess to you that we have brought a blemish upon the cause of the Redeemer, and that those cruel alienations which have now come to light, have had the effect to ruin souls.

While we cannot admit that any of our faults have justified you in remaining a single moment in your impenitency, we fear they have been the occasion of it. We have been to the Savior for pardon, and we now come to you and beseech you to forgive.

And now, dearly beloved friends, having relieved our souls by this united confession to you, though deeply unworthy, we cannot refrain from offering our united entreaty that you would come to our dear Savior's feet. Wicked as we are, still our souls are pained by your impenitency. As neighbors and friends, we have found you kind and amiable, but our hearts bleed for the perils which hang over you. We long to see you on the march towards the heavenly world. We have prayed for it, and we shall continue to pray for it. May you and we together become fellow Christians on earth, and dwellers together in heavenly light!

February, 1844. Confession when Rev. Mr. Wickes held a meeting in that place.

MADRID, COLUMBIA VILLAGE, March 16, 1844.
MY DEAR WIFE:

You will perceive by this that I am at the place of battle. I had a very tedious journey, calling on friends at various places on the way. It was neither sleighing nor wagoning, and two or three times came near turning over. But the good hand of the Lord was over us and kept us from falling. And I found myself very much fatigued and worn out, but commenced the meeting here on Thursday evening. A pretty good congregation out and very good attention, but there is a good deal of rubbish to be removed out of the way. Yet I do think there may be much good done in the name of the Lord. But it is a hard place and nothing but the power of God will accomplish anything here. And now do pray for me here and for this place. The Lord is alone our helper and God has helped us in days past and if we will only look to Him and lie at His feet, and not having any of the things of this world to shut out our prayers from Him and thus lose sight of the great work before us. An extract, March 21, respecting the work of the Lord in Columbia Village.

March 21, 1844. The Lord is with us here. Much to be done that is not yet done. Some have made a consecration of themselves to Christ, we hope, but I pray God it may be increased an hundred fold. Br. W. has got where he never was before. He says he never took so great delight in serving God before, and can bless God for what He has wrought in his own soul. I rejoice to see it, and I do pray that I may possess more and still more of the spirit of my Lord and Master.

Another extract respecting Columbia Village, May about the 20. May. The meeting at Columbia Village, Madrid, was a long one. It is a very hard and obstinate place, but the Lord has done indeed great things for them. It has made a shaking among the Universalists and infidels of every class. There were something like one hundred hopeful conversions. Among them were merchants, doctors, mechanics, teachers of music, farmers, etc., and the work seems to move forward yet. To God be all the glory and the honor for it is due to Him. Truly the Lord is good to those who will trust Him and labor for the souls of men. I have often thought that nothing would separate me from my family, but a cause so glorious as this. But while I do love my family I do love the cause of Christ more. May the Lord smile upon you all. Love to all.

As ever, your husband,
L. A. WICKES.

WADDINGTON, May 20, 1844.

MY DEAR AND AFFECTIONATE PARENTS:

Your kind letter I received while I was in Madrid. It is one of the greatest sources of delight to me to sit down and have my mother talk to me, and I *guess* it would be so if father would talk. I sometimes think I love my parents more than the other children do, but perhaps such is the feeling of each of us. I hope it is, for God has commanded us to honor father and mother, etc., and may they ever be honored. I have been in this place since the first of the month. The Lord is in the midst of the people, and opposition has been raised and kept up. Husbands forbidding wives going to meeting and parents forbidding children. One man the other day told his wife with oaths and curses, that if she did not come home (as she was conversing with me at his sister's) he would horsewhip her!! All he wanted, he said, was to break one club on my head, and yet they are on the way to heaven, all of them!!! There is an unprecedented ignorance among those who pretend to know a good deal. The Episcopal church have had the moulding of the face of society here. And more ungodly influence there could not scarcely have been exerted. For their iniquity is covered up under the mask of the religion of Christ, and so the Christian religion has been brought into disrepute. Whereas, if it had been under the name of irreligion that these things had been done, they would not have had so baneful an influence. Some young men the other day, wanted to know why it was that Christ died, after hearing a sermon on the suffering and death of Christ. And they were young men twenty and twenty-three years of age. So had their eyes been blinded by the course of instruction which had been taught there. Universalism has a strong hold here and many of them are most vile and sinful; but I trust there is a redeeming power to save this wicked place. How long I may remain here I cannot say, but I have attended meeting every day since the 4th of March, and preached every day but one. To God be all the glory given. Truly I am a great debtor to God for all His kindness to me and the constitution which He has given me. How much we do need an humble and quiet spirit to lead us in the path of light and love. May the Lord smile upon you in your declining years, is the sincere prayer of

    Your affectionate son,
      L. A. WICKES.

CHAPTER XIX.

SECOND MEETING AT MASSENA AND AT CHATEAUGAY.

MASSENA, Jan. 23. 1845.

MY DEAR AND AFFECTIONATE WIFE:

BY this you will see that I have got back to the old place of our first visit to this part of the county. It has been with a great degree of reluctance that I have come here. Still it may be for the best. But the abominations which are practiced—and in this part of the county—are awful! The Millerite excitement has been like the locust of Egypt—has eaten up every thing that is lovely and kind. Here is a part of the holy band; also a community who, under the mask of religion, have their spiritual wives. They are now divided into two parties, and each have their minister and leader. The Episcopal and Weslyan Methodists each have classes and ministers. They are not agreed. The regular Baptists have also a church and a good minister, Elder G. His three daughters were hopefully converted at West S. They have two Universalist ministers here; one keeps a rum-hole of a tavern; the other is the one who wrote me a line at N. that I answered publicly, before the church. The Congregationalists have a small church; they are old and dead in comparison. They have a small, neat, brick edifice and might live, indeed, if they would. They now have two singing schools in the place; one dancing school; Universalist preaching every other Sabbath. And the wicked and ungodly are made so hard by such a motley mess that hope looks very dark, indeed, of doing much good. I can tell in a few days what prospects will be. But now let us lie humble before the mercy seat; and may we so live and act that God will smile upon us. I closed the meeting at East Stockholm on the Sabbath, the 29th, with a very good state of feeling. They wanted the meeting to continue, but I could not stay. Left my sleigh there, or rather at Brasier Falls; made several calls on the way. Mr. B's little daughter is now poorer than ever. She truly is a sufferer, though she bears it with Christian resignation. I saw Mr. R., from Waddington. He appears quite well, and seemed to feel much for the souls of his neighbors Truly, how good the Lord is! And may we ever be found at the feet of Jesus, to adore and honor Him, and take a course that will advance His cause, and which will secure His approbation, and that our God shall not be evil spoken of. I find some feeling here among the impenitent, which is of an inquiring nature; still they are much prejudiced against the Christian religion, from the horrid actions of the professed friends of it. Let us watch and pray, and cast all on His arm. And may God smile upon us, and prosper His own work! Love to all.

Your husband, as ever,

L. A. WICKES.

MASSENA, February 17, 1845.

MY DEAR WIFE:

When I last wrote you I could not tell what I should do about staying at this place another week, but such is the interesting state of things here, that there is not much doubt that I shall remain here during this week, so that the calls are so pressing from Chateaugay that I probably shall not return home until after I have been there. And it may be some time in April before I can get around. The Lord's will be done! And I will inquire for His will. The Lord is with us, we hope. Nearly every day for ten days past there have been more or less that have bowed at the foot of the cross. Two of N. P. sisters have been hopefully converted, and two or three of her cousins. Last evening (Sabbath) there were about seventy forward for prayers, and a majority professed submission to God, and the work is deepening every day, and obstacles are giving away before the chariot of the Lord. O! may heaven ride forth from conquering to conquest, until all bow at the foot of the cross of Christ. But to accomplish this a great deal has got to be done. The Lord owns and blesses suitable means, and may His people all be willing in the day of His power. Pray much. Write, without fail, immediately.

As ever, your husband,
L. A. WICKES.

CHATEAUGAY, Franklin Co., March 14, 1845.

MY DEAR AND AFFECTIONATE WIFE:

I had a very tedious journey; made some calls; found friends generally well. I arrived at East S. in season to attend the young peoples' meeting on Tuesday evening. Wednesday I fixed my wagon, preached in the evening, and Thursday started for this county. I am in sight of Lower Canada and the St. Lawrence River. I reached here about half past six in the evening, tired, pain in my breast and arm, and faint hearted, and half wished that I was at home. I found Bro. M. waiting for me with many fears and many sorrows that I had not come, but was very much relieved by my presence. I board with a Mr. H. He is a Presbyterian; his wife a Baptist; his sister Episcopalian; the hired girl a Catholic. No family worship until now; nor is there an altar to the name of the Lord to be seen or found in the whole place. The first evening there were some sixty persons present, and while preaching, a man cried out at the height of his voice, "O, Lord!!" He is a crazy man. They have a meeting house about thirty-six by fifty, two stories high, and will seat about five hundred persons. But the state of society is most wretched and vile. Yesterday we had meeting in the afternoon and evening.

March 15th. Fourteen present in the morning. The crazy man cried out again, and very much frightened some in the house. Last evening there were about seventy out. Mr. H. set up the family altar, and we had a prayer meeting and each prayed except the Catholic. But things are very dark and discouraging; but my hope is in God, and in Him will I trust. He will not let me be put to shame. This evening there was a singing school in the church, and the meeting was dispensed with to let them sing. One reason why I would consent to it, is on account of my health. I have taken a severe cold, so that I find it very difficult to talk or pray, and a constant pain in my breast, so that I have felt it to be duty to hold up a little while. But, the Lord helping me, I will go forward still with the work until I must stop. But I will wait until after the Sabbath before I close this sheet.

Monday morning, 16th. Was quite a blustering day, but the people said they had a large congregation, though I thought it was small—their house, I think, not half full. Many, they say, were in who are never seen in the house of the Lord. I preached all day. There was quite a a good attention, and some feeling. They are quite an uncouth and rough looking set of people. And if "it is not all gold that shines," perhaps that which does not shine may be gold, and may yet reign in the golden city; and there may abound blessings to those that earth would disdain. They seem to listen to what is said, yet there is very poor preparation indeed here for the work of the Lord, and most of the people are glued to their houses. They say this is a real gambling hole. The first Judge of the county resides here, and is reputed to be a gambler and scarce never attends church. O, what a set of rulers our nation has got! "When the wicked bear rule, the people mourn," and it is a wonder to me if they will not wail and lament as well as mourn. But may it please the Lord to avert the storm that may be gathering over us, and let us be found at the foot of the cross, and lie humble before Him. I find that my heart is prone to wander from the Lord, and He only can keep me in His hand; and O, may I ever be found in Him, and of His righteousness partake.

The people of God have much to do; to watch and pray, lest in this time to try men's souls they forsake the rock of their salvation. Tell the children to love the

Savior, and tell all to lie humble before God, and may the Lord smile upon you all.

Your husband,
L. A. WICKES.

An extract.

CHATEAUGAY, April 16, 1845.

MY DEAR WIFE:

Since I wrote you the Lord has appeared for our help and has truly been our deliverer. There have been a good many backsliders brought to bow at the foot of the cross, and a goodly number of sinners have given up all to the Lord, as we hope. The number I cannot say. There have been some conversions of persons as old as fifty-five and sixty. There are the *most men* affected, as there is by far a much larger class of them impenitent than of the other sex. The community seems to be on the move, and a large number attend in the evening, and something of a number in the day time. There have been some cases of interest. In the village there have been some four or five family altars erected to the Lord, and quite a number in the town. I believe I mentioned Dr. B. had relatives living here. Some of them are what are called hard cases. We hope that three or four of his connection have bowed at the feet of Jesus. A cousin of his by marriage, is a backsliding, drinking, gambling, Baptist preacher. Keeps tavern, but has made some little confession, and burnt up two packs of cards, but is not yet, it is thought, what he should be. One physician, we hope, has given his heart to God; and another physician's wife, two merchants, and one wife. I know not what the Lord will do yet. I do pray for greater things, and I do pray God that He will show His mighty power in bringing hard hearted men to humble themselves. I find, in some respects, this one of the most difficult places that I ever labored in, viz., the want of *moral* principle. They seem not to feel moral obligation at all; yet the Lord may show them their vile hearts and make them feel their awful condition. And my only hope is in Him; He can turn them as the rivers of waters are turned—the cause is His. Brother M., of N., has been here and spent a few days, and has done much good. It was the former place of his labors and they think much of him—and he is worthy of their esteem. Pray *much* for *me*. The people of Lawrence want that the meeting in that place be deferred until about the first of June, if I can. But I do not know what I shall do. I was expecting to return in two weeks, but I cannot tell. We have a good turnout notwithstanding bad traveling. There have been as many as eighty forward for prayers at a time, and most of them men. May the Lord have mercy upon them! But O, the wickedness of this place! I have not time to point it out. Love to all.

Farewell,
L. A. WICKES.

An extract.

April 25th. The meeting is *now* quite *interesting*, and there have been quite a goodly number hopefully converted, and brought into the fold of the Saviour. The meeting has been crowned with the blessing of God. To Him be all the glory and honor. The Saviour's promise has been truly verified: "Lo, I am with you alway; even unto the end of the world."

L. A. W.

MASSENA Jan., 1845.
MY DEAR AND AFFECTIONATE PARENTS:

Birthday letter to parents. By this time I suppose you are often saying that Lewis has forgotten his birth-day letter and why do we not hear from him, and a good many other things which would take me a long while to answer. But I would say that since I wrote you from West S. I have preached every day but two and nearly all the time twice a day, besides a meeting each day for inquiry and prayer. And besides I have written about one hundred and twelve quires of paper into letters and I have not got around yet. Neither have I heard directly from Albany.

CHATEAUGAY, Franklin Co., N.Y., March 19, 1845.

The above I wrote at the time of the date, and since that I have been all the time engaged one day and another. I plead guilty to the charge of negligence, though I have been busy, yet I might have taken time to have written a few lines. I think the time I wrote you was about the first of my meeting in West Stockholm. Since that time I have held some four long meetings and been allowed the privilege of seeing the hopeful conversion of at least three hundred and fifty souls. To God be all the glory. And it has been in the midst of discouragements which could not be imagined but by those who were on the ground. All the evils of Millerism, Spiritualism, wifeism, church contention, singing school jealousy, slothful professors, Universalist ridicule, ignorant superstition and unbelieving professors. And so many are the obstacles that none but a God could help forward the work. So gloriously did God work that the politician note of warning was not sounded, nor heard, and the winter has passed with meetings every day and all day. "And the Lord has overthrown the horse and his rider." The subjects of the work are from the men of threescore and fifteen, to the child of eight and ten years of age. Nearly all classes of persons and many who have never been into the house of the Lord. Truly, what hath God wrought for us. To His name be all the glory and the honor, for His own right hand has done the work. After closing at Massena, I started for home and spent about three days at home! since the 7th of last October. And then I started for this place. I am now 130 miles from home and 200 miles from A., within four miles of Lower Canada lines, and a wretched hole it is. They have a small village of some twenty-five or thirty families and not a family altar here except in the family where I board, and that has been erected since I came here. And all manner of wickedness seems to be carried on here. And this people are extremely ignorant, with the exception of a very few. The first Judge of the county resides here, and is reputed to be the leader in the gambling line. Of all the congregations I think this exceeds all I have seen of late. Rough, uncouth, real bushwhackers, and among the rest Dr. B. has an uncle and a cousin or two here. One of his cousins was into meeting the other evening but could not wait until he got out of church before he must light his pipe and begin to smoke. They say he has not been known for a long time to visit the house of God before. I shall try and see him for the Dr.'s sake and for Christ's sake. On my visit home I found all well. It is the Lord's mercies that we are spared and His loving kindness to us is great. The Lord has sustained me thus far, and I want to lie at the foot of the cross and honor God in my whole life, and I wish not to hold my life dear unto myself, that I may finish my course with joy. And my life be such that it may be an honor to my parents, my family and to the church of God. I hope my dear parents are enjoying much of the presence of God, and all the brothers and sisters. Oh, for a family like heaven, to be always doing the will of God, and yet meet together in the Paradise above. Love to all. I am as ever,

Your eldest son,

L. A. WICKES.

———

CHATEAUGAY, April 2, 1845.

MY BROTHER CROSS:

You will perceive by this that I have arrived on the battle field of the North. I passed you about two or three o'clock in the morning of the day I expected to, when I saw you last, having made a stay at home of three days! And found my family quite well, and enjoying the comforts of life except religion, which I found in rather a low ebb. Oh, may God have mercy upon them. I arrived in this place on the 13th of March, and was sick, tired and faint-hearted, within three miles of Canada, in a village of some twenty-five or thirty families, and where there was not a family altar in the whole place, or was not when I came here and I know not that there is but one now. But I pray God He will give us more. The church is in a miserable state. Down at the lowest ebb. But few that have been in attendance during the day time. In the evening there is a goodly number out. The state of community in this place is miserable, and moral principles have been very low; and in many, scarce a vestige of moral principle left for them to feel or to be governed by. Yet, after all, there is a chance to work and teach and instruct as well as exhort, and indeed they must have and learn it or nothing permanent can be done with them. They have been scorched over here by the wildfire of the Miller excitement, of the world coming to an end, and many were quite religious while the hour was rolling on for the world to end, but as the world did not come to an end their religion has ended. Oh, how many we have reason to fear have built upon a false hope. I found it to be a very difficult post to fill, to get the mind on the right object to lead the sinner to Christ. But the Lord has appeared and some souls have given pleasing evidence of a saving change of heart. One man that was about fifty years old, who had been a most wicked and vile being, and one who knew enough to know and do better. Oh, may God keep him! There were about forty forward for prayers last evening, and the most of them were men from eighteen to fifty years of age, and several told us they now gave their hearts to God and His cause. One among them, a lawyer. He had been trying to survey, *but he could not run a straight line all he could do, he felt so bad,* and he could live so no longer. There have been a goodly number of back-sliders brought to bow and take up their cross and follow the

Savior and confess their awful wanderings from the Lord. The region is full of these creatures who once indulged hopes. They were the children of God and some have lived so that no one would know that they scarce ever thought of God. Oh, when will God's people ever do their duty and live before the Lord all the time a life of devotedness as becomes the children of God? How glad I shall be to see the time when the people of God will make the religion of Christ their life's business, and do all in their power to advance the cause and bring souls to bow at the foot of the cross. It is such blessed work that I wonder how any man can do anything but live for the Lord all the time. But alas, I find I have a very treacherous heart to deal with, and have to be on the look-out all the time, lest the devil get the advantage of me, and then he will come behind with his crafty devices ere I am aware. I find there is much to do in this whole region. I wish you was here with me. I want some help very much, and can you not leave and come out here? My health is poor, and I have to put on all the ambition which I can command to get along. The minister is a good man, but he wants more strength in a dead lift. This is my first meeting in this county (Franklin), whether I shall stay in this county is uncertain. Remember me to Deacon White, Allen and Walker, and all. Tell all to pray for me and this place. How many have come to Christ since I last saw you? Brother, let us ever be found with our fisher's coat on, looking to Christ for help, and relying on His blessed promises. "Lo, I am with you alway, even unto the end of the world." Matt. 28:20. Write me soon. Love to sister C.

Your brother in haste,
L. A. WICKES.

CHATEAUGAY, April 25, 1845.

MY AFFECTIONATE DAUGHTER :—

I have been wishing you would write to me and let me know how you are busying yourself, and I thought I would write to you and tell you about things in this place. I will begin by saying that I board with Mr. H., a merchant in this village, and Mrs. H. has assigned me a very pleasant well furnished parlor, and what makes it more so, is we have a good many seasons of prayer. And I have often wished you was here to mingle in them. But this does not seem to be the mind of the Lord. My sleeping room is the room over the parlor with all necessary conveniences. While it is pleasant, yet it is my own little family that I find not there. I there take a journey home and visit you all and can imagine I see you fast asleep as it is about midnight when I retire. But I cannot speak to you, so I ask our heavenly Father that He will indeed protect and guard you in all your slumbers. And so also I want you to pray. I will now tell you about the place and people. I went some one hundred and fifty rods the other day to see the place where the army had their quarters (called camping) during the last war. They had nothing but log houses called barracks, which are all torn down and burned up, still a part of their chimneys remain and I counted about thirty-five of them and all laid out in order. They cleared off a large field of land for a parade ground, that they could learn how to kill one another. Oh, how cruel is the art of war! While they were here there were many of them died from yellow fever. I visited the place where they were deposited. But there were no traces of the grave, as it was all ploughed over and covered with crops and no monument to tell where they lay! I had many curious thoughts. Many of them I suppose were fathers and husbands, yet no kind wife near them to administer the cordial to their parched lips, and no affectionate daughter to wipe the death sweat from the brow. How many wives and children were made destitute by the ravages, and often saying why does not my father come home? But to the grave they have gone. Yet, the slumbering dust will awaken, and if they were among those who love God, He will remember them. And though *our country* may let the place of the soldier's tomb be forgotten, yet not so our heavenly Father when we will serve Him. And I thought, shall I have to lay my bones by the side of these and my own daughter never know where her father's grave is? Well, we will be consoled by this one thought, viz., the Lord knows where we may lay and can bring us up at the last great day. But the great thing is for us to live so that when we arise we shall not have to look on a useless life in the cause of the Redeemer. And may it be your happy lot to dwell with your Savior. Read Dan. 12:1-3, and ask your mother to teach you the meaning. There used to be a system of wickedness here which has had a sad influence on the rising generation as well as the original perpetrators. There was reputed to be a great many wolves in this part of the state, and the people wanted to free themselves of the destroyers. There was a bounty bid on the head of every wolf of sixty dollars. Twenty dollars by the town, twenty by the county and twenty by the state, and the people went into the business of catching them. When a man caught a wolf he had to take the head to a magistrate and the magistrate cut off the ears and then gave the man a certificate, and with this he would get his money. And they killed dogs and took them and got a bounty on them. And they finally went so far that they would get the magistrate drunk and then tell him they had caught some wolves and get him to go out in the night in the dark and cut off their ears and they would have a young calf or two or more and call them wolves and get their premium on them. So that the farmer's tax sometimes was one hundred dollars a year. And they had to take their oath that they had killed the wolf and by thus doing they have made themselves liable to state prison. And it is said that some of them got sixteen hundred dollars a year, when they had not killed more than one or two wolves, but had taken other quadrupeds. And some of them do not like it because I tell them that God will bring them into judgment and there it will be known. And nearly every one of those who were engaged in it are poor and miserable beings, and lost all their property, fulfilling what Solomon says in Proverbs 13:11, 20 and 21st. Let all remember that there is a God and still He lives, and they must meet Him. All this seems to be in the way of their coming to the foot of the cross. Oh may the Lord show them their sins.

The meeting here is now quite interesting; there have been quite a goodly number hopefully brought into the fold of the Savior. Ann Wilbur, cousin to D. and S., has just been into my room and been trying to pray and return to her Savior from whom she had wandered. Do you pray when none but God can hear and know how much you desire to be useful in the cause of Jesus? Give my love to all.

Your affectionate father,
L. A. WICKES.

CHAPTER XX.

MEETINGS AT BURKE, LAWRENCEVILLE AND MOIRA.

BURKE, Franklin Co. N. Y., May 17, 1845.

MY DEAR AND AFFECTIONATE WIFE:

A letter from Burke.

I SUPPOSE you are asking what has become of your husband. I can say I started for home some two weeks ago and got as far as here, and then, by the earnest request of the friends and church, I stayed by the day until now, and may stay longer. But in all probability shall not be here long, as they have nothing but a school-house to meet in, and that is wanted for school. And I shall probably start some thirty miles towards home and stop at Lawrenceville and hold another meeting, and commence week after next. There have been hopeful conversions nearly every day that I have been here. To God be all the glory and the honor for all the mighty deeds He has done! The last night of the meeting at Chateaugay there were one hundred and sixty persons forward for prayers, and eighty-five rose and spoke of their delight and determination in the service of God besides some twenty-five professors who also wanted the privilege of speaking of the goodness of God, so that our meeting did not close until after midnight! And then we had to really choke them off. It would have done your soul good to have been there. The minister here has missionary aid from the H. M. S., for the people are poor. But if I can do them good, and lead souls to honor my Saviour, it is all I ask, and God will take care of us so long as we obey and follow Him. To-morrow I expect to have to preach in a barn, as there is no house that will hold the people, and O, may He who was born in the manger be present with us, for His mercy and holy name's sake, and grant His blessing to us!

May 21st. Since writing the above I have not had time to say more, but have labored all the time, and we hope there have been quite a goodly number of hopeful conversions. To God be all the glory and the honor for all His mighty acts, and for the goodness which He has shown to this people! I have finally found it impossible for me to come home before my meeting at Lawrenceville. Remember me to all friends, and tell them to pray for me and this region, and so let us live that the Lord may smile upon us all, and let nothing keep us from the love of God, and from holding free intercourse with the Father of our spirits. Kiss the children for me.

Your husband, as ever,
L. A. WICKES.

LAWRENCEVILLE, June 2, 1845,

MY BROTHER CROSS:

I was expecting to see you at consociation, but such is the state of things here, I find it will be out of the question to leave here. I hope you will find it among the consistent things of your life to come out here and spend one week at least. I do want your help a little, and I will help you as much. If you come out to attend the installation of Brother Cutler, on the first of July, why cannot you stay? I hope, brother, you will find it consistent with your arrangements to so do. There are some things which look encouraging here, while there is much to discourage. We hope there have been a few hopeful conversions, and quite a number of backsliders reclaimed.

Mr. Cross.
Lawrenceville.

Brother, pray for me, and for this place; pray much for me that I may have that meek and humble spirit which a minister of Christ should have. Why is it I must carry so hard a heart all the time? All things have some feeling but this hard heart of mine! With the expectation that I shall see you, I will write no more; but when I see you I will tell you all.

Your brother in Christ,
L. A. WICKES.

LAWRENCEVILLE, June 17, 1845.

MY DEAR WIFE:

There is but little done here as yet. I think it is one of the most discouraging fields of labor that I have ever been in. There are a few that we hope have given their hearts to God, but nothing seems to give way; and yet there is some feeling among the churches. Yet the obstacles in the way are very great indeed. I do pray that good may yet be done. May we keep our hearts low before God,

A short extract written after leaving Burke

and watch and pray, and keep humble and prayerful till the light of His countenance beams upon us, and we may yet witness the displays of His power. O! for faith that works by love, that purifies the heart, overcomes the world, and brings the speedy blessing down, for Jesus' sake. I must close. Tell the children to be kind and good and pray for a new heart, and to serve God with all their soul. Pray much for this place.

Your affectionate husband,

L. A. WICKES.

A short extract.—June 29th. Lawrenceville. Says he had a cold, tedious ride to that place, and arrange-ments had been made for his board at a tavern, and nothing very encouraging here as yet. Last Sabbath a crowded house and the opinion was that the place would be too small for them soon. "Well," (he says), "the Lord has got a great house for us, and O! may we sit at the foot of the cross, where the Savior can smile upon us.

There were conversions at the Tavern.

Love to all. Pray much.

L. A. WICKES.

STOWS SQUARE, July 28, 1845.

MY DEAR PARENTS:

Cheap postage does not help write letters at all, do you think it does? It takes just as much resolution now as it ever did and I think a little more. You will perceive by this that I have finally arrived at home once more with my dear family after an absence of between four and five months, and in fact I have scarcely been at home for better than nine months (only three days) and nothing but the work of the Lord would have kept me from my home. But when I see souls bowing at the foot of the cross daily, and giving honor to the Lord, I had rather be in such a place than in the midst of mere earthly bliss and no Savior in it. But it is heart sickening to see the state of the church in this whole region. The very price of blood is and will be found on the hands of those who are stationed on the walls of Zion. To see them all wrapped in sleep and doing nothing while immortal spirits are fast going into eternity, is awful beyond description and the people love to have it so. And the great dearth there is, they put all on the sovereignty of God as a cloak and an excuse for their indolence. I often feel that I am the most guilty of all, for my heart is so hard, that I see the cause dishonored and yet I feel no more. Since I left home in March the Lord has graciously been with me, and His blessing has followed much of the labors that have been put forth. When I could hear of no revival in any direction, yet the Lord was with us and sinners were daily brought to bow at His feet, and the cause of Christ has been advancing in both the counties of Franklin and St. Lawrence. The Lord in answer to prayer and by His Holy Spirit has worked, and several hundred of our fellow men have been brought to bow at the feet of Jesus. And among them are persons in nearly all the ranks of life, as well as ages, from the man of 85 years to the child of 8 and 10 years. And many of them were persons who had gone far in sin, and spent most of their time ridiculing the things of religion and making this world their God, and among others who had bowed before the Lord the inebriate has found the waters of life pleasant to his thirsty soul, and which will be a living fountain in many of them. We will give all the glory and the honor to Him who has done so much for us. Yea, He is worthy of more praise than all the powers on earth can express, and my prayer is that I may ever consecrate all I have to the service of the Lord. He can create and He destroy. My voice is quite poor since I closed my meeting, I think it is poorer than when constantly laboring. I shall not probably engage in any meeting for a few weeks. As to my future course I cannot say what I shall do. I sometimes think of "settling down" as folks call it. Yet I cannot see it to be my duty as yet. It has been a peculiar train of Providence that has placed me in the field of labor where I now am placed and I dare not take any course which would be displeasing to God. And all I wish to know is, what is duty to the cause of God, and I will do it. I do ask your prayers and your counsel that God would open the path of duty plainly before me, and I will gladly walk in it. All send love to all.

Your son as ever, write me soon.

LEWIS A. WICKES.

MOIRA, Franklin Co., Nov. 17, 1845.
MY DEAR PARENTS:

I have been here some six days. It is a place of some refinement, and some intelligence. Not a large place. They have a new church just dedicated to Almighty God, and the service of the Lord we hope has commenced indeed. The meeting has been held as yet only afternoons and evenings, and the congregation is filling up quite fast, and the interest is increasing to some extent. Things were very dark indeed when I came. There was quite a division and excitement about Calvinism and Arminianism! So both parties were about fighting the cause of Christ, and the devil laughing at them. But I am in hopes they will get down at the foot of the cross of Jesus, and be brought to work together and forget their party names altogether, for, I find the more men love the Lord and engage in his service, the less they care about the "mint, anise, cummin," Matt. 23: 23, and use of religion. While these may have their appropriate place, yet they are not the whole nor any of the absolute essential parts of religion. And when I find men making this the great thing, I find they are very low in spirituality. Tell all to pray for me and this place. Love to all. Remember me to Cousins Rodney and Sidney.

As ever your son.
L. A. WICKES.

P. S.—18th.—The meeting is becoming rather interesting and this morning I have been out visiting and find some very interesting cases indeed. And yet there is much to be done. Some of the impenitent are quite thoughtful. Oh, that the Lord would visit them with His renewing grace, and which He is willing to do if they will only submit to Him to be saved by grace divine.

Your son.
L. A. WICKES.

November 24. An extract. DEAR WIFE:—The meeting is now becoming quite interesting. Two or three evenings ago after family worship, two young ladies came into my room and desired me to pray for them that they might be made to see their hearts and become Christians. We bowed in prayer. And they have appeared very thoughtful indeed until last evening, when they both bowed and called upon the name of the Lord, and there hoped they gave themselves to God. One of them is daughter of Mr. L. with whom I board, her name Sarah. And the other, a friend of hers, who lives in the family when she is not engaged in teaching. Last evening was the first opportunity given for rising for prayers and some eight or ten rose. I have not held meeting all day as yet but shall commence to-morrow. Mr. Reed, the minister, is not with us but a part of the time; he resides about seventeen miles from here, he left for home this morning, to kill his hogs! So that I am alone most of the time. Sabbath we attended the Methodist quarterly meeting. I preached the sermon. After which we had the Lord's supper. I think there is more union among the people than when I came, and an appearance of good being done. Still I find that much of the work has yet to be done. And much that must be done now or probably never. Five o'clock P. M. I have just returned from meeting, but few out, but a good degree of feeling. S. and her friend both spoke and several rose for prayers. After meeting I spoke to a young lady and she burst into a flood of tears and wanted I should pray for her, which I did. The young lady called upon God and hoped she gave up all to the Lord. While I was praying Sarah came back into church and brought two of her cousins in with her and bowed with them in prayer, and they felt to surrender all to the Lord who died to save them. Thanks be to His holy name for the gracious manifesta-

Nov. 25. tions of His spirit on the heart. Tuesday morning. Dear Wife. The Lord was in the congregation last eve., and truth took hold of the minds of men. (Text Mark 2, last clause of 17th verse.) They have had so much of every thing here that many are afraid to move, lest they should find themselves overpowered by some delusion. Men are in attendance at the meeting that have never been known to go to meeting at all and and are quite serious. Both the physicians are very thoughtful. Pray for them with all your soul. I will hold my sheet open till after meeting to-day. 6 o'clock eve.—I have just closed a season of prayer with a company that came into my room. Several to day have chosen the Lord to serve Him, and some three or four family altars have been reared for God, and to His name be all the glory. I have much to say but no time to say it, as I must mail this. Pray for me and this place. Love to the children.

Your husband,

L. A. WICKES.

Dec. 11, 1845.

An extract. P. S. I have but a moment to say the Lord is with us. There has been some sixty or seventy forward for prayer, and some very interesting cases of conversion. And my room has been thronged for several days, and the work is spreading, and deepening. It now is meeting time, and I must close. Our friend Mrs. H. of Malone, is now in my room, and sends her love to you. I am requested to hold my next meeting at Gouverneur. Think it is probable I may. To-night the Lord was in the midst, and truth took effect. Thank the Lord. Praise His holy name. Pray for us.

As ever yours affectionately,
L. A WICKES.

Being the thirty-sixth anniversary of the life of Lewis Alfred, oldest of ten children of Jonas and Sarah B. Wickes; and the nineteenth year of my Christian life through the Redeemer's blood, thirteenth of the gospel ministry, and fifth of my exclusive labors as an evangelist, according to the grace of God given unto me, and of whom I am not worthy to be called His child.

MOIRA, Franklin Co., Dec. 8, 1845.

MY DEAR AND MOST AFFECTIONATE PARENTS:

This morning thirty-six years ago (as you say), you remember—I do not—and the events of that morning and its consequences so far, you have known. Little did you know or even think what you was holding in that lap, or nursing upon that breast. Then it was that you watched over me; then it was you thought of me. I think then I had no praying father or mother; I was the first of impenitent parents. But thanks be to God, after I was born, *they were born again.* And well do I remember the first time my father assembled us, a family for his family devotion. And when he bowed his knee to call on the Lord in the log house at what was then called "the West." And I stood up straight as a *candle*, and thought if *I* could not pray better than that I would not pray at all. Then my young heart was filled with anger, and I said to Brother H. I would not stay at home if there was going to be such work as that. But, oh, my folly! and, oh, my wickedness! I trust a Saviour has pardoned, and my parents also. But what changes since, and how checkered has been life. Sometimes with prospects of delight, and then dark and dismal clouds, that seemed to threaten all hopes. But still the sunbeams of my Lord have shone again, and life appears once more. The two past years have been peculiarly years of trial to my soul. But in the midst of all this the Lord has very kindly looked upon me and granted me His assistance. During the last year I have taken a longer respite in my labors than I have before for thirteen years. I have preached during the year about four hundred and fifty sermons, and attended about three hundred prayer and inquiry meetings. I have held eight different protracted meetings in as many different places, which have lasted from three to eight weeks, and there have been about five hundred and fifty to six hundred *hopeful* conversions. And many of them, perhaps, are not the children of God. O, may He search and see and open their own eyes to the things of eternity, as well as a correct view of their own hearts. Yet, in justice, I must say that I had the most pleasing evidence of their being born of the spirit of God. It is God that has done it: to His great name be all the glory and the honor for the wonders He has wrought. I have, during the year, traveled about fourteen hundred miles, mostly in my own private conveyance. I suspended my labors for three to four months on account of my health, and during that time I did more mechanical labor than any time since I commenced my preaching, only preaching occasionally on the Sabbath. I had restored my health, but a severe cold has brought on my hoarseness. But I feel I cannot stop my labors. So you have a synopsis of my past year. I am sorry that it is no better, and that I have done no more good in the cause of the Lord. But if I know my heart, I do most solemnly wish to be engaged in the cause of the Redeemer. Since I wrote you last the Lord has graciously smiled upon this place, and quite a goodly number have come to Christ. Some of the most influential persons in town are among the number. Two physicians are subjects of this work. Thank the Lord. Two young ladies came to my room after family worship (one the daughter of Mr. L., with whom I board,) and wanted I should pray for them. We bowed in prayer; in a short time, we hope, they gave all to Christ. On going out of church in the afternoon a young lady was weeping in the aisle; after speaking a word or two with her, pointing her to the Savior, we bowed in prayer, and while we were praying, Miss L. (above) came back into the church and brought five or six others, and fell on their bended knees, and there, we hope, several gave all up to the Lord. And they have gone to work for the good of others. Thus the Lord has put His own hand to the work, and smiled upon His own truth.

December 9th. Last eve we had a crowded house, and the Lord was in the midst of us. I preached from Ezek. 33: 11, "As I live," etc. At the close there were somewhere about sixty presented themselves as subjects of prayer and hope. A large number gave themselves to the Lord to be His in a covenant never to be broken. To God be all the glory and the honor, for it is His due. A deep feeling is pervading the whole community. Do pray that God will make this day of my life the emblem of each day of the year. I ask earnestly let me be the subject of your prayers. Perhaps you have not a child that with so much propriety can say, pray for me in the station in which I am called, with so great a responsibility resting upon me. Love to brothers and sisters and all.

As ever your son,
L. A. WICKES.

MOIRA, Dec. 16, 1845.

MY DEAR WIFE:

I have just this moment received yours of the ninth. I have been rather unwell for a few days. I have but little ministerial help. The work is going forward. Maj. Lawrence (with whom I board), I trust, has become a praying man. This morning he took lead in the family devotion. And there have been some twelve or fourteen family altars erected here. And the work is spreading far, and, I think, deepening. There have been somewhere between forty and fifty hopeful conversions, and my room is thronged almost as much as it was at Adams. Pray for this work, especially for me.

After meeting, half-past seven P. M.—The Lord is in the midst of us, and moving on the mass. A good number of married people rose as subjects for prayer, and rose as an evidence of their giving all to Christ.

Text: Ps. 57: 7, first clause. And may God seal it upon the hearts of all. But I am extremely tired. I want you to live near the Savior. Love to the children, and tell all to pray. In haste,

Your husband,
L. A. WICKES.

MOIRA, December 29.

MY DEAR PARENTS:

The bearer of this, Hon. Judge S. Lawrence from this place, I introduce to you, is a member of the Legislature, a member of the M. E. Church, and an active Christian. A brother to the Mr. Lawrence, with whom I have boarded during this long meeting. When the meeting commenced the Judge's three brothers, heads of families, were impenitent. He commenced asking prayers for them and their families. And we hope that each of those brothers have become praying men. And the wife of one of them (the others were professors), the only son and daughter of one family, two daughters of another family, three daughters and one son, if not three of the other family. To God be all the glory. You will find him an agreeable guest. I hope you will give him a cordial welcome. As I have but a moment to write, you must inquire of him about the meeting, and he will tell you, and also about the prospects here. He will like occasionally to go with father to the Bethel. We hope there have been somewhere between eighty and one hundred hopeful conversions, and the work is now increasing, and extending to others over a large tract of country, and promises to be a great ingathering of the harvest of precious souls. I had intended to have started for home this morning, but such is the state of things here that we could not close, and am holding on by the day. A delegation from the church in Malone wishing me to go there. I think now probably I shall go there first, then to Gouverneur in St. Lawrence county, before I return home, to save travel, and time is precious. Remember in prayer. Love to all.

Your son,
L. A. WICKES.

MOIRA, January 2, 1846.

MY DEAR WIFE:

I have only a moment to write, and don't know but the stage may be here before I can finish this. And I can only just have time to say that such is the state of things in this community, that it seems almost impossible for me to leave this section of country. The whole region is on the move, and all are inquiring what these things mean, and whereunto will they come, and such is the state of things that I have concluded to go from this place to Malone, which is thirteen miles still further from home. They sent out a delegation of four men the other day after me, and such is the state of feeling that I have thought it my duty to go there, and therefore I shall not be home for a few weeks. I commence there next Tuesday evening, the 6th inst, the Lord willing, and I hope I shall have your prayers now as well as all of the others. The Lord was with us yesterday, and it was one of the happiest New Years days that this community have ever seen here, and the Lord brought some fifteen or twenty souls to bow at the foot of the cross, and this week has been a glorious one. I cannot say how many have been hopefully converted to God in all, but somewhere not far from one hundred and twenty or one hundred and thirty, and things are now ripe for a mighty shaking among the dry bones. I will write more particulars from Malone. In haste.

As ever your affectionate husband,
L. A. WICKES.

CHAPTER XXI.

MEETINGS AT MALONE AND GOUVERNEUR.

MALONE, Jan. 20, 1846.

MY DEAR AND AFFECTIONATE WIFE:

YOUR long looked for and kind letter was very thankfully received last eve, and I hasten to reply. I have but a moment to say a word as I must hasten to church in season this morning. I do very much regret that I could not meet the Association to-day. But such is the state of things here that I feel it would be sin against God for me to leave. The work seems to be getting hold of a class of persons here, that all other means have been unable to reach, and the whole affair would apparently come to an end if I were to leave. The whole region is on the move. The work of God commenced in Moira, has spread into the different towns, and many have turned to the Lord. In the towns of Bangor, Brandon, Dickinson, and Bombay, there seems to be indications of good. There have been seventy-five and one hundred persons forward for prayers at a time here. To-day is a day for *fasting* and *prayer* and humiliation before God. Oh, for more of that broken-heartedness before God myself—I do hope you will pray for me much. But Christ does care for us, and "his own right hand will well sustain the children of His love." And to study to be like the Son of God in all things is my great desire; Let Matt. 5:11, be our support. It is time for meeting and I must close. May the God of peace rest upon you, and all the children, and the whole family. Love to Father and Mother especially. Write often if short. I want to hear about the meeting. There have been quite a number of hopeful conversions. To God be all the glory.

Your husband,
L. A. WICKES.

MALONE, Feb. 13, 1846.

MY DEAR WIFE:

Yours was very thankfully received. I have but little time to write. You are aware how it is. My room is continually thronged. The Lord is truly in our midst. There have been sometimes one hundred and one hundred and fifty forward for prayers at a time. The most of them have been youth of the first families, generally from sixteen to twenty-two or three years of age, some quite interesting cases indeed there are. The other churches have not taken much interest in the work as yet, though a few there are who have. The number of hopeful conversions I cannot say, not far from one hundred. There are very promising young men among them, and sons of the first talent in the county. A large number of clerks in the stores have become subjects of the work. There have been some few heads of families brought into the kingdom, and some ten or fifteen family altars set up. To God, be all the glory for all that He has done. Mr. Woodruff their minister is a fine man, and one that takes hold in every place, and one which I think will be a lasting blessing to this people. I was carried the other day to the poor house for the purpose of preaching to the paupers, and a good time we had of it. There are three or four hopeful conversions, and since then there have been some three or four more, and one of the daughters of the keeper of the poor house. Some members of the factory in the place have bowed at the foot of the cross; also, quite a number of the students of the Academy. To God be thanks and honor given. The glory, Lord, is Thine. Since I have been here I have spent one Sabbath at Moira, and administered the communion to the church, and twenty-two were received into the church fellowship; it is now nearly doubled, probably many accessions will be made. Yesterday I went out to preach the funeral sermon of Mr. Abiram Lawrence, brother of the one with whom I boarded. It was a consolation to me that God had made me an humble instrument of leading one soul to the Lord, whom we hope will praise the Lord through the ceaseless ages of eternity. If there is nothing else my dear wife that would prompt us to be separated, will not the thought of being co-workers with the Savior in salvation, and seeing friends in Christ and reign with Him in glory. Does it not adequately repay for all the deprivations which we are called upon to make? I have of late looked much at the object of our life here. It is to get men and women to heaven to honor God,

<small>His object in life.</small> and there can be nothing of greater worth, nor more worthy of all our efforts. The Lord will

strengthen and bless those that put their trust in Him—
pray that the Lord will raise up faithful witnesses in all
this northern region, and especially here in Malone.
Say to A—— her two last have been received, and she
improves much. I wanted her to answer the questions
I proposed to her. E—— does very well; let them write
often. Tell S—— to be a good child and love her Savior.
Remember me affectionately to Aunt W——. I have
had an earnest call to go to Clinton County. Pray God
to direct.

     Affectionately, your husband,
       L. A. WICKES.

      MALONE, Feb. 17, 1846.
MY DEAR AND AFFECTIONATE PARENTS:

Your kind letter was received and I hasten to reply, as
I know you feel a deep interest in my welfare and work.
The place where I now am is one of the largest places
there is in this northern region. There are four different
church edifices in this village, and the Universalists meet
in the court house, and the jail is under them (emblematic
of their condition). There are three factories, besides
furnaces, and one distillery! It is a place of considerable
business. They have an academy, and other schools. It
is a place of a good deal of refinement, and yet there is
much abomination, and much opposition to true principles of piety, and even of morality Yet, truth is mighty
and will prevail. There has been quite a good work
wrought here, about one hundred and fifty hopeful conversions, and some very interesting cases too, mostly

among the young, and young married people, and a few cases of those past middle life. I shall leave here on Monday, if the Lord will, for home, and spend only about a week, and then return to Gouverneur to spend a little time in that contentious place. Since I have been here I have been out to Moira twice, once to administer the Lord's supper, when twenty-two united with that little church; and then I went out to preach the funeral sermon of Mr. A. L——, (Brother of the Judge at Albany). He was a subject of the work there, fifty-five years of age. He lived to see his children all brought into the kingdom of Christ, and closed up his career of Christian life, and entered into rest. It has been a source of consolation to me that God should, through my instrumentality, lead him to repentance, now that he has so soon removed him from the family circle on earth to the family above. It is the Lord's doings, and may it be sanctified to the bereaved, while we adore the riches of His grace and give glory to the Savior. If I can only be the means in the hand of God, of leading my fellow men to Jesus, and then see them rise to dwell above, and praise my dear Redeemer, it is all I ask. And let me have the true spirit of my master who came to seek and save the lost. I know that I am unworthy of any such favors, yet I do trust that Jesus owns me for His, and will through His abounding grace at the last receive my soul into His embrace. Since the 11th of November I have preached two sermons a day, besides all the other talking which I have had to do. Except mornings, my room has been thronged with anxious ones. I get little time for writing. Pray much for this region, and for

Your unworthy son,
L. A. WICKES.

GOUVERNEUR, March 11, 1846.

TO ORRIN LAWRENCE, ESQ.:

Dear Brother in Christ; I take a moment to redeem my pledge made to you and the dear family, to write to you after I had been at my home. I found the traveling quite hard after I left your kind and hospitable roof, and only reached Lawrenceville that evening. In Antwerp I visited several afflicted families. I arrived home on Thursday noon, safe and sound, except I froze one cheek a little, and the end of my nose. I found my family in tolerable health. I commenced meeting here last week on Thursday evening. There was a congregation of about one hundred out, but the state of society is most wretched and miserable. They have two Congregationalist churches, one Baptist, and a small Methodist, in connection with the Academy. The First church will have nothing to do with the Second church (I am laboring with the Second church). The First church would not read a notice of the meeting, and some at least determined not to do anything to help the work along. I am sorry, for they stand in their own light, and will bring darkness upon their own souls. The meetings have become as interesting as I could expect from the state of things, as it was a very dead time in all the churches here. Some of *all* the churches attend the meeting, and are active in taking part in the work. The house has become so full that we have to crowd the pulpit stairs, and an increased interest seems to be awaking upon the subject. The impenitent appear to feel considerable for their soul's welfare. I do pray God they may bow humbly at the foot of the cross. It is very painful in such a state of society, that professed friends of Christ feel thus toward each other. But perhaps the arm of the Lord will soften their hearts, and they will once become like the Savior—they will love one another. I mean to endeavor to do all in my power to reconcile things, and bring them to a happy termination, if possible. I do earnestly hope you will all remember me and this place in your prayers. That God will glorify Himself and His cause by pouring His spirit upon us all. That His people may lie humble at His feet, and the impenitent may yield to the sceptre of love. I have often to think of the hours spent in the stone house, and the blessings and mercies from heaven's hands which were poured upon us there, and while I regret I felt no more for souls, yet I do thank God that He ever allowed me the privilege of ever coming under your roof. Though I never can repay you for all the kindness which I have received from your hands, yet in the judgment, I trust, when Christ shall gather up His jewels, you will be rewarded among the number who shall rise to praise the Savior who have been born to Christ in that west room. My heart does swell with joy now, at the remembrance of those hours, and it will be more joyful in full realization in the world of glory. I do hope that each of your dear family may be among the blessed throng at that last great day—I hope that all efforts will be made to keep up the prayer meetings, and the regular appointments of the church. Remember me affectionately to your own dear family, together with all the beloved friends. And may God smile upon you all, is the prayer of your

Brother in Christ,
L. A. WICKES.

March 6, 1846.

MY DEAR AND AFFECTIONATE WIFE:

I will commence now a brief journal of my present meeting. I found the traveling much better than I expected, through rather hard a part of the way. I called at Brother Stimsons; met a few friends; had a season of prayer, and on I came; reached G— about sunset, and made my home at Brother Pond's. I found that invitations had been given to all the other churches to come in and co-operate. They were read by the Baptist and the Methodist churches. But Mr. B— of the First church refused to read the notice. I hear that they think Brother P— insulted them by giving them the notice—so you have a clue to their feeling. I tried to preach in the evening from Rom. 8:9, last clause. There were some one hundred persons out, and some from each of the churches, several even from the First church. The state of things here is very dark. My own soul seems hard. A severe headache all the evening. Yesterday no meeting in A. M., in P. M. about twenty out to prayer meeting, and not much feeling among the churches; two or three impenitent in. In the evening they had an oyster supper.ball. Yet about as many in as the evening before, and some feeling, and my health better than the day before. No meeting this morning, and must go and call upon some families of my old acquaintance. Oh, how much we need to pray and labor for the good of souls. Evening, half-past 10. To-day there have been some more in attendance, and some more feeling. I visited Mr. H's family, saw Mrs. F. there, but little feeling on the subject of religion. This evening saw Mrs. Fowler and Susan (formerly of the Oxbow), they were at the meeting. They now reside here; they were very urgent I should call upon them, which I shall do the first opportunity. I saw Mr. P. Horr; they have united with the Baptist church again. This evening the congregation about doubled, and a goodly number of the old church was in. I do pray their hearts may all be subdued and made humble by divine grace, and so may I get low before God. But I must close for to-night. The first week of spring is gone, so time passes away, and hearts of stone cannot go back. O, may I improve the moments as they pass. To-morrow's responsibilities are coming on apace. O, for grace to meet them! But another thought is in my heart. What will my family do? How will they spend the day of the Lord? O, for a change on the Square for His glory, may God clothe us all for His honor and glory. I heard this evening that Brother B— is holding a protracted meeting in B.; just commenced; nothing special at present. May the Lord protect us all, while we lie in His arms.

11th. I have not had time to write since the last date; my health is about as when I wrote, though at times I find it very difficult to speak. But the Lord's will be done. The meeting has become more interesting. A larger number of persons in attendance, and more feeling. Last Sabbath the house was crowded full; it will seat about three hundred persons. Truth seemed to take hold. I presented the characters of Abraham and Eli. Monday I was out at Richville, and saw our friends there. Dea. W. has come out there to-day, and seems to get hold upon the arm of the Lord in some measure. There are a few colored people here, and no one feels disgraced in having them sit promiscuously in the congregation. The church here have some very strong ones in it. Some of the sisters are the real praying ones, and seem to lay all upon the Lord's arm. I am of the opinion that if Christians do not take hold, they will see when it is too late for help. I have just called upon some of the old church, and they do not know hardly what to do or say. They evidently feel that they are occupying a responsible station, and the blood of souls will be required of their hands, and yet they have taken and sustained so high ground of opposition to the Second church, that it is hard work to come to where they ought to be. But they are about full, and I think they will be soon filled with their own way and that will be bad enough now, I assure you. There is a large class of young people here that are under their influence, and they are ripening very fast for destruction.

They have had one dance since I have been here, and this evening they have an exhibition at the Academy, and the whole community are turned out to see and hear the boy speak. Our congregation was only about one hundred and twenty or thirty, as nearly all the young people were at the Academy; and from a great distance around, they are just returning home, now fifteen minutes to eleven at night. I must close for to-night, as my room is cold, and I am taking cold. Thursday morning. The Lord has protected once more, and the mercies of God are continually with me. One week this morning I left home for this place. How rapid time does fly! God and all nature are on the march, and so may I be found. And now may we see the need of being more watchful than ever, of lying at the foot of the cross, and being more like Christ. Let not the world nor any thing find in us a sordid nature. And let not the thought of a *place* (an earthly home)* be to you any but a help towards heaven. Let us not provoke God to depart from us by our forsaking Him. This world is nothing as long as we rise above it, all is well. But when we become entangled in it, we shall be sure to have enough of it. "For the backslider in heart shall be filled with his own ways." So let not the children have their expectations raised on such a vain show of things, on expectations they will be all joy and delight—For their hopes may soon be cut off. I can very easily see there are many disadvantages which will arise to us. The opportunities for improvement may be small there to what it will be in other places. And so also there as to church privileges, these two will be greater than all others. I may be taken away in a little time, and I want they should be provided and prepared for any exigency. My great anxiety is to know what God will have me to do, and when I know that I know He will help me through—Oh may my feet be directed in the path of rectitude—Pray much, yea renewedly before God. Love to all. Remember me to Aunt Waters, and tell all to pray for this place and for me. May the Lord direct in all things.

Your Husband,
L. A. WICKES.

GOUVERNEUR, March 21, 1846.
MY DEAR AND AFFECTIONATE WIFE:

Yours came to hand last eve. The meeting is getting quite interesting now. There have been somewhere

*He purchased a small place at Stows Square to which his family was moving when this was written.

between 15 and 20 hopeful conversions, among others is S. F. The other churches begin to come in a little, and several conversions in connection with the families of the Baptist church. They see that the Lord is evidently in the midst of us. The first church evidently feels that they are in a bad predicament. The house is pretty well filled every evening, and considering all things, quite well in the day time. Those we hope who have given up all for God, appear very well, and are quite strong, and seem to take delight in the cause of Christ. And there have been a good number of backsliders brought to bow at the foot of the cross and renew their covenant to the Lord. There is much opposition from the wicked. One brother had his harness cut the other evening, but not so as to prove fatal, as he found it out before he started for home. Still the opposition is giving away to truth. Last evening there were over thirty forward for prayers, and they seemed to feel that now is the accepted time. One of them is a reclaimed drunkard. Now *pray* much that God would overrule this work in the salvation of many precious souls, and to His own honor and glory. The cause is His. May we be His willing consecrated instrument, just what He wants us to be. When I shall be at home I cannot say. But soon as consistent with duty to God and His cause. Love to all. Pray much for this place and for me.

In haste, your husband,
L. A. WICKES.

GOUVERNEUR, March 30, 1846.

MY DEAR WIFE:

I suppose by this time you want to know what we are doing. I write so many letters east, west, north and south that I cannot tell when and where I begin and end, and so I have forgotten where my last closed to you. But for a few days the Lord has been with us. There have been between thirty and forty hopeful conversions. Several heads of families brought to bow at the foot of the cross. You will probably remember R. S. of this place (the Abolitionist). He, his wife, daughter and son have all come over on the Lord's side. I have been to see H. W., he is in poor health. I am afraid he will never be any better. He has been out to meeting

April 1. once or twice and was forward for prayers, and had some feeling. His wife is a fine woman, and feels very deeply for him, prays with him, seems very anxious about him. But what may be his fate I cannot tell. I shall probably call upon him in the morning. Last night the house was jammed full, and when we sent the congregation away, requested such as desired prayer to tarry, there were seventy or eighty came forward, and more than two-thirds of them young men, and some of the hardest cases there are in the place. There seems a giving away of the prejudice in minds of the old church. But they have a most dreadful account to give for the awful responsibility they are exerting on the minds of many of the impenitent whom they hold under their own hand, and try to discourage them from attending meetings. But may God show them their hearts. But I want a heart to be more like Christ, and bear all things for Jesus' sake. This afternoon there were six or seven we hope gave up all for Christ. To His name be all the glory, and the honor and the praise for all the wonders He has done. The Baptist brethren take hold some and God is greatly blessing their families. Two of the converts were baptized yesterday, Monday evening. I preached this evening from Luke 15 : 10, and the Lord helped me. There were some sixty men and forty women forward for prayers, and a deep feeling pervaded A goodly number who had been careless submitted to the Lord. A young lady who told me to-day she did not wish to be a Christian now and with whom I had some plain talk, to-night came forward and cried aloud and we hope for mercy (she had been very rude and vain), but to-night she was all dissolved in tears of tenderness and sorrow. A young man who formerly lived in Antwerp, Mr. I., gave up all to Christ as his Savior; two young ladies from the Quaker settlement have been reclaimed from their wanderings, daughters of the merchant S. at that place. They appear well. I find it is no small obstacle in the way that they have to come to the Second church. The opposition has been so great that those who do come have to be fully persuaded in all their course, and so makes them more decided than ever. It

April 1. is midnight, I must retire. April 1st. I called on H. W., his health is very poor, we had a season of prayer and he promised the Lord he would do his whole duty. He came out to meeting in the evening and told the congregation that he would serve God and said he wanted they should pray for him. His wife's twin sisters we hope have given up their hearts to God, and prayed with us, may it prove a genuine work of grace, and they show themselves to be the true followers of Jesus Christ. Opposition in some is giving away, and the work is spreading over the town, and there have been some very interesting cases of conversion. Brethren here feel like getting low before God. April 2nd. Yesterday and last evening was a good day, several hopeful conversions and quite an increase of feeling, the house is crowded so that we have to make seats. I cannot say anything about how many conversions there have been. But there is much to be done yet. H. D. S. opposes the meeting very much, and says he will not own any thing done in the meeting. But if the Lord blesses the means used for the salvation of sinners for whom Christ died, to His name we will ascribe all the glory, and be thankful that He can use us as instruments to do His will. The appearance of things here is such that I do not much expect to get away immediately. Brother Pond and family join in sending love to you. Pray much for me and this place.

April 2.

As ever, your husband,
L. A. WICKES.

APRIL 4, 1846.

DEAR WIFE:

The stage went before I could have a chance to mail my letter, and so I say a word or two more. I had an interview a few days since with Rev. Mr. B., and I find him to be a most unpleasant and disagreeable opposer to everything good that does not come to his standard. He said I came to this place to pull myself up into notoriety by taking hold of the skirts of his coat! Wonderful! What an exalted privilege that would be! Poor man, he is to be pitied for his stupidity. Oh, for a soft and tender heart towards him. When he got penned up and could not say more, then he would indulge in the outbursts of "fools," "ungentlemanly," etc. He is in trouble, I cannot but think, and I do pray God that he may see his sin and repent of it. His church begins to get into the work of the Lord. Yesterday they had their regular Friday meeting, and those who had been in attendance on the meeting could not hold on any longer, and broke over their bounds, men and women, and he found himself penned up in rather close quarters. I know "God can make the wrath of man to praise Him," etc. I have heard from Malone. The Lord still is carrying on His work there gloriously. Some eighty or more have been examined to unite with the church, sixty have united. Pray much. Live at the feet of Jesus. Let nothing be done through strife or vain glory. I want my dear family to enjoy the stated means of grace. What is an abode on earth in comparison with an inheritance in light? I must close. I have taken a severe cold and my nights' rest is broken and tedious. But all is right. Love to all.

Your affectionate husband,
L. A. WICKES.

An extract.

GOUVERNEUR, May 27, 1846.

An extract from an account of the work of grace in Gouverneur, dated May 27th, 1846. Taken from the Baptist Register, volume 23, No. 17, May 29th, 1846.

Such was the situation of this people. In a church of something over two hundred members, there were thought to be but few family altars on which the incense of prayer ascended to God. Our prayer meeting only had a name to live, and this was so poorly attended that its vitality was somewhat called into question, while few frequented the public worship of God on the Lord's day.

About the first of March (the time we commenced our labors here) Mr. Wickes of the Congregational order began a series of meetings with the Second Congregational church in our village. Though we could not approbate all his course, he presented much gospel truth, directed the sinner to Christ as the only ground of justification, the only hope of salvation. It was soon apparent that God was accompanying the truth to the hearts. The change in the moral aspect of things is truly astonishing. Our sanctuary is filled to overflowing. Our prayer meeting and lectures are nearly every evening, and full, solemn and interesting. The work is still progressing. Such was the instrumentality that whatever of this work is genuine must be of God. To Him be all *the praise both now and forever.*

Your brother in Christ,
J. H. WEBB.

CHAPTER XXII.

MEETING IN OSWEGO.

OSWEGO, JAN. 20, 1847.

MY DEAR BROTHER:

Letter from minister in that place.

GOD willing, I mean to endeavor to prepare the way among my people. I mean, I hope to *preach* and *pray* and labor to the end of introducing Zion's King emphatically among us. We have had two sermons of interest within two years, but not at all commensurate with our necessities. Many are perishing in sin around, and comparatively but little is doing directly for their salvation. I write you to advise you of my wishes and plans, and to ask you to come and spend a few weeks with us, commencing about the first of December. *Can you do so?* This is an important field. We need a thorough breaking up. I wish to calculate in God's strength for a siege that may result in the capture of the place. I need your assistance or the assistance of some one much, and my mind for some time has been turned to you. In

God alone is help. But we must show our belief in that doctrine as supposed by corresponding labor. Write me soon. And if it be the Lord's will, may you come full of the blessing of eternal life.

With esteem and affection, yours truly,
C. JONES.

OSWEGO, Jan. 14, 1847.

LITTLE EMMA. An extract.

In a letter to his little daughter E. gives her a short history of his journey to Oswego. The places at which he called. The number of inhabitants. The churches he passed. The persons on whom he called. His arrival at Oswego, was welcomed by Mr. J. the minister. Preached that evening though fatigued and almost sick. About two hundred and fifty persons were present at meeting. In the morning took a walk, found much worldly business, a village of six thousand inhabitants. Probably many wicked, some of them at least And a great many things, are very discouraging. Closes by praying that the Lord would bless her and all the dear ones at home. That all may love and serve the Lord, with expressions of affection.

L. A. WICKES.

OSWEGO, Jan. 14, 1847.

TO REV. G. CROSS, DEA. WHITE, WALKER, ALLEN, AND OTHERS:

I hasten to take a moment to drop you a line. I reached home the night I left Richville, about eleven at night after a tedious and lonely ride and walk (for I found considerable bare ground.) It was lonely for I thought much of those dear friends whom I had left behind, and the hours of seven and nine, I could almost see them bowing around the altar for prayer, and spirits mingling together. I took an addition to my cold, and was about sick, but could not be still. I left for this place on Tuesday morning amidst many misgivings of soul, and reached here last evening about six o'clock, and found things in a most wretched and disturbed state in the church, difficulty between members and minister; and carried so far that they have thrown up a request before the presbytery to have the pastoral relation dissolved. Though a large majority of the church have been and are still strongly attached to their minister, and will consent to no such dissolution. But such is the state of things here that if I had known before I came what I know now, I do not think I should have come. Perhaps I should have done wrong. And even now I hardly know what duty is, I have been a great mind to get into my sleigh and leave. But it rains, and the roads are nearly bare for four or five miles out, and I must stay a little at least. Oh how I need faith in the Lord Jesus Christ. It is an important field of labor, and much ought to be done. There is population of about six thousand, and much wickedness is to be found here. It may be God will regard His own great name and honor, and many may be led to the Lord Jesus Christ. I do hope you will most earnestly remember me and this people at a throne of grace, and especially often call upon the name of the Lord for me. Remember the hours of seven and nine in the evening. Tell all to pray. I do not forget you. I do love to bear you to the throne of grace that God will help and sustain you. Say to those dear young converts look to Christ earnestly. Seek after duty and do it, and joy and gladness shall be yours. Time fails to write more now. Let me hear from you all. Pray for me, and mine, and for Oswego.

Your brother in Christ,
L. A. WICKES.

OSWEGO, January, 14, 1847.

MY DEAR WIFE:

You will see what I have written to E., I have only time to add that I find things in a very bad state here indeed, a part of the church want to get rid of their minister, and have circulated a subscription accordingly, and the whole has been thrown before their Presbytery for their decision, some do not like brother J. because he takes his stand on the subject of abolition, and preaches against all the popular sins of the day, and I find there is considerable commotion about him, and there is such a state that if I had known about it before I came I think I should have felt it was my duty not to have come, at least at this time. Though it may be for the good of all. Yet I find it is hard to get the minds of people off from their old and besetting sins. The morals of this place are dreadful indeed, and nothing but the power of God can reach the ear of this people. And I find after so long a time that they are far from being anywhere ready or prepared to take hold of the work of God, or even to commence meeting in the day time. Do pray much for this people. It is an important field of labor. Much good or much evil must follow this meeting, and let us lie humble before the Lord. It may be God's will to think upon us, and He will give us His salvation and confer life upon souls here. May God protect us all. I am very comfortably provided here as to room, etc., but I feel poorly prepared for the work before me in soul or body. I have found much delight and consolation in reading the forty-sixth Psalm. Oh for the faith which the Psalmist of Israel had. Let me hear from you.

Give my love to all. Pray much for me.

As ever your husband,

L. A. WICKES.

An extract.

OSWEGO, February 1st, 1847.

MY DEAR WIFE:

I catch a moment this morning to drop a line to you. As to the state of things here. They are worse and worse. I find that they had assumed a very bad state before I got here, between the church, or a part of them, and their minister. And one party says "if we don't have a revival the other will drive our minister off," and the other says if they do we shall have to keep him, and the motives of both to be equally wrong, and the feeling wicked. While there are some who are seeking God's glory and honor. And they had a case of discipline of a wicked member, and just got through with it as I got here or the week before. It was a *presbytery trial*, but some of the presbytery had their eyes open, and presbytery set aside the whole of the case, and the brother is restored, and the church has to go over the matter again. I find the difficulties in the church are such that it is almost impossible to bring things to an humble and cordial agreement between them, some say this meeting was gotten up for the purpose to reinstate their minister into the good favor of the people, and that if they come in they would be considered as sustaining the church in their course, and so there is an awful pull-back. I shall wait but a few days more to see the real state of things, and what prospects there may be before me. It is meeting time and I must go. Half past ten, evening. With the various reports before me I have taken two different expressions of the people for the continuance of the meeting, or whether they would have one, and have each time had a decided expression of the people in favor of it. I have then concluded to hold on. There have been previous to this, somewhere between twelve and twenty hopeful conversions and quite a large number of backsliders reclaimed. I thank God for it. To-night there were about forty forward for prayers. Some of them backsliders, and five or six professed to give themselves up to the Lord. This is the second time I have given opportunity to come forward for prayers in the church. We have generally resorted to the basement of the church where the meetings are held during the day. The text I preached from to-night was Prov. 8: 36. Thus in the midst of all our discouragement the Lord does and has appeared as our helper and defense. To His name be all the glory given, for His hand hath done the work. Still the church is in a very unpleasant and dead state, and none of them feel as they should in view of all the work that is before them. There have been some three or four sailors converted we hope. I believe if the people of God were where they ought to be, there would be a great break up here and much good done, might be seen here accomplished. Tues. afternoon. I would just say to-day has been a good day, and there seemed to be much brokenness of heart among the church, and others. What may be the final result, God only knows. I pray it may be for the furtherance of His cause, Pray much for me and for this place, and that "God would bring order out of confusion, light out of darkness."

Your affectionate husband,
L. A. WICKES.

OSWEGO, January 15, 1847.

DEAR AND HONORED PARENTS:

Half-past nine, just returned from evening meeting will drop you a line. I left Richville, St. Lawrence County, on the 6th instant. We had a good and glorious work. It was as hard and as laborious a meeting as I have ever engaged in. We had but little good going, and the mud was awful, and I had to travel about much on foot to get around at all. There were some as interesting cases of conversion as I have ever known in my life, and as clear cases of conversion as I ever knew in any meeting or revival. Among them were several men from sixty to seventy-five years of age. One man who had been one of the boldest in sin, and been trying all in his power to lead others astray and was rather an infidel, was in such distress, and yet determined to resist the spirit of God, that he felt there was no mercy for him, and begged of Christians to pray that if there was no mercy for him, that God would lay him in the grave, for he was only making his damnation more dreadful and aggravating. But the Lord, we trust, did have mercy upon him, and he came like a lamb to the foot of the cross. Many were so cut down that they cried out in the congregation, "what shall I do."· There was the earnest cry for mercy, and they found peace and hope in believing in the Lord Jesus Christ. One young man rose with his hands over his face and cried out "what shall I do, I can stand it no longer." We hope he found Jesus precious to his soul. Some individuals where the cries for mercy were truly heart rending only for their stubbornness in not being willing to give up, until it seemed to be like giving up of the ghost. There were something over a hundred that gave pleasing evidence of their being the Lord's. To His name be all the glory and the honor, for His hand hath gotten the victory. I will praise Him for what He has done. My soul shall magnify the name of the Lord, and I feel that if I shorten my days let me die laboring for the souls of friends and for whom Christ died. I have a constant cough, and I sometimes think that I am on the last days of my life. God can sustain me even yet. I reached this place on the evening of the 13th, and find things not very encouraging to work with prospects that are around here. It is an important field, and one where much good or evil may be done to the cause of Christ. I am laboring with the Second church, Rev. C. J. is their pastor, and reputed to be a good and faithful man. I feel entirely incompetent to the task before me, my only hope is in the Lord of hosts. The forty-sixth Psalm has afforded me much consolation, yet I do want more of that living confidence in the Lord, and that holy reliance on His eternal hand. I think I can truly say "Prone to wander, Lord, I *feel* it." Still to His dear cross I would cling as my only help and support. I do earnestly hope that you will remember me in your prayers and this place, that the arm of the Lord will be made bare for salvation, and His great name may be honored. I came into this place with a determination not to have it known that I had any connection around here. But yesterday after meeting, a gentleman asked me if I had any connection in L. (about eighteen miles from here), I told him I supposed I had some distant connection. He wanted to know if Mr. B. was a relative of mine. I told him he was. He said he thought he saw a family resemblance, and that he had often heard Mr. B. speak of a nephew he had in the north, etc. And so I am found out. I may be here some three or four weeks, and I may be here but a short time, and I suppose they don't care much about seeing me. And mother taught me when I was a *little* boy, "always to let my absence be where my presence is not wanted." And I think it is time when I am a *big boy*. Though if duty to the cause of my Savior calls me, then I shall go.

Remember me affectionately to all. Let me hear from you soon. May I ask again, pray for me.

While I remain still your son,

L. A. WICKES.

OSWEGO, Feb. 9, 1847.

DEAR PARENTS:

I have but a moment to write this evening. I have had the privilege of an interview with Uncle C., and he tells me he expects to visit A. in a few days, and I thought I would just say that the Lord is among this people, and so is the devil in all his mighty strides, though he is a conquered foe. And all his army will be broken. I find much to do to keep my own heart any where near right. But I do try to conquer all. I think I never was in a place that opposes so many obstacles to the work of the Lord as I find in this place—especially among the professed followers of the Lord and Saviour. There are a great many who are very serious and who seemingly, are near the kingdom of divine grace and regenerating love, but not strength to bring forth. There have been somewhere about forty hopeful conversions since the meeting commenced among them, and backsliders reclaimed, and several sailors and boatmen, and some very hard and obdurate cases; and while God in His infinite mercy is visiting this place, I do hope you will pray for me and for this people. Uncle C. will tell you how things appeared to him, and what he saw and heard while here. I received a letter from home. They write of good being done there. It is somewhat encouraging, and for a blessing on that place little E. writes me that she hopes she has given her heart to the Lord, and loves to pray and serve the Savior. I do hope and pray she may ever be the humble child of grace. She also mentions the conversion of some five or six others in the neighborhood, but not in connection with the old society. May prayers be made in their behalf.

Let me hear from you soon, and pray for

Your son,

L. A. WICKES.

OSWEGO, Feb. 15, 1847.

MY DEAR DAUGHTER:

I was glad to get a letter from you. I am very glad you have told me about the meetings which you have, and of your mates becoming Christians. And you say you hope you have, too. I want you to tell me when you became a Christian, and what makes you think you are a Christian, and all about it. Tell me all about it in your next letter. And love the Savior. And if you want to be a happy girl, be a kind and affectionate girl, and try to be useful, then you can be happy, and such happiness will be lasting and will afford you joy in the last. Since I wrote you there has been a coming up to the help of the Lord in this place among the professed followers of Christ, though not all, only in a small proportion. May the Lord be your guide and protector while life shall last, and lead you into all truth, for Jesus sake, is the prayer of

Your affectionate father,

L. A. WICKES.

Love to all.

OSWEGO, Feb. 15, 1847.

MY DEAR WIFE:

I find this to be the most difficult field of labor that I have often found or have been placed in. Taking the minister and his church, together with the state of society here and the moral training which has been, or the no training at all, still the Lord has proved our deliverer. There have been some interesting cases of conversions. Some men who have been bold in sin and wrong, and who have seemed almost to defy the mighty God, yet the Lord has brought them to bow at His feet. There have been hopeful conversions to the number of about sixty; but what is that in the midst of such a population. The faith of God's people has been and is quite small, and if it was not for the thought that I have friends praying for me far away, I know not how I should possibly get along: I should soon leave here, and I hope to now very soon. But it seems as though the work had but just commenced and opposition to it seems to be giving away, and religion to be the chief topic of conversation in all their circles and conclaves. I do pray that the Lord will turn sinners to Himself by scores and by thousands. (You did right in paying that tax, but it was too much. But you know the Savior paid the tax for Himself and Peter, though it was wrongfully levied on Him. Let us suffer wrong rather than to do wrong, and evince the spirit of our divine Lord. And that we may have a conscience void of offense toward God and man.) I am glad to hear of the work of the Lord among the people. I do hope they will let the Lord work by His own power and glory, and not trouble Him by their unbelief and isms.

Uncle C. was here a day or two since from L., attended a meeting and preaching; said to a friend he had got amply paid for all his stay, and went away with the intention of trying to get me to go to L. and hold a meeting, but I think it will be very doubtful, indeed, about my going there, though the will of the Lord be done. I must go to the ministers' prayer meeting this morning, and I must close for the present. The weather here is very peculiar and changeable, so that people who

are predisposed to a cough are very much exposed, indeed. May the Lord protect our little family, is the prayer of
Your affectionate husband,
L. A. WICKES.

OSWEGO, March 1, 1847.
MY DEAR AND AFFECTIONATE WIFE:
I received yours on Saturday last, and then did intend to start for home this morning, but they have put another slice on the meeting, and one that keeps me here only a day or two, and perhaps a week, so I hasten to return you an answer immediately. Yesterday I preached to the converts; there were something like ninety of them seated together, and the most of them are interesting cases, indeed. There are several heads of families that are among the subjects of the work, and quite a goodly number of family altars have been built up; and old ones are rebuilt. The scene which was before the people was such that they could not bear to stop so, and begged me to stay a little longer, as there was quite a deepening of the work for the last week, and some quite interesting cases of conversion. May the Lord still smile for His great name's sake, and still bring many more to bow at His feet. I have heard from Richville; the work of the Lord is still progressing in the various neighborhoods around there. * * * *

CHAPTER XXIII.

BIRTHDAY LETTER, 1848.

BEING the thirty-ninth anniversary of the days of the life of my pilgrimage, and the twenty-third year of my hope in Christ, and the sixteenth year of my ministry, fifteenth year of my married life, and the fourteenth of my being a father!

STOWS SQUARE, December 8, 1848.

MOST HONORED PARENTS:

Yesterday our oldest daughter said, to-morrow pa will write to grandpa. I ran in to sister Anna's and she said brother Albanians will be looking for that birth-day And so I suppose my parents will look for a letter. But if they only looked upon my life as I do, they would rather it would be hid until the time of the final revelation of all things, and when, too, may God prepare me to give up my account. For then not only my life with all its acts must be revealed, but all the motives that have actuated me will be known. And may it please God that I may know them now, and not act ignorant of all the heart. I find it quite a trial to give my anniversary letter, because the opening of a door to that disgusting thing called egotism (what *I* have done), and yet also that even when I have entered and feel no such thing in my own bosom, yet to others it may appear very much so. And these together have sometimes induced me almost to not write another letter. But I may hope in the last of these that my parents will pardon me, and they will use a little of that *charity* which "covereth a *multitude* of sins," and will reprove and point out to me my errors and all my wrongs, for I find often that when I have passed by in review I find myself often to have been in the fault, and yet others may see more than I can or do at least see. It is seldom I find a *friend* that will tell me my faults. While my enemies are sometimes uncharitable and cruel, yet

> "Mine *enemy* is oft my *friend*,
> Though wrathful and severe;
> He helps to perfect that great end,
> For which I linger here."

And I will try to learn from all and improve upon all that I learn. When I commenced dating this letter I was astonished to see how fast time had fled, and how old I was, indeed I had to cipher it out to convince myself that I was so old, and I have come to the conclusion thirty-nine years have rolled into the *eternal* world, and are locked up among those things which *were*, but are past and gone. And truly I can say that it has been now "like the Indian's arrow," not only that *life* has gone so fast, but that each of the events in that date so long ago did take place. The day and time of my *uniting* with the church at first I did not recollect, but I think it was in the fall of 1826 but am not certain. It was a day that I shall probably remember until eternity shall pass, still the date I had forgotten. The events of the year that has passed are nothing unusual. My labors have been very hard, but in rather a new manner for me. You have already been informed that I have preached half of the time in Denmark for some over a year. I went there of my own accord, without any invitation from them. They were living almost without hope and God in the world, and only one or two family altars in the place. No meetings of any kind. The Sabbath was a day of recreation among them, and for miles it was one vast desolation. They had had a house that was built some years ago for a church, and where they had met for worship. This had now been sold for a *dairy house!* and there was no place to meet to worship. There were a few females who felt they could not have this state of things remain. I finally secured an old academy to preach in, but when the Universalists heard I was coming they offered their house (for they have one there). I preached one Sabbath there, and then there was no more place for Jesus' blessed truth to be spoken there, for they would want the house themselves. So I gave notice that I could have the old academy, which was hired for a select school by an impenitent young man, and but few came, still I continued my labors on during the winter, and the house began to fill up, and some moving among the dry bones. But directly the select school closed and the building must return into the hands of the owner, and he a rumseller, and on Sabbath morning as I was about entering, the deacon came to me and wanted to know if I was coming any longer; I replied, that certainly I was. He shook his head and said he was sorry. I asked why. He answered Mr. B. the owner of the Academy was afraid it would be burned and he had concluded not to have any meetings there, and if I only gave notice that I could not come any more things would pass off very well. But if I continued to come and there was no place to meet in, it would make a great disturbance in Denmark, and they would censure him very hard. I told him if that would make a disturbance then I would make a disturbance. If I could get a barn or even a door yard to preach in I should continue to preach. Just at this moment an impenitent man came up and ascertained what was the theme of conversation, and he said I will go and see if I cannot get it, and soon returned with an affirmative answer. I then continued but a short time before the Lord moved upon the impenitent and backsliders to start for a meeting house. The old Academy became so full that all could not get in. The church is now about finished, a neat tidy house, and large enough to accommodate all. And I have labored with my own hands to procure bread for my own family, while I have been laboring with that people for comparatively nothing, while I have refused calls where I could have had a competent salary, and only because I knew something must be done for them. And while I have been depriving my dear family of many of the comforts of life, I trust in Jesus I have been giving to others the bread of everlasting life. There are a few who have a heart to do but are poor, and they have been turning their hands to do all in their power to get a house of worship. There have been some few souls that have been hopefully brought into the kingdom of God, and some have died in the triumph of faith. To God be all the glory and the praise. A part of my time I have been preaching in Champion and Carthage where God has seemed to smile in a measure. In all, my preaching, lectures on

Temperance, Anti Slavery etc., number about two hundred. This is I feel rather small to what it should be. My family I have felt were calling upon me for more of a heavenly frame, and yet how far short I come from doing all I should. I do feel more the want of more converse with God. Though at times I do have some blessed seasons of communion with my Savior, though not all that sweet communion as in some seasons past. Our Heavenly Father knows what will be for our good. All send love. Remember me to all and ever pray for your eldest son,

L. A. WICKES.

STOWS SQUARE, 1848.

DEAR BROTHER AND SISTER:

With the various duties of life and their constant calls, I find myself wafted along through time almost unperceived by me, so that I do not think how long it is since I wrote until I take a march backward, and truly it has gone, "Swift as the Indian's arrow flies" and tarries for none, and to improve it should be our every duty. I find that every day brings its duties with it, and to defer the duties for another only makes the work of to-morrow more abundant, especially in the things of religion. I reason that if God spares me to see the opening of morning dawn, it is because I have a work to do, for if my work was done I should be called away. Then my duty like the faithful steward is to ask what that duty is, and inquire with an intention of *doing it*. We had better not know *His* will than when we have known it to turn away in negligence. Did you ever reflect on the beautiful eulogy which our Savior pronounced on those who obey His laws? I think it one of the most beautiful that can be found (Matt 12: 50) "He that doeth the will of my Father which is in heaven the same is My brother, sister and mother." How great is the honor which He has put upon us to allow us that exalted station. And how much greater is the humility which He has exercised to condescend to put Himself on a level with us! Still how sweet the expression. How full of meaning, of heavenly meaning. To be allowed to call the "Prince of glory" brother. To be admitted into the family circle of the God of glory. To be inmates of the mansion of bliss. Truly may it be said, "'Tis love beyond degree". But let us not forget the *condition* of this exalted privilege: "To *do the will* of my Father which is in Heaven". He tells us Ps. 40, and Heb. 10, his own character was to do the will of God, and not only to do the will of God, but "*Delight*" to do it. I trust dear brother and sister this is your delight. For unless it is our chief delight to keep His law we cannot take pleasure in those who do thus keep it. And yet the Christian life is one of progressiveness. That we are to look forward unto the perfect man and woman in Jesus Christ. And that we, like the Psalmist, be satisfied when we awake in His likeness, and not be afraid of getting to be too holy, or conquering sin too much. I have had a good many thoughts since looking at your likenesses, they are frail things but still they may remain when you are gone, and this is probably the reason you had them taken. Many and dear are the associations of life, and when friends leave us it is not the image that is the most dear. Nay it is the moral character which is the most to be loved. Yet when life has been useful and virtue shown in all its beauty, it is that a view of these features may review in memory the whole character. Then how important that we live a life of usefulness, that like Abel yet may speak. Mary (in the Gospels) left no delineation of her features, nor the color of her hair, yet how sweet does the record of her devotion to her Saviour, make her appear, when it is said she wiped His feet with her hair. O what a contrast to the vain pride of this world. May the Lord grant that we may all have her humble spirit. Write soon and let us know all. And all serve God so that we may meet in glory is the prayer of your brother,

LEWIS A. W.

To Mr. T. Lord and Jane Lord.

CHAPTER XXIV.

MEETINGS AT BOONVILLE, BROWNVILLE, LA FARGEVILLE, AND LETTERS TO PARENTS AND MOTHER AFTER FATHER'S DEATH.

BOONVILLE, January 19, 1849.

DEAR BROTHER CROSS:

I HAVE only a moment to write and let you know my whereabouts. You may be surprised to find that I am here. But so it is, I am now seated in your brother John's house, where God has made bare His arm. I have been here a little over two weeks, and awful dark has it been in this place. But the Lord has truly made His appearance among us. Last Monday your brother said if I would go some three miles to see some that were quite deeply convicted he would go along "to hold the horse for me." So we started. We found that four young men whom we had prayed for the evening before had gone out to get some of their mates and comrades to go to the Lord with them. We called at one or two houses, and then went back where we first called, some six impenitent ones who were cut down to the very earth, and after talking a little while we bowed in prayer. I asked your brother to begin and he did so, and the Lord helped, and so we all prayed, and salvation came; I prayed and all followed me, and it was a feast; all, we hope, gave themselves to God. There have been somewhere about thirty souls that have bowed to Christ. Some that the first night that I was here were engaged in the ball-room, to-day we hope have given all to Christ. To God be all the glory given, and the honor. The minister, Mr. N., is a *young man*, rather *poor health*, but a willing spirit. And nearly all the labor comes on me. I should be glad to meet you once more on the battle ground. The meeting I think will not be a two-months meeting. But yet we cannot say how long. And your brother says that you said that you would come if you knew when they had a meeting. Tell the dear people in R. to pray for me and for this place. And urge daily their request before God. The bell has rung and I must close. Your brother and family send love. Pray that God will direct me in my field of labor. Love to deacon W. and all the rest of the friends. And remember me to sister Cross and the children.

As ever yours,
L. A. WICKES.

BOONVILLE, January 22, 1849.

MY DEAR AND AFFECTIONATE WIFE:

I had hoped that by this time I could start to embrace home once more. But such is the state of things that I find that I cannot, and I know not when I can. The Lord is truly with us. While there is a good deal of feeling and a few have come to Christ in the village, among which are L. H. and A. C., and some twelve or fifteen more, the most are out of the village. Nearly all of one school district is brought to bow at the foot of the cross. The work has commenced among the young men. Last evening there were about sixty forward for prayers. And most of them hoped they had given all to Christ. Among whom are several school teachers. To God be all the glory. Some who the first time I was here were in the ball room, are now seen in the praying circle calling on the Lord. But there is a most powerful opposition. And there is a disposition to run into infidelity. I have to do nearly all the labor connected with the pulpit and much out of it. Brother Northrop, their minister, complains much with his throat and is quite feeble a part of the time. We have had meetings only part of the day and evening, and I do not know as I can get any more. I am afraid that they are so covetous that they will grieve the Spirit away from them. Some of the members of the church are even counting *how much* it costs them every day to go to meeting, and what it may cost them in the end. Still this is not the case with all. There is an appearance of an abundant harvest. And may God grant it may be the case for Jesus' sake. I am rather fearful that I cannot be at Denmark next Sabbath. I shall write to brother Wait to supply them if he can and I will come as soon as I can. I feel much anxiety about them, and hope that God will overrule all for His glory and His honor.

Tell Emma and Sarah to be good children, love the Savior and do not forget their Bibles.

How does Aurelia do, etc.? Love to all.

Pray much for your husband,

L. A. WICKES.

BOONVILLE, January 23d, 1849.

MY DEAR DAUGHTER:

To his daughter A. E. Wickes, attending school at Denmark.

I thought you would like to know what we are doing here, and though I have but a moment to write, still I will improve the moment. The Lord truly is in the midst of the people, and many are the souls that hope they have bowed at the foot of the cross, among which is your former friend L. H. and Mr. C.'s niece, A. The Lord has most graciously visited the whole place and many have turned to the Lord. There are several that at the first night of the meeting were in the ball room, and are now seen bowing at the feet of the Savior asking for mercy and pleading for sinners. While there are a goodly number in the village that hope they have given all to the Savior, the work is mostly in the country around. Last evening there were one hundred persons forward for prayers and more than twenty spoke and hoped that they had given up all to Christ, and the work seems only just begun. I have wished that you were here, but such is not the case, and we must be at the disposal of our heavenly Father. I hope, my dear daughter, that you do not forget to bow your knee to your Savior all the time and look to Him for help, and make the Savior your only guide and help.

There is nothing I desire more of you than that you make the life of the Christian your great aim, and while you apply your mind to your studies, and make all the improvement you can, I hope you will feel that all must be done for the glory of God. I can not now say when I may be home, but I will be at D. as soon as I can. I wish you would let me know all that is doing in D. Do they have good congregations in the church? May the Lord be your constant guide, is the prayer of
    Your affectionate father,
      L. A. WICKES.
To AURELIA E. WICKES.

   BOONVILLE, Oneida Co., Jan. 31, 1849.
DEAR PARENT:
 You perceive by this that I am some twenty-five miles nearer you than I have been before for some time. I have been for about four weeks holding a series of meetings with this church. The meetings are held only afternoons and evenings. There have been some one hundred who profess hope in the Savior's love. They are from eighty years old down to ten and twelve years. Let us ascribe all honor and glory to God, who alone is worthy. Their minister is a man of feeble health, and is not able to be out to meeting but a part of the time, and all the labor nearly comes on me. With a bad cold and hoarseness I find I am almost used up, and feel somewhat inclined to stop. But such is impossible, while the whole region is on the move. May God give me strength equal to the labors which he has put upon me. And

pray for me that God will direct. I write in haste. Please excuse this scribbling. Love to all inquiring.
While I remain your son.
L. A. WICKES.

BOONVILLE, February 6, 1849.

MY DEAR WIFE:

I catch a moment to drop you a line and let you know how things move here. I did intend to start for home yesterday, but such was the state of feeling that it was an almost unanimous request that I should tarry longer. I preached on the Sabbath to the converts; there were over one hundred seated together, and were of all ages, such a scene as Booneville never saw before, and while they saw it they felt they could not for a moment be satisfied with what they then saw, and it was one of the most painful parts of it that others should be left behind, and they felt they would do all in their power to advance the cause. I then concluded to stay and do what I could for the cause here. The church has not taken hold as a general thing, and there is a sure help only in the few. Yesterday there was quite a number of new cases, and this afternoon we had to have prayer three times at closing the meeting, and there were some, we trust, brought to bow at the foot of the cross. To God be all the glory. My fear is now that I cannot be home before the Sabbath, and what will poor Denmark do? If I can come I shall, and do what I can to get away consistent with truth and duty, and it will only be the great sense of duty that will keep me here

Pray that God will direct me for His holy name's sake and I will cheerfully obey. I do not know of any one that I can get to supply my place in Denmark if I do not come. Tell all to pray much. The bell is ringing, I must close. Love to all. In love and haste,

Your husband,
L. A. WICKES.

BOONVILLE, Feb. 18, 1849.

MY DEAR WIFE:

You see I am up at this late hour, half-past eleven o'clock, to redeem my promise. To-night there has been a general move among many who have before stood aloof and opposed, and it has taken hold of the village people. There were some thirty-six entire new cases forward for *prayers*, and one lawyer. The village school teacher (one of the ball characters), one fancy painter, and one tailor (ball character), hoped they gave all to Christ to-night, with some others. And the prospect is now that I *shall not* be able to be at home in season to attend that *wedding*, and must very reluctantly give it up.* Perhaps I may be at home in season, but they had best not depend on me, for I might entirely disappoint them. You see how I am placed now. And let me ask you to pray much for me that God would lead me into the path of

---

*This was an answer to a request to attend a wedding on the 21st, in D., who would feel very much disappointed not to have him perform the ceremony. When the request the day previous came there had then nothing very special taken place, though there was some moving out around the village. He felt he needed unerring wisdom to return a negative answer.

duty and of God. Oh, how I need His Holy Spirit to guide me in the path of right, and to fill my soul with His spirit. Give my love to all.

Affectionately,
L. A. WICKES.

BOONVILLE, MARCH 2, 1849.

DEAR WIFE:

Do you think I am never coming home? I have been on the eve of starting every day this week, and every day new obstacles seem to oppose themselves in new cases of conviction and conversions, so that nearly all opposition is done with, and some of the most stubborn and hardened cases have yielded and turned from hatred to love of the Saviour. The work is now going right through the village. Several of those who were engaged in the ball have been led to Jesus the crucified Savior. You would rejoice to be here and participate in the work of the blessed Lord. How long I shall stay I cannot say, but I am now inclined to say I shall be at home on Monday or Tuesday of next week, at the farthest. My voice is almost as poor as it has been at any time in my previous labors. I have had all the preaching to do as yet, though they promised me if I would stay they would take hold and preach, still they are not able to do much; a weak set as to body. Some fifty or sixty conversions since I returned, and I do not know when I have held a meeting so long and the interest continue to rise as now. The lower part of the church is crowded every

night, and about three-quarters full in the daytime. To God be all the glory and praise for what He hath done. I am anxious to do what I can and get home, still I know God will take care of us. But I must close and go
March 3. out a visiting. I must be constantly on the go. As I commenced the meeting by visiting the fore part of the day, all think I *must* do it, and it is harder for me than having three meetings a day. Perhaps I may have time to add more before the mail goes out and will not close it yet.

3d. I was so constantly engaged that I had not time to mail this, and there being no meeting to-night I will write you a few lines more. The Lord is still among us. There have been a number of hopeful conversions to-day, one an awful profane, swearing infidel. He was truly made to tremble before God. To God be all the glory, the praise and honor. On the 22d of February I gave an address to the Washingtonian Society and got almost a hundred signers to the pledge. But I must close. Pray much for us. Tell the little children to be kind. Love to all.

Your husband,
L. A. WICKES.

Meeting at Brownville, commencing April 11, 1849. —Mr. Wickes had had a call to go to Brownville. On his way thither he arrived at Watertown, where
An Extract. he found his dear old friend, Prof. Whitford, lying at the point of death. A council of physicians had been called, who said he could not live twenty-four

hours. The afflicted family urged Mr. Wickes to remain with them through the trying ordeal.; he accordingly rode to B. and filled his evening appointment, and returned to his suffering friends after the service, the distance being about six miles. Prof. W. passed away the next morning about seven o'clock, leaving the wife and only remaining daughter very sad and lonely, as a short time previous they had buried their only son and brother. Mr. Wickes was requested to preach the funeral sermon upon the next day, which was the Sabbath. It was a peculiarly trying place for him. He went back to Brownville and preached in the afternoon and evening. Some feeling was manifested; two arose for prayers, and one individual arose and confessed. He preached again Sabbath morning and in the afternoon attended the funeral and preached: "The Lord helping him," from I Thess. 4: 14, Revs. Brayton and Snyder in the pulpit assisting him. A large assembly were present. In the evening he again returned and preached in B. Some interest was manifested, but not as much as he had expected, and there were some disheartening occurrences followed. A ball was gotten up among other obstacles. "That, you know," he wrote to his wife, "is necessary in these days to the opening of a revival of religion (*i. e.*) if we judge from other places."

The following extracts from a letter tell a little more of the results of the meeting.

BROWNVILLE, May 4, 1849.
DEAR BROTHER AND SISTER CROSS:

For more than a week I have been trying to get a place to write you a few lines. But I found it impossible. It was either some one sending for me to visit the sinner, or else some one calling to converse with me, and to know what *they* should do to be saved. And talking and praying all the time until ten and eleven o'clock at night, and then I was too much fatigued to write to any one. *   *   *   *   *

There had been a meeting held here evenings for some six weeks before I came here, though I found things in a much less interesting state than I expected. There had been some few conversions, and the church had been made more faithful, and difficulties had been settled, and brethren were made to be faithful with each other. There have been quite a goodly number of conversions, and many backsliders reclaimed, and the work seems to be increasing and deepening all the time. There have been some quite interesting cases of conversion. To God be all the glory. * * * But I must break off and go and see some anxious sinners; may the Lord have mercy on them.

Saturday, 5th. I catch my pen a moment more before I have any calls. The Lord was truly in our midst yesterday and last evening. Truly God was in our midst. There was among others, one of the ring leaders in balls and parties brought to bow at the foot of the cross, with an humble confession, all broken and bathed in tears. I do hope to see much done in the cause of Jesus still in this place.

Pray for us that God may be our director and that we may be His willing subjects, for His great name's sake. You have probably heard of the death both of Mr. Whitford and of his son. The first Sabbath that I was here I had to go to Watertown to preach his funeral sermon. Thus father and son have both been taken away, and truly they are an afflicted family. Truly, how peculiar are the dealings of God, and "His ways past finding out." I pray God it may be blessed to all of us.

Tell Nettie to love and serve the Lord. Be more like the Saviour; and Delia to live for Jesus, and God shall be her helper in every place. Johnny, be a good boy and make father and mother happy. But other duties call and I must close this hasty scribbled sheet. Remember me affectionately to all the dear friends in B. Let me hear from you soon.

With Christian love I am your brother in Christ,
L. A. WICKES.

LA FARGEVILLE, Jefferson Co., N. Y.,
November 19, 1849.

DEAREST MOTHER :

I have just heard from home, informing me that father has gone to the salt water for his health. I have wanted to hear from you very much, in your loneliness, and it must be a trial to you, his absence and his ill health, to have all this upon your heart. Still, dear mother, God has carried you through trials and borne you up when no arm but His could sustain you. We would be resigned to the will of the Lord. Yet affections still cling around those we love. But, in the midst of all, there is a sweet consolation in the thought that Jesus will do all things right. I have been here only about three weeks, and preached every day. When I came here everything was then most forbidding, that there could be apparently. But the Lord has appeared for our help, some thirty or forty hopeful conversions, and all of them appear quite well. There were about eighty forward for prayers last evening. Quite a number of heads of families have been among the number of hopeful converts. To God be all the glory for His hand hath done the great work. Remember me to C. and F. I wish F. was here, I think she would love to see the work of God, and be a sharer in it. In haste but in much love.

Your Son,
L. A WICKES.

LA FARGEVILLE, Dec. 4, 1849.

MY DEAR AND AFFECTIONATE WIFE:

Things here have been quite encouraging for a few days. Last week was a very hard week, although there were some all the time coming to Christ, yet the work was up hill. Their temperance meeting was very bad business, and very much diverted the mind. There was such a bad spirit, etc. And things have all the time been hauled up to keep the mind diverted. There have been somewhere between eighty and one hundred hopeful conversions. To God be all the glory given. I have been quite at a loss what I should do or when to leave. But have concluded to go to Depauville to-morrow, and am in hopes that my stay will be short. Depauville is about seven miles from here, and the prospects are rather favorable, though I know we cannot possibly tell what may be. I do not anticipate anything without the blessing of the Lord. May God direct me what to do for His name's sake. Let us watch and pray and live for heaven and for Jesus. So that we may have His favor. And "His favor is better than life." Dear wife, if God can make us the instruments of bringing souls into the kingdom of Christ, let us indeed feel that we will rather suffer the privations of this life, for God will hold us up, " He will never leave nor forsake those that put their trust in Him." Write immediately.

Your husband,
L. A. WICKES.

December 4, 1849.

Dear Sister E.:

I wrote to daughter A. from here a few days since. Since which the Lord has greatly appeared for our help, and many souls have been brought to bow at the foot of the cross. Last evening there were about eighty forward for prayers, and there are some thirty or forty that hope in the Lord. And you would have seen, if here, a most melting time. At my room after the noon meeting, there were ten young ladies that came to converse with me. We bowed in prayer and had been on our knees but a short time before there was a room full crying out for mercy all around. Some of the most hopeless cases to human view that were in the community. There are several heads of families that have bowed at the foot of the cross, and the work seems only to have just commenced. And it seems impossible for me to get away. To God be all the glory and the honor for His great name has done all. No human arm could do the work that has been accomplished, and seems to be doing. Oh, how good it is to be allowed to work for the Lord, and see souls brought into the fold of Jesus. We have just heard from father, he has gone to the sea shore for his health, but it is poorer since he left home. I fear for the result. Pray much, may the Lord be our guide and all. I must close. Don't fail to write immediately. In haste.

    As ever, your brother,

        L. A. WICKES.

Dec. 4, 1849. In an extract from another letter of the same date, he writes, the state of religion is very encouraging. I now board with a Brother L., formerly from L. He had built him a new house, and the young people had been making their calculations to have a house warming. But they had a different one from what they expected. I commenced praying with two young ladies that came here to see me about their souls' salvation. Before we got off our knees there was a whole circle for prayer around the room, and indeed more than could get into the room, and they were the very ones who were desirous of having a house warming. And four souls hoped they gave up all to God. And as one young man expressed it, we have had a "heart warming" instead of house warming. And the work seems only to have begun. Some who have not been to meeting for years have been brought to love and honor the Savior who died to redeem their souls from the pit of woe. To God be all the glory given. I want more of His presence and spirit, to lead me in the path of duty. May the Lord direct. Pray much for me. Love to the children.

Your husband,

L. A. WICKES.

LA FARGEVILLE, Dec. 8, 1849.

Being the fortieth anniversary of my life, by the grace and mercy of God to me a sinner, through Jesus Christ my Lord.

DEAR AND RESPECTED PARENTS:

Last Birthday letter Dec. 8, 1849. I am so situated to-day that I have but a short time to write to you on this my anniversary. Yet I will pen a few lines to meet your expectations. Is it possible that I am an old man forty years old? I used to think a man of that age was an old man, but now I have got there I scarcely know where to put myself. But I am just what I am, and that too by the grace of God, and may be called a sinner saved by grace. And I pray may my remaining days be all for the glory and honor of God. I have kept you advised of all the events of the year so much that I have not much to pen to you. I have not all my memorandum with me, so that I cannot state the particulars of the past year fully. I have only preached some three hundred and eighty sermons, attended some one hundred and fifty inquiry meetings and visited I know not how many families. There have been only some three hundred hopeful conversions and backsliders reclaimed. This is a small number I feel indeed, and a poor report this.

Yet I do feel that God has in His mercy been my helper and my all. His hand has done the work, and to His name be all the glory and the honor. He shall be praised for all His mighty works among the children of men.

I sometimes think on account of my hoarseness I will give up my constant labors. But still I do not feel that it would be pleasing to my heavenly Father. I want to do my Savior's will for His name's sake, and to advance His cause and lead souls to Christ. Oh, it is a blessed work. I have been from home only about five months this year past, excepting for only a day or two at a time. So that you see I am not quite as bad as formerly to be absent. I am really anxious to hear about father's health. I know you must be in great affliction and filled with sorrow; yet I know our compassionate Saviour will do all things right and we shall know by and by what now is dark to us. Pray much for me that God would lead me, and that I may ever be willing to walk in the path of right. With the kindest regards to all. The Sabbath before I left L. twenty-five united with the branch of Christ's vine and probably as many more will very soon. How is our sick father?

Your eldest affectionate son,

L. A. WICKES.

STOWS SQUARE, Dec 22, 1849,
Saturday, 2 o'clock, P. M.

MY DEAR AND AFFECTIONATE MOTHER:

I have just returned from Clinton where I had been to get the sick ones home, and the moment I reached

After death of his father. Written to his widowed mother.

home with them, the children handed me the telegraphic dispatch announcing the death of that ever dear and kind parent. My first thought was, I will take a fresh horse (as all the stages have left for to-day) and start for Utica, and reach Albany by Sabbath noon. Then I felt, how can I break God's holy day? Would that dear father approve? I felt I should be treading on the very sanctity of that dear parent's memory, and, besides, I might not reach there in time for the funeral. I went to see what Sister A. M. could do, and she says that she has not the preparations ready either for herself or her babe, and it would be impossible for her to go. She was very anxious I should go, and for our dear mother's sake. But she agreed with me that it would *not be right to travel on the Sabbath*, and that in view of the great regard which our dear parent held that day, it would not be advisable. So I felt that I would stay with her and not leave her alone. I may, perhaps, visit you in a few days, but cannot tell. It would be the joy of my heart to mingle with you in this hour of sorrow, but I have thought that, perhaps, I might do more good to wait a little time and then assist in arranging your temporal affairs. But enough of this. Your letter came after I left for C., so that I did not get it until after I returned home. I had felt a great anxiety to see father ever since I received sister Julia's letter to A. M., and should have done so if it had not been for the sick about home. But all will be right. And now, my dear mother, I know not what to say. My heart is full. I cannot weep for him back again. No, no, but oh, the home is gone. I think of the living and their trials. You speak of your working hard and toiling all day through life. You have, dear mother, and perhaps there is none of your children that know it better than *myself*. There are scarcely none of them that can remember you in the log house of only one room and no cellar, and only rough boards for a chamber floor, and a ladder to ascend. When your oldest son would have to run of errands in the winter barefooted, and toiling with the needle until midnight, and even longer, to save the little that we had; and do your washing before light by the light of a *pine knot*; and from that time to this, God truly has helped you. And shall He, dear mother, forsake you in such an hour as this? Will He not help you? Shall He not be your guide and your all? Has He not promised to be the widow's God, and to protect you in these very times of trouble? May the Lord be your guide and support, and feed you with His manna, and lead you in all the way of love.

The sick which I brought home are as comfortable as I could expect. I hope this will be improved to our good and the glory of God. All our afflictions, for the present, seem grievous, but we know that it is the rod of a kind Father, and that all things work together for good to them that love God.

Dec. 23. Sabbath afternoon. To-day has been a time lonely to me. The storm last night shut us in and the Sabbath we have spent at home, and the most of the time in private and social prayer, and in meditating upon the scenes at your home. I long, I sigh to be with you, but I have thought, too, of the kindness of the Lord toward us. Oh, how sweet to remember that our Savior can feel with us. I have been thinking of Him at the grave of Lazarus. He did not chide when with those orphan sisters because they gave vent to their troubled spirits in tears. No, but mingled with them in their sorrow. O, how much there is in those two words, "Jesus wept." He mingled his tears with the lonely and showed them that He felt with them. And so, dear mother, He can feel for us, and we can go to Him with all our affliction with the assurance that He will feel for us, and will cherish our request for help. I suppose by this hour that you have returned to your lonely home, or remained at home, while by others he was borne away. But while others are and may prove, indeed, very kind, yet, dear mother, you have a promise now which you could never plead before, "I will be the widow's God," and His promises are sure. He will provide and supply all your wants. Let us hear from you soon, and tell us all about the funeral. All join in love and in affliction. I now subscribe myself as never before,

Your fatherless son,

LEWIS A. WICKES.

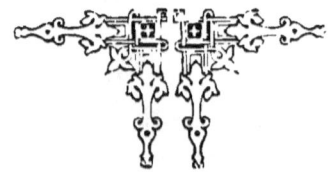

CHAPTER XXV.

MEETINGS IN DEPAUVILLE, CAPE VINCENT.

DEPAUVILLE, Feb. 4, 1850.
Monday Morning.

MY DEAR WIFE,

THIS morning, I catch a moment to let you know how things prosper here. The work of the Lord has been on the increase ever since I came here, and the whole community is on the move. God has broken in upon the head ranks of the Universalists, and one of the J. family has given up all to Christ. I was called up at midnight to go to his house and pray for him. On Saturday I preached to them from the two thieves on the cross. Among others, all three of the physicians of the place were forward for prayers. All got up and spoke. One of them declared that he had ever been known as a Universalist, and that now he still held to the same; but he did not think that he had lived a practical Christian. If he could not do it, he would give up his Universalism. I think he will find it hard business to mix the two. Yesterday we had a perfect jam. There were between three and four hundred seated in the slips. There were two hundred seated in the aisles, and about a hundred in the orchestra. God helped me to preach all day. Morning, Luke 24: 26. "Ought not Christ," etc. Afternoon, Judges 5: 23. "Curse ye Meroz," etc. When at the close nearly every person in the house rose in covenant that they would come up to the help of the Lord. In the evening the house was as full as ever. Text, Isa. 1: 2. At the close of which I should think over one hundred rose for prayers. After which the choir sat and sang in a plaintive tone "Show pity, Lord." There was no chance to make any move, but I requested them to sing the first and last verses of "Alas, and did my Savior bleed." And that all in the congregation who did really give themselves to the Lord to serve Him, if they did adopt the sentiment of the last verses, to rise. There was a deep sigh like eternity all over the house. When no sooner than the choir struck the last verse, the whole congregation (with the exception of possibly forty) sprung to their feet as if each were the only one to rise, and each wished to be the first, with their handkerchief over their faces. After they had finished the last verse, I repeated that if any had risen not understanding it to mean a consecration to God, and as such were expected to do the duties of a Christian, they could sit down while the choir repeated the verse. But not one sat down while the choir sang. O, what an hour was that! God only knows the heart. Time must develop the whole. To God, to God, be all the glory for His hand hath done the work. At about eleven at night, as I was fixing for bed the man that I mentioned to you before, whose wife had given up all to the Lord, and he had felt so bad about it etc., came to my room and as he entered, said: "I want a physician. I have such a load on my heart I cannot live. I went to bed, I could not lie there; I had to come and get some one to pray for me." We talked a little and bowed in prayer. He gave up all to Christ, we hope, and went home rejoicing in the Lord. I thank my heavenly Father for His great kindness. And let us lie humble before Him. But I must close to make one or two calls this morning. P. M. We have had a good meeting. Several hopefully gave up all to God. And yet there is much to be done. And there is great danger of their being carried away in a mere whirlwind of ecstacy. (I mean professors.) But there is one power above all others for our help, and I do hope and pray that God will indeed be our strength. And may I be humble at His feet and crown Him Lord of all, for He alone is worthy. Half past ten in the evening. I have just returned from meeting. The house was crowded to overflowing, so that I could make no move in changing the house, but to have them *rise* for prayer, and then they could not kneel the house was so crowded, but some forty spoke afterwards, and Mr. J. the Universalist, rose and said he would lead a different and praying life if he could live a Christian Universalist, but would renounce his faith as a great error if he could not; and requested prayers for his whole family. O, that God may take this work in His own hands, and bring order out of confusion. How many have given up all to the Lord I cannot say. But there are many who are not yet brought to bow at the foot of the cross. Let us ever look to God for help, for Jesus' sake. February 12. An extract. As they have been after me from Chamount, six miles from this place, I shall not of course go to R. I am glad they have got Brother B., as I could not get there in time.

How long I shall stay here I cannot tell. The work keeps spreading. There have been several interesting cases of hopeful conversions. Some cling to error of whom it was hoped better things. But yet God's spirit is still striving with them. The Universalist minister is quite faithful in his labors to make men more like the devil, and seems to be fearful that all will be lost if they forsake Universalism. They had a meeting on Sabbath evening. Some got up and talked, told how happy they were, and how the gospel saves swearers and all. But God may overrule for His glory as it opens the eyes of people to see their awful condition, without a new heart or love and at the same time say they are prepared for heaven. May the Lord have mercy on them.

DEPAUVILLE, February 20, 1850.

MY DEAR WIFE:

My health is not quite as good as when I first came here. I did intend to close here last Sabbath, but such was the state of feeling they wanted the meeting to continue. There have been over one hundred hopeful conversions and backsliders reclaimed. The house continuing to be crowded every evening and well filled every day. And an advance in interest since the Sabbath. The only way they can make any great expression of feeling is by holding up the hands. Last Sabbath the house was so perfectly jammed that when they took the expression for the continuation of the meeting, there was a universal holding up of the hand and some of the impenitent held up both hands. How long I shall tarry here I cannot say. I shall have to be at home on the 4th and 5th of March, to attend to the Turin business.* Let us have more of the spirit of Jesus in our souls, and make heaven our great aim, that we may finish our course with joy. I hope the children will be very industrious and learn much for their good and ours. I must close. Love to all.

Your poor but affectionate husband,
L. A. WICKES.

DEPAUVILLE, March 14, 1850.

DEAR BROTHER WICKES:

I shall never forget the morning you left Depauville. The language of your last prayer here. Since you left we have been trying to serve the Lord. You had been gone only half an hour when C. F. came to see you start, he felt bad because he did not see you. Directly after Mr. W. came over and said "is it possible he has gone," he could not restrain his feelings. I then thought it was time to start and let the people know you had gone. I then went and distributed the cards you left. The first house I went in was Brother F.'s, there we had a season of prayer. Then I went to Deacon G., and I prayed with them, all uniting. Went from there to Mr. M., and when on the steps heard prayer. Left and went to Doctor S., then heard prayer, and left again, going by Doctor I., heard him praying, so when I came back, got opposite of Mr. F., stopped in the street, heard him praying, and

---

*He was guardian to a fatherless young lady.

likewise Mr. W. It did seem as though the people were worshiping God. The meetings since you left, have been well attended on the last week. This week I have just returned after a short absence. The converts take up their duty well. Brother W. did not preach last Sabbath, he was sick. The house was well filled, but adjourned to the Methodist house. Brother B. was a good deal embarrassed, but with all, there was a good meeting. In the afternoon went to Brother L. to a prayer meeting, house full, a good meeting. In the evening prayer meeting in the M. E. Church, a good meeting again. I tell you Brother Wickes, I never expected to see such a time in Depauville. When I look and see the change that has taken place in this village, I cannot but exclaim, to God be all the glory through our Lord Jesus Christ. My prayer is that you may always be, while on earth, turning souls to the Savior. Brother C. F. sends his love to you, and I might ask who don't. You have certainly got the prayers, if not the hearts of the people. I have been to La Fargeville, and the inquiry has been, have you heard from Brother Wickes, you have the prayers of the people for your immediate recovery. Dear Brother, there is not at present anything in respect of the converts to write discouraging, but all do their duty. The young people have a prayer meeting, and the house is well filled. There is a good deal of sickness around the village, but none of the people that attended the meeting, as I have heard of. Many individual friends send love, praying for your recovery to health. Pray for us. I remain yours in the bonds of Christian friendship,

ABEL COLMAN

Mr. Wickes came home to attend to the court business in connection with his guardianship, remaining about two weeks, and going to Cape Vincent, from which he wrote.

CAPE VINCENT, March 20, 1850.

MY DEAR WIFE:

I catch a moment this morning before the mail leaves to give you the history of my journey. We arrived at Mr. C.'s about 11 o'clock, and stayed there until after dinner. When we took buggy and started on in the storm. We stopped in Watertown a short time, Mrs. W. not at home. We then came on to B. in the mud. The frost out of the ground so much, that they were laying plank on the road between B. and W. It stormed very hard indeed, and began to grow colder. Called upon Brother Wood. He gave his consent to have me come here very reluctantly, and then I must call and see the brethren at D. I did so, and they felt it would be cruel indeed for me to come past them. But I finally did come. We had a plank road from D. about five miles and then in the mud half a hub deep, and so hard that the horse would go only a few rods before she would stop. About a mile and a half from D. is the village of L. on P. river, a village of some twenty-five or thirty houses, but no church at all. We arrived at Chamount* about seven in the evening, and put up with Rev. Mr. Camfield, who very courteously entreated us. I found I had taken cold in my neck, and a severe pain in the small of my back. I bathed myself with spirits of camphor, rested not very well, and in the morning I rose with a severe head ache,

---

* Pronounced Shemo.

the worst I have had for a long time. Chamount has got to be quite a village. But morals have not advanced much. They have a stone bridge nearly completed across the bay, which cost them about $5,000, which now has the appearance of being very durable. The next morning I had to foot it a part of the way, and the going was very bad. I reached here about twelve o'clock, having called once on the way and washed my head again with spirits of camphor; and when I reached this place I found my head some better. Found things here in a very interesting state, and yet not that attendance in the afternoon which I expected. Meeting at half-past two in the afternoon was very poorly attended, two male members, four female members, and six converts, and two ministers. I felt strangely, I can assure you, with all the description which we had of the state of things to meet only a few in this time of interest. I walked around the village after meeting, and retired to my room in the Rev. Mr. I.'s house. In the evening there was a house pretty full, say some three hundred persons out, and a good attention. After which there were two hopefully brought to bow at the foot of the cross. I have given you a brief history up to this morning. I feel better than I did yesterday, and nothing is yet unfavorable to myself. April 9th. I have watched the mail for the last few days to hear from you. The developments which have made themselves manifest since I wrote have astonished me beyond degree. If I had known them before I left home you would not have parted with me for this place. There was a division of the church in regard to getting help, and the minister did not want help, only just because the

The last letter while at his last meeting.

church would have it. And I have not been able to get him to preach a sermon since I came here. I supposed all the time it was because he did not feel able to, but I found it was because he thought the church did not want to have him. And I had this thing to settle between them. Brother L. felt they were treating him unkindly, for they sent him for me, and supposed that as such it was all harmonious, taking things as they were. I then told them they were treating me and the people in D. and the cause of Christ wrongfully, and I should leave. Then all began to beg me not to, for the work would be at an end, etc. There were new cases of conversion daily, and the work spreading all the time. With the view of closing I preached to the converts last Sabbath, when there were about one hundred hopeful converts seated together. The church, and the wicked, and all were surprised to see the number. And they do all appear very well indeed, of all ages and all classes. To God be all the glory given for all that He has done. There are some who have been R. Catholic, Universalists, and would-be Deists, etc. I thank God for all His kindness towards all this people. Then, as is always the case, the Lord opened the hearts of the people to desire more, and they took an expression to have me stay longer. I felt reluctant so to do, but I finally consented thus to do. Hence this letter. The people in Dexter feel very anxious, and yet I am very fearful that hope deferred maketh the heart sad, and do not know what will be the effect. But I must close this with a word to the children, which was dated March 23.

Yours affectionately,
L. A. WICKES.

Finish of next letter. Spend your time usefully, and try to make each other happy. And improve all the time you can in your books, and may God be with you, and you love the Savior, is the earnest prayer of your affectionate father.

L. A. WICKES.

Hope to be home in a few days. Love to all. Pray much.

CAPE VINCENT, March 23, 1850.

MY DEAR CHILDREN:

I trust before this you have received my letter descriptive of my journey to this place, directed to your very dear mother. The village contains some six hundred inhabitants. Quite a number French and Canadians. The moral influence is not very good. Infidelity has a very strong hold upon the minds of the people. Men, and women too, deny the Bible and the existence of God. They have two church edifices, Episcopal and Presbyterian. The Presbyterian is of stone, with the woodwork and steeple on the outside painted a light brown. It has quite a large porch. Session room over the porch that would accommodate some seventy-five or more persons. This church has fifty-four seats which will hold six persons each, (Sarah, how many will that seat?) besides an orchestra that will hold fifty, perhaps more. The pulpit in the back end of the church with an ordinary sofa in it, and the floor of the whole church carpeted. It is situated on Main street, which runs east and west nearly a mile long. It faces the north and is quite a pleasant location. Morning of Monday, 25. Since writing the above I have taken a walk out. I went upon the river, as the ice was still across it or nearly so. I went into one of the stores, and it is a hell upon earth. Drinking, and gambling, and swearing, a most miserable hole. I would not dwell in such a hole as that for all earth calls dear.

I have some fears of the powers of infidelity that are so prevalent here. But still I know that the Lord's arm is very strong, and there is no arm like unto His, and it is His own course, and He will "make the wrath of man to praise Him." There seems to be an increase of feeling here, though I found things different from what I had anticipated when I came here. I found that there were very few who attended the meeting except professors, and but few of them. The church is now quite well filled, and some forty forward for prayers last evening, converts and all. One of them has just been in to see me, by the name of H., a man sixty years of age. He appears very well. His wife, his only child and her husband, have given up all to God. Blessed be His name. My health this morning not quite as good as usual, but hope for the best. Monday evening, half-past ten. I have just returned from meeting. I will spend a few moments in writing. At the meeting this afternoon there were some six or seven hopefully converted. It was the most melting time I have seen in a good while. This evening there were somewhere between fifty and sixty forward for prayer, converts and all, and nearly all of them hopefully gave up all to Christ. To God be all the glory. I wish my dear children were here to enjoy it with me. I do sometimes feel that I cannot consent to be absent so much and you not have the privilege of the means of grace. I feel that it is robbing you of the greatest blessings to shut you out from the stated means of grace. But let us truly look to the Savior for His guiding hand to lead us according to His will and He will guide us for our good.

STOWS SQUARE, March 14, 1850.

DEAR MOTHER:

I have been home only a week and been confined to the house most of the time since my return home. My labors were so fatiguing that it brought on some of my old complaints and I have been obliged to lie still for a few days, though I find it is very hard work for me when they are all saying, "Come over and help us." Such is the state of religion in all the region where I have been laboring, that I have most urgent calls from eight different churches, and the spirit of God is awakening sinners in all that region.

The meeting I last held continued six weeks, and would have gone on longer but I had to come to attend Surrogate's Court. The meeting was in a most blessed state when it closed. Between the afternoon and evening there were some forty persons came to my room for prayer and counsel, and several for the first time called upon the Lord. That evening there were some one hundred and eighty came forward for prayers; after which I gave an opportunity for such as hoped they had given all to Christ to speak, and then one hundred and ten got up and spoke, and I had no chance to close the meeting until half-past eleven o'clock and then all seemed loth to leave the place. Some went home weeping, some went singing, and some went praying. And all feeling the work must not cease. There were from one hundred and thirty to one hundred and fifty hopeful conversions, and from the child of twelve to the man of seventy. Most of them were youngerly people, and the majority were males. To God be all the glory and honor, for all that has been done is by His might, for Paul may plant and Apollos may water, but God alone giveth the increase. I do feel that it is a privilege to be allowed to work in the vineyard of the Lord, and be instrumental in leading souls to the paths of peace. Let the world have its riches and boast of its glory, but give me the glory of leading souls to Jesus Christ, and be counted a fool for Christ's sake. I shall probably leave home again as soon as I am able, and for how long I cannot say.

If my health should not prove good, I then shall take another course. But may the will of the Lord be done in my heart and in all of us. C. and all the rest send love to you and all.

Your son,

L. A. WICKES.

CHAPTER XXVI.

COPENHAGEN AND LAST SICKNESS.

AFTER the close of the meeting in Cape Vincent, he came home and staid about two week, trying to recruit his health by out door labor on his little farm of twelve acres, not all paid for. He was in constant reception of letters urging his presence in different directions. He preached two Sabbaths in Copenhagen, the last time taking his wife with him. This was on May 5th, 1850, the text on Sabbath afternoon was from Mark 6: 12. "And they went out and preached, that men should repent." While in the desk he felt in such pain that it was noticed, and when questioned why he did not stop, he said, "I thought it might be the last and tried to finish the work." He went to his boarding place, and the results will be found in the following letters:

COPENHAGEN, May 7, 1850.
DEAR SISTER AND CHILDREN:

I suppose you looked for us home yesterday, and wondered some why we did not come. I will tell you. Your pa did not feel well Sabbath morning, but preached twice, and came back sick to Mr. Kilburn's, where we staid Saturday night. We sent for Dr. S. but he was not at home, *we* tried to doctor him all night, but he did not feel any better in the morning, so we sent for the doctor again, but he had not got home. Then Mr. K. called in the Dutch doctor. He attended faithfully to him through the day, yesterday, and this morning he brought Dr. S. with him, and they both say he is not able to ride home now. And Dr. S. says he ought not to go home until next week, but we hope much sooner. His disease, congestion of the lungs, bilious stomach, and general debility. We are in the midst of the kindest of friends, but you know we came away without bringing one extra garment, thinking we should be home by Monday. (Here several necessary articles were named to be put into a valise, and pa gave some directions about some necessary work, etc., and telling all at home to do the best they could, to send to us by the bearer of this letter.) I trust through a kind Providence we shall not be detained here long, though pa is quite weak now. The pain in his lungs, head and back are somewhat relieved, except weakness he complains of pain between his shoulder blades, and his blister on his stomach. He thought he ought to be bled, but the doctors thought not best. He vomited some, but we gave him a cathartic, which operated copiously. Of course he will be necessarily considerably prostrated. You shall hear if there is any unfavorable change hereafter.

Your affectionate sister and mother,
C. WICKES

COPENHAGEN, May 8, 1850.

DEAR CHILDREN:

Sickness. No doubt you are wishing to hear about your dear pa. Yesterday he was under the influence of a cathartic and another blister; rested some the latter part of the night. This morning I thought his symptoms all were favorable, but he seems considerably exhausted after writing a short letter to Mr. Coleman. He has some fears that the seat of the inflammation on his lungs is not broken up. He coughs very little, expectorates some, not quite as easily or freely as yesterday. Talking tires him exceedingly. Countenance at times indicates jaundice. Has not had his clothes on since last Sabbath night. The German doctor went to Adams yesterday, returned to-night. Dr. S. called last eve. We expect him again to-day. They agree in their practice. But the Lord only can make any means efficacious. If he has a work for us in Copenhagen or anywhere else, I trust He will prepare us and give us strength to perform it, and when our work is done may we be ready to go where none shall say I am sick. I was glad of the things you sent. Friends are very kind. I do not know as we could have gotten a man in the county as good a nurse as Mr. K. P. M. Pa's pulse ranges about 100. Dr. has not been in to-day. Cannot say that I think he is materially worse though he appears a little more feverish. I have been anticipating if the weather would be good we should return home this week, but we will try to be content with what seems best. There was a female prayer meeting, and a very good one. It was appointed last Sabbath. I did not then think of being detained here so as to attend it. If we do not go home will write again. In the meantime be good children and pray that the Lord will take us all under His special care and grant what will be for our best good. Love to all.

Your affectionate mother,
C. WICKES.

8th. Mr. W.'s symptoms all appeared better. The doctor left him to visit other patients at some distance; was absent all night. After all had retired, Mr. W. arose and wrote a letter, then woke his wife, who was asleep on the sofa near his bedroom, wishing her to address the letter and see it mailed in the morning; he then retired, but was restless the remainder of the night and the next day. Instead of having regained his rest and renewed strength, he felt an extreme debility, loss of appetite for any food; felt some discouragement, as he could not ride home. Still hoping all for the best, anxious friends were ready to anticipate and meet every want which they could. The doctor returned hoping to find him convalescent, but found him in rather a feverish state. Dr. S. also came in to see him. They concluded he was having a relapse of his bilious disease. They immediately commenced taking him through a pretty severe course of treatment to break up the bilious symptoms, which they thought made him appear so feverish. This added to the prostration of his nervous system. He continued to exhibit the same feverish state until the 14th, when a council of physicians met. After some consultation it was then thought a course of *salivation* would break up the disease, and his naturally strong constitution would enable him to regain his health. His attending physicians pursued the advice, but "man's ways are not as God's ways, nor his thoughts as God's thoughts." His nervous system became so exhausted it seemed advisable to send for the dear children to visit him, as he might not be able to communicate or know them. When they first came in he appeared to know and smiled to see them. They staid all night. He was not unconscious, but a stupor came over him, mostly during the night. The little daughters were taken to his bed in the morning and he was told they had got ready to leave and go home. He replied, "Will they not stay all night?" not realizing that they had staid through the night. He then seemed to be sensible of their presence. He desired them to always be good children, remember to keep up the family altar, then kissed them good-bye and immediately relapsed into a stupor. They never heard the loved voice of their dear affectionate pa again. Nothing but the precious promises of our blessed Savior could sustain at such an hour. He continued to sink notwithstanding every effort to revive and raise him up, except when after moments of extreme pain he was relieved, he then would thank the Lord for the respite from pain. The last night he suffered much from bodily pain. On Sabbath morning he gave up all hopes of recovery; he called and wished to see his dear wife— commended her and the children to the Lord, unable to say more. About nine o'clock A. M., May 19, 1850, while the bell was calling the people to assemble at the church where he stood and delivered his sermon, just two weeks before, he was summoned to join the assembly above and worship in the presence of the Savior whom he adored and so faithfully served while here on earth. On Tuesday, the 21st, a large concourse assembled at the church in Copenhagen, where the Rev. Mr. Spears preached an appropriate funeral sermon from John 13: 7. Jesus said, "What I do thou knowest not now, but thou shalt know hereafter." His remains were then conveyed to and interred in the family burying-ground at Stow's Square. His bereaved family received many letters and tokens of condolence from those who had been benefited by his instructions and prayers.

"The memory of the just is blessed." "He that winneth souls is wise."

DEPAUVILLE, May 14, 1850.

DEAR BROTHER WICKES:

The opening of your letter caused me a good deal of pain. Oh, brother, your family have claims on you. I believe it is your duty to have some care of your health. I don't know as I should find fault with you, for the Lord has promised to be with all those who put their trust in Him. I believe "it is safer to wear out than rust out." But then I think of your family. We here sympathize with you in your affliction, and pray that the Lord will make your afflictions a blessing to yourself and family and the church of our Lord. There is still a good state of feeling in this place. Our Sabbath-school has commenced, and there were over one hundred scholars present last Sabbath to recite.

When I mentioned your sickness in the school it produced a great feeling. Oh, I wish you would come here and see us when you get better, we all want to see you, it would do us good, we love your Captain, or I think there are some here who do. Remember the Fourth of July; we shall soon make the arrangements for the same. E. M. has been very sick and there was very little prospect of her recovery, but to day she is some better. You have the prayers of all the people here for your speedy recovery. Mrs. C. and mother send respects to yourself and family.

                Respectfully yours,

                          ABEL COLEMAN.

In haste. Write soon.

CHAPTER XXVII.

FUNERAL SERMON, AND TESTIMONIALS.

EXTRACTS from a sermon by Rev. G. Cross on the death of Rev. L. A. Wickes, preached at Canton Falls, May 30th, 1850, at Richville, June 7th, at Lisbon June 16th, and by invitation delivered at Denmark in presence of his family the same fall.

Text, II. Cor., 11: 23. "In labors more abundant." It has been customary in all ages, the history of which has been written, for men of serious thought, to remember with gratitude to God, those who have been benefactors to their fellow men, both in church and State. This is required in Scripture and not censured if not degenerated into the idolatry of "worshiping the creature more than the Creator." In the history of the church we read of marked instances where the people of God have paid great respect for their dead whose services had been owned and blest of God in ameliorating the physical and moral conditions of man, especially those who have labored for the good of His common Zion. I may be permitted to say that my long and endearing acquaintance with my dear brother Wickes does require of me, public attestation of his personal and ministerial worth, and which was purely by the grace of God.   *   *

The great object of the Apostleship of Paul, was the salvation of souls and confirming Christians in the truth.

This blessed work called forth all the energies of his mind, in it he was "willing to spend and be spent," to accomplish which, he did "not count his life dear unto himself" so that he might finish his course with joy, and the ministry which he had received of the Lord Jesus. In this he labored, and in it he died; when he ceased to labor for Christ, his soul went from the martyr's stake, home to glory.

The review that we have referred to, was of the life of one who was an inspired man; one who sustained an extraordinary relation to the church universal. Still we believe that the words may be used by us on this occasion appropriately, for the reviewing in a brief manner, the ministerial life of our lamented brother Wickes.

Let me say in particular that it is a cause of gratitude to the great *head* of the church, that our brother was so fully prepared for so extensive usefulness in our *Master's* vineyard. It is given but to a few, to be so peculiarly endowed with ministerial gifts, by which much good was accomplished in the way of immediate effect to those who enjoyed the privilege of sitting under his ministry only for a few weeks, to many of whom it was a "savor of life unto life."

I. *He was abundant in his studies.* When time permitted he was studious to acquire all knowledge which was necessary for the faithful discharge of ministerial duties. He believed and practiced on the principle that it was not commendable for a minister to attempt to communicate to others what he did not understand himself. It was his invariable rule to acquire distinct and intelligent views of any subject which he intended to present to others, and to make all knowledge which he possessed subservient to the great object of presenting truth. The fund of knowledge which he had acquired was taxed constantly for the purpose of elucidating truth, that his hearers might understand and embrace it. But aside from human science, he was an industrious and devoted student of the Bible. Not only did he make it a text book, but a devotional book. By its precious contents he strove to nourish his own soul, and by so doing feed others with the same spiritual manna. And when time would permit, and as far as the subject on which his thoughts were fixed, required, he was a critical reader of the Scriptures. Very few of his discourses were weak for not having them well strengthened and fortified with scriptural quotations. The doctrinal and practical proof texts drawn from this source occupied their proper places in his sermons.

To accomplish this, he searched from page to page, and did not rest satisfied till he had found and incorporated in his skeleton, or manuscript, every passage of Holy Writ which proved the doctrine or practice under discussion.

He possessed a very great facility in turning from passage to passage, and thus file in quotation after quotation to prove the point he wished to urge on the attention of his hearers. (When some complained, that for this, his sermons were too lengthy, when at Canton his elder brother, Rev. R. Pettibone, wished him to continue the practice, for it was the *truth* that converted sinners.) When engaged in protracted efforts, it was his custom to read the Bible systematically, that he might bring out from its rich treasures things new and old. He obeyed the command, "Search the Scriptures," that he might divide aright the word of truth. He studied the Scriptures, I repeat, that he might preach them. All who have listened to his sermons do testify that he brought to view many passages, that are not usually sounded by the ordinary blowing of the gospel trumpet. This was acknowledged by his older brethren in the ministry. With it striving to obey the command given to Timothy by Paul, "Strive to be a workman that needeth not to be ashamed," yea to be an able minister of the New Testament.

II. *He labored more abundantly in prayer.* This armor of conquest seemed to be always on him. Always ready to meet every spiritual enemy by it, or to assist the pilgrim in any situation in which he might be placed. By this gift he would discover to the disconsolate child of God the pillar of fire by night and the cloudy pillar by day, that he might go on his way rejoicing. The gift that was given to him by the great head of the church, the spirit of supplication, was of a wrestling kind. He seemed to have passed it maturely, while as yet he was not regularly inducted into the ministry, and he ever improved it to the edification of those who listened to his earnest entreaties at the throne of grace. How the heart was moved! It melted down by the soul-stirring pathos of his depicting supplications. It mattered but little how cold, dry and formal the feeling that might pervade, when the spirit of prayer was on *him*, the souls of the pious would be moved, and the lukewarm stirred up, and the impenitent would listen and often melt before its softening influence. Verily he labored abundantly in this gift.

He acted on the resolution of David: that at morn

ing, noon and evening, he would bow before the Lord and supplicate His favor. (The Rev. R. P. spoke of his being heard early in the morning pouring out his heart in prayer to the mercy seat.) Such was his habit that we may say of a surety, that in improving this gift, he departed not from the altar of devotion. He might at times have been too personal, but it was zeal that prompted to the effort, that he might discern, as far as human effort could, between those who do good and those who do evil. I would not exaggerate or eulogize beyond the truth, but it is my conviction that the gift of prayer bestowed on our departed brother and willingly improved by him, has done much instrumentally, for the past twenty years, to irrigate the thirsty hill of Zion with rain and dews of heaven, throughout the whole region where God in His providence has called him to labor. Under God, it has often broken up the thick and gross darkness of the mind, dispelled the dark clouds of unbelief, and turned the thoughts of the impenitent within that they might see their own vile hearts; and by the same means, how often has the compassion of God been manifested. The expiring, bleeding Savior portrayed as dying on the cross for sinners, with outstretched arms of mercy! So far as the form is concerned, how many cases he has presented to the mercy seat? How many times he has bowed the knee before the "Father of our Lord Jesus Christ" to beg of Him for pardon and salvation, that the feet of the impenitent might be taken from the horrible pit and miry clay, and set upon the Rock of Ages. It was his custom to pray for faith, that he might have his confidence unshaken in God, especially in his efforts to do good. His labors in this gift are closed.

He sleeps in Jesus; he needs not to pray. That entreating voice is hushed in death; those imploring eyes closed in the long slumber of death, and his voice will remain silent till the archangel shall bid him rise for greater services in a more ample sphere than earth. But the spirit that has fled has been doubtless attuned to praise, yet it sings but one song, and that is, "The song of Moses and the Lamb." And as he wakes no more to pray nor to entreat, let those whosoever heard him pray, remember that it was not for naught in the mind of God that they had the privilege.

III. *He was abundant in preaching the word.*

I declare this before many who can bear witness that I lie not. It was not only his prayer that he might "rightly divide the word and give to each their portion in due season, but to give line upon line and precept upon precept." And he labored night and day that he might be a faithful steward to the household of faith for his Master. Whatever of talent, or science, or acquisition, he readily brought it and laid it down at the feet of his Redeemer. His gift was not locked up by him like money in a chest; or as a lamp, trimmed and put under a bushel; but was diffused abroad, or placed in a conspicuous place, that all might be benefited. He dwelt under the canopy of devotion while preaching. He went into the desk after earnest prayer for the divine blessing to accompany the word dispensed, and when the seed of the word was sown he looked to God again that it might take deep root in the heart and bring forth the fruit of salvation; and he desired soon to return to scatter abundantly more of the precious word of truth.

His labors in various sections made him personally

acquainted with incidents which were skillfully used by him, and that often with great effect in impressing truth on the minds of his hearers.

The history of David informs us that he brought all the spoils which he acquired by conquest and devoted them to build the temple of God. So should every minister do with the spoils he may win, make all subserve the one great purpose of enforcing truth. On this plan our deceased brother ever labored. As far as human mind could scan, nothing escaped his notice; by observation and reading he gathered materials from the land and from the ocean, from the battle-field and social circle, from the learned, from the unlearned, from the lightnings that play on the bosom of the angry clouds, and from the thunders that roll in its forked pathway, from the devastating tornado and the gentle zephyr and favoring breeze, from the huge mountain and the bubble on the water (under the ice*), from the joy of recovering a lost child, and from the fear of, or an actual plunge over Niagara's awful cataract, from the deep distress of a soul from a sense of sin and from a soul rejoicing in the love of Christ, from the living and from the dead, from things animate and inanimate, and above all, from the law and historical facts of the Bible and the full gospel of Christ —from the happy pair that dwelt in Eden and from its pleasant bowers, from the tragical scene of Cain and Abel, from Enoch walking with God, from Abraham

---

* When a youth, one day, while on the river, walking on the ice he saw, as he supposed, a piece of silver looking like a twenty-five cent piece. Elated at the idea of obtaining it, he hastened to procure a tool to extricate it from the ice, and, upon breaking it up, found to his disappointment, it was only a bubble!

pleading with the angel of the covenant, and from his offering in faith his son, and from Moses pleading with God and Jacob wrestling with the angel, from Joshua's pious resolve to serve God and Gideon's overthrow of the Midianites, from Elijah ascending to heaven and Elisha curing Naaman, from Nehemiah building up the walls of Jerusalem and Esther going before the king to plead for herself and people, and from the patience of Job and the devotions of David, from all the force of the language of the prophets, from the austerity of John the Baptist and the zeal of the apostles, from the infinite motives drawn from the life and death of the Son of God, by the attractions of His cross, His burial and resurrection, and from all the pointed passages that treat of the depravity of the human heart, and that speak of the sorrows of the lost and happiness of the redeemed. These all were used by him to instruct and enforce truth. Though sometimes in a mirthful manner, yet as often of the solemn and melting, often of the most encouraging description to the child of grace, that he might gird his soul for a new conquest by grace. He usually succeeded by the Spirit when God's people asked for bread not to give them a stone, or for an egg not to give them a scorpion, not to conduct to the stale putrid cistern rather than the living overflowing stream of salvation. There was, by grace and gifts bestowed, in his administration, much to comfort and edify the pilgrim in his march to the Canaan of rest, much to rouse the backslider in heart and to convince the impenitent " of sin, of righteousness, and of judgment to come." His gift was of a rallying kind. He never enjoyed himself better than when he was associated with praying people and had the sacramental host around him moving on to conquest. Few ministers preached as much as he did, by day and by night. It is well-known to the public that for several years his labors continued as an evangelist, with but little cessation. He has labored in protracted efforts as much as three years of continued labor since 1841. In such meetings he usually preached fourteen sermons in a week, making in all two thousand one hundred and seventy sermons in the time specified. This is as near as I can estimate by the facts in my possession. I do not say that it is to a fraction. I think it true on the whole. This would be more than ten years of ordinary preaching at the rate of four sermons per week. Besides this his exhortations and instructions around the anxious seat and to the promiscuous assembly was usually as much as an ordinary sermon each day and evening. We may add to this his seasons of prayer in private, in the social circle, at the opening and closing up of religious services, and for the anxious, whom, except in a few instances, I never knew him, and may venture to say, nor others ever knew him to leave till he had prayed for and instructed them to come to the Savior. Probably he preached to or addressed public assemblies between six and seven thousand times while he was laboring in his Master's vineyard on earth; probably some three thousand times more than ordinary preachers in the same time. When he labored statedly in one church he was very active in conducting the Bible class and Sabbath-school, and the benevolent institutions of the day were plead by him with success.

His was a warm heart towards every cause which had for its object the amelioration of the human family.

The principles of peace, purity of heart and life, the cause of temperance, and freedom from oppression in all its forms were deeply rooted in his soul, while the conversion of sinners to God was the first object of his life. "He that winneth souls to God is wise." (Letter from his widow.)

He labored extensively in the counties of Jefferson, Lewis and St. Lawrence, and some in Franklin, Oswego and Oneida. There are but a few towns in the three first mentioned counties where he was not generally known as an evangelist whose labors were blessed of God to the conversion of many souls, few inhabitants in these towns who usually attend religious worship that had not heard him preach.

It is not for me to say how many expressed a saving change of heart in the meetings conducted by him. I may say, that within the bounds of charity, he has witnessed the conversion of three thousand souls in meetings held by him and other meetings which he attended, while a candidate for the ministry. But the great day that will reveal the secrets of all hearts, can disclose the true number saved by his instrumentality. In a physical sense, as well as moral and religious, we can see that it must require a large amount of labor to perform so much ministerial service. To have journeyed from county to county and from town to town, and in all seasons of the year, carried forward so arduous a work as efforts which he was engaged in required. "He must have been in *labors* more *abundant*."

You may think lightly of such labors, you may say that they were eclipsed by human imperfection. Let us think soberly for a moment, and let candor and true judgment prevail. Let facts speak, let truth utter her voice, and we shall learn that the Lord spoke to a very great degree by such means. So that hundreds of souls have been converted to the *truth* as it is in Jesus, by them, many of whom are now rejoicing in heaven. We dare not say that on the whole evil has been done. Who will say that God has cursed and not blessed? "Wisdom is justified of her children." Has not the manna by these means fallen around our tabernacle? Can we wish that it had not been given to us? Rather let us think that it came from the good hand of our God. If the ratio of doing good as recorded by one is true, "that if one soul is converted and that one is the means of the conversion of two more, and let this ratio roll on a thousand years, the sum would amount to 60,000. Reckon according to this ratio, and the labors of our departed brother, with a starting point within the bounds of charity, would amount to the startling sum of 90,000,000 of souls saved through his instrumentality, or his labors laid the foundation for this amount of good. I make this statement not to boast of the dead, but to show how the Lord can bless; and who will say that He cannot thus by small means, when He has set in His statutes the promise " that one can chase a thousand and two can put ten thousand to flight," and that those "who turn many to righteousness shall shine as the stars in the firmament forever and ever." I may say of Brother Wickes, that he was an *instructive preacher*. A practical preacher by doctrine and practice. He was a wise preacher. His discourses judiciously selected. He was a plain preacher. His hearers could understand him. He was faithful to expose sin. He was an animated preacher. The great compass of his voice made him touchingly eloquent. He was a successful preacher. His soul was formed for friendship. In his domestic circle he was kind and affable. So in the social circle. His brow was scarcely ever knit with anger, but to rebuke sin. He was a man of great moral courage. In this quality he exceeded in his profession. I never knew him to quail before the transgressor. In all his labors he sought to find out acceptable words. *He is gone!* The candle has been removed from its place in the sanctuary. The laborer has been called out of the Master's vineyard. The form of a good man has passed away from before us. One who was extensively known. Of friends he had many; so of enemies, it might be said for righteousness' sake. Did he not pray and labor for Zion? Was not the Lord with him *by His spirit?* True his abundant labors could not save him; nor others meritoriously. "It is not by might nor by power," etc. "Paul may plant and Apollos water," etc. He was a reaper and a gleaner in God's harvest field. He gathered good fruit for the people of God. He always came down from the land of Canaan bearing on his shoulders fruit as pleasant as the grapes of Eschol; and with what adroitness he would give them to his hearers. Christian friends, when shall we have another Christian teacher like him? God may yet be kind. May He raise up laborers after His own heart and send them forth into His vineyard. But let us be grateful for past favors. He has given us much good instruction. "Being dead, he yet speaketh to us." The voice from the grave seems to say, "Remember the words that I declared while I was yet with you." Has he not stood with us in the awful front of the battle by God's command, and like our great statesman who rose to speak and was struck with death, and breathed his last in the capital of the nation, so our brother was preaching in the pulpit when the last summons came by sickness that terminated his earthly existence. As our two great statesmen died on the 4th of July, the Nation's birthday; on the day they loved, so it was on the Sabbath morning that he closed his eyes forever on the light of the sun, to sleep, we hope, in Jesus. He was cut down with his armor on. " Blessed is that servant who, when his Master cometh, He shall find so doing." He shall appoint him ruler over much; and what shall I say to those persons present who believed not under the preaching of our departed brother? He held three different meetings in this place, almost every impenitent person residing here at the different times that he was here, heard him declare the word of life. Do you blame us for introducing him to you as the servant of God? We do feel grieved to-day that you did no more attend to the words which he spoke, as well as others who have visited us as the servants of God. We would weep tears of pity, for the hectic flush of the sure and fatal disease of sin is yet on your cheeks, that betokens eternal death. Is there no physician that can heal you? None, except ye believe. But did not our brother faithfully converse with you on the important subject of your soul's salvation? Did he not use many arguments drawn from the law and gospel, from heaven, earth and hell to convince you of your need of accepting of the offers of the Savior? He will never come to Richville and Lisbon again to preach to you, but he will meet you at the judgment seat of Christ and be a witness against you, and this by the appointment of the Lord. Once more, in this manner he speaks to you. We come with the news of his death, with his coffin and winding sheet, with his pale countenance, which you have seen so smiling, and beaming with love, and ask you to remember his words.

> "High in the temple of the living God
> He stood amid the people, and declared
> Aloud the truth, the whole revealed truth,
> Ready to seal it with his blood. Divine
> Resemblance most complete: with mercy now
> And love, his face illumined, shown gloriously;
> And frowning now indignantly, it seemed
> As if offended justice from his eye,
> Streamed forth vindictive wrath! Man heard,
> The uncircumcised infidel believed.
> Light thought, mirth, grew serious and wept;
> The laugh profane sank in a sigh of deep
> Repentance; the blasphemer, kneeling, prayed,
> And prostrate in the dust, for mercy called.
> Such was his calling, his commission such.
> Yet he was humble, kind, forgiving, meek,
> Easy to be entreated, gracious, mild;
> And with all patience and affection, taught.
> Rebuked, persuaded, solaced, counseled, warned,
> In fervent style and manner.
> A skillful workman he
> In God's great moral vineyard: what to prune
> With curious hand he knew, what to uproot:
> What were weeds and what celestial plants,
> Which had immortal vigor in them, knew,
> Nor knew alone, but watched them night and day,
> And reared and nourished them, till fit to be
> Transplanted to the paradise above.
> Oh, who can speak his praise! great, humble man!
> He in the current of destruction stood,
> And warned the sinner of his woe; led on

> Immanuel's soldiers in the evil day,
> And with the everlasting arms embraced
> Himself around, stood in the dreadful front
> Of battle high, and warred victoriously
> With death and hell. *And now has come his rest,
> His triumph day.*"

"And I heard a voice from heaven, say unto me: Write, blessed are the dead who die in the Lord, from henceforth, yea saith the Spirit that they may rest from their labors, and their works do follow them." Brethren, let us pray, that our acquaintance with our brother may be renewed where parting shall not be known. May God bless his bereaved family, for His Son's sake, to whom be glory and dominion in earth and heaven forever and ever. Amen and Amen.

The following is an extract from the minutes of Black River Association:

SISTER WICKES:

The Moderator having announced that since our last meeting it had pleased God in His providence to remove from us our highly esteemed and much beloved brother, Rev. Lewis A. Wickes, the following minute was adopted: Inasmuch as we are called upon to record the death of Brother Wickes, who, after a brief illness, departed this life in joyful hope of a blessed immortality, at Copenhagen, Lewis County, the 19th of May, in the 41st year of his age, and the nineteenth of his ministry, having labored nine years in the churches at Stows Square and Antwerp, and a little over nine years as an Evangelist in the counties of St. Lawrence, Franklin, Oneida, Oswego, Lewis and Jefferson. Therefore

Resolved, That the churches in this region have occasion to mourn. And as an Association we feel deeply afflicted in the dispensation of Divine Providence, which has removed from our fraternal intercourse and from an extensive field of usefulness a dear brother, who had but just passed the meridian of life, and who manifested a single-hearted devotedness and an untiring zeal in the work of his high calling, until from the pulpit he was summoned to his final account, and that while we bow in humble submission to the will of Him whose ways are unsearchable and who doeth all things well, we regard the event as a voice from our Master, saying, "Work while the day lasts; be ye also ready."

Resolved, That while we extend to the bereaved family and relatives, in their deep affliction, our affectionate remembrance and tender sympathy, we also rejoice that God, in His abounding goodness, has so richly commingled their cup with the consolations of His grace, and that we most earnestly commend them to Him who has not only promised to direct the steps of those who commit their way unto Him, but to be "the widow's God, and a father to the fatherless."

Resolved, That a copy of these resolutions be sent to the family of the deceased, and also to the editors of the "Independent" and the New York "Evangelist" for publication.

 (Signed)   H. H. WAITE,
           Register for Association.

www.ingramcontent.com/pod-product-compliance
Lightning Source LLC
Chambersburg PA
CBHW032041220426
43664CB00008B/811